Painted Poems

RAJPUT PAINTINGS *from the* RAMESH *and* URMIL KAPOOR COLLECTION

Painted Poems

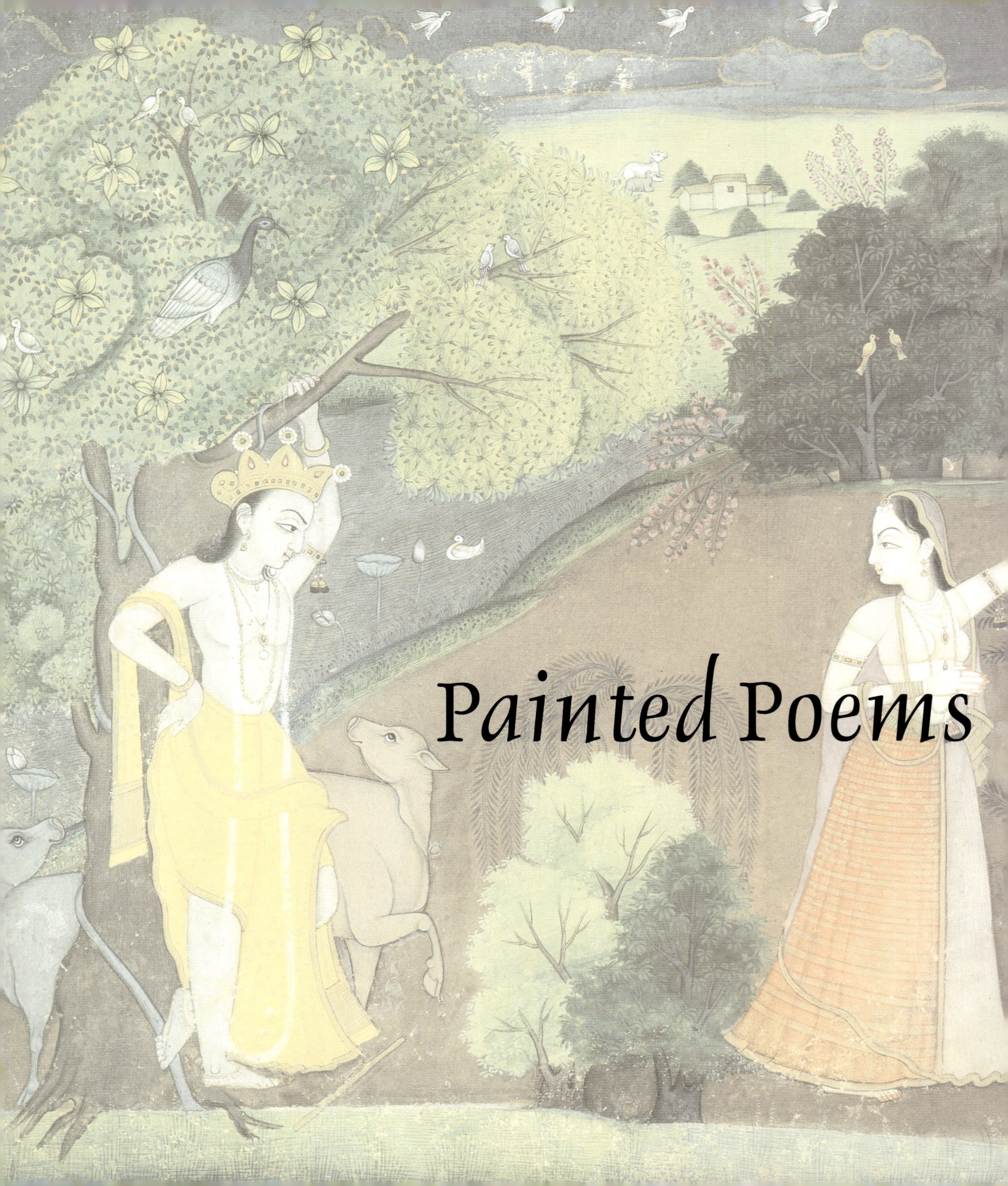

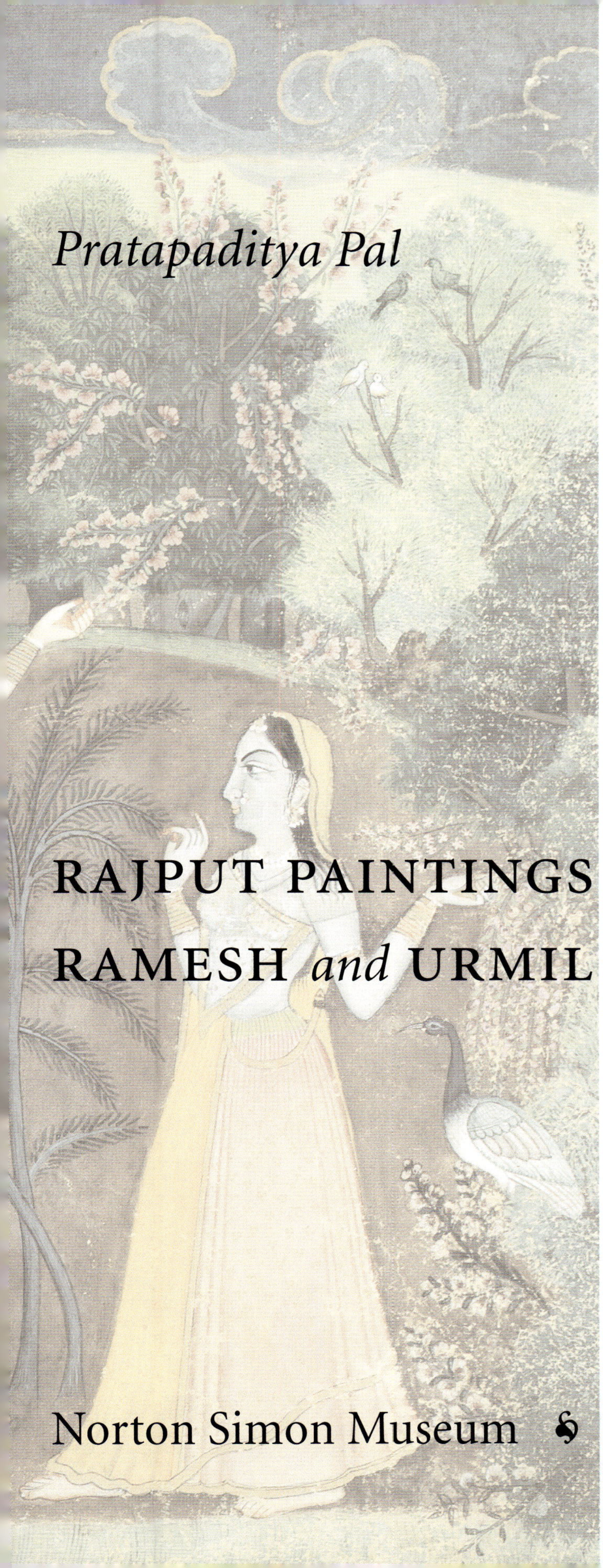

Pratapaditya Pal

RAJPUT PAINTINGS *from the* RAMESH *and* URMIL KAPOOR COLLECTION

Norton Simon Museum & Mapin Publishing Pvt. Ltd.

Published in conjunction with the exhibition
PAINTED POEMS: RAJPUT PAINTINGS FROM THE RAMESH AND URMIL KAPOOR COLLECTION
at the Norton Simon Museum, April 2–August 23, 2004.

Diacritical marks have been omitted.

Publication coordinated by Christine Knoke
Photographed by Antoni Dolinski
Edited by Jean Patterson
Designed by Lilli Colton
Processed by Reproscan, Mumbai
Printed by Tien Wah Press, Singapore

FRONT COVER: *Krishna Converses with a Messenger* [48] (detail), Himachal Pradesh, Kangra workshop, c. 1800
BACK COVER: *Ladies Worship Krishna and Radha* [54], painted by Harinarayan, Rajasthan, Jaipur, c. 1900
P. 1: *Camp Scene with a Feast* [FIG. 2] (detail), Mughal, c. 1610–20
FRONTISPIECE: *The Captive Krishna* [47] (detail), painted by Prag Chand, Himachal Pradesh, Kangra workshop, 1775–1800
P. 6: *Krishna Upholds Mt. Govardhana* [30] (detail), Rajasthan, Kota workshop, 1750–75

411 West Colorado Boulevard, Pasadena, California 91105 USA
www.nortonsimon.org

First published in India
in 2004 by Mapin Publishing Pvt. Ltd.
TEL: 91-79-755-1833/755-1793. FAX: 755-0955
EMAIL: mapin@icenet.net. www.mapinpub.com

Simultaneously published in the United States of America
in 2004 by Grantha Corporation
EMAIL: mapinpub@aol.com

Distributed in North America by Antique Collectors' Club
TEL: 800-252-5231. FAX: 845-297-0068
EMAIL: info@antiquecc.com. www.antiquecc.com

Distributed in the United Kingdom & Europe by
Art Books International Ltd.
TEL/FAX: 020-7953-8290
EMAIL: sales@art-bks.com. www.artbooksinternational.co.uk

Distributed in Asia by Nickleodeon Books Pte. Ltd.
TEL: 65-6338-5924/6338-3740. FAX: 6338-4213
EMAIL: shafinah@singnet.com.sg

ISBN: 81-88204-32-3 (Mapin)
ISBN: 1-890206-69-5 (Grantha)
LC: 2003116902

Table of Contents

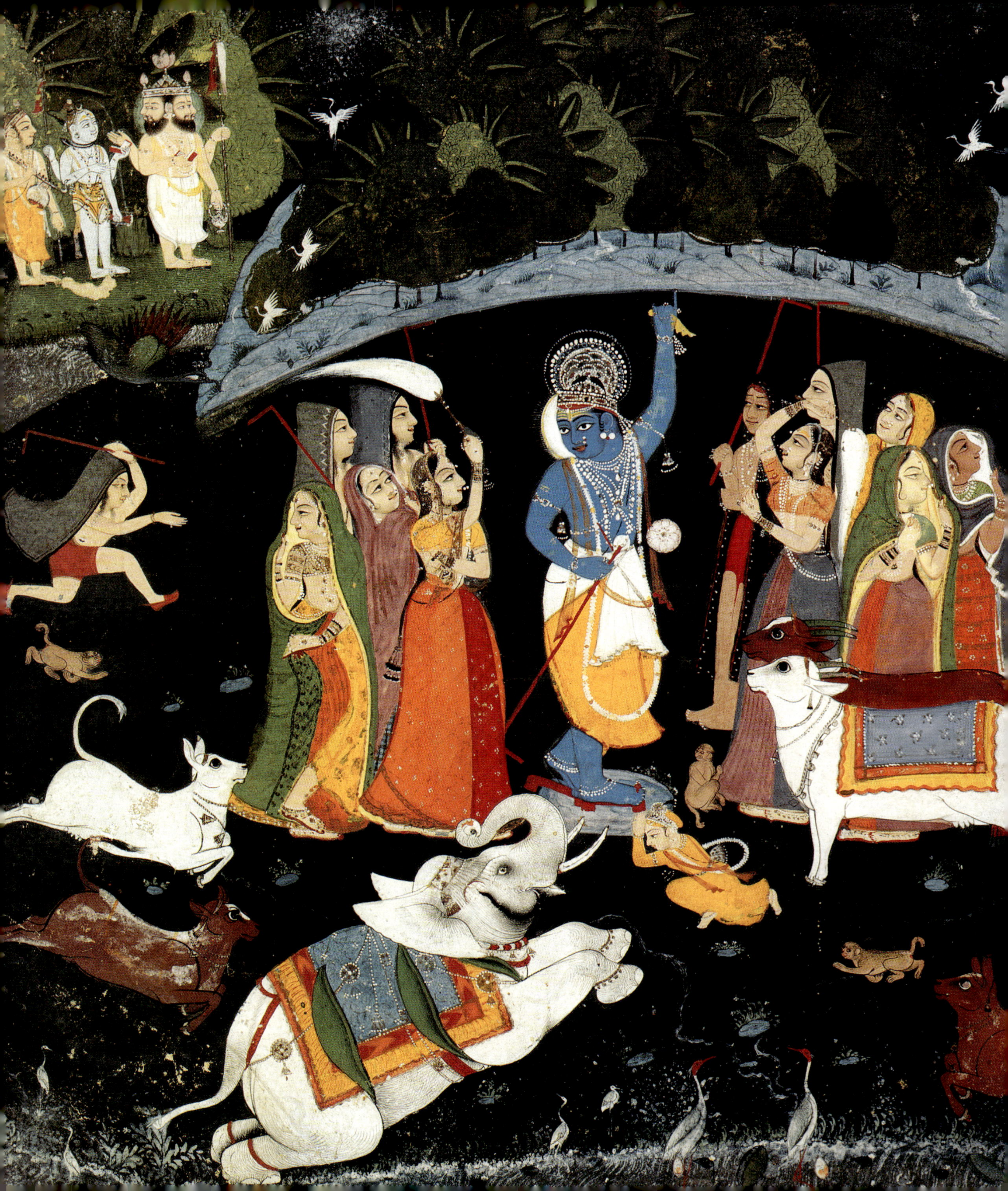

Acknowledgments

IT IS WITH GREAT PLEASURE THAT WE PRESENT the following group of eighty Indian paintings in an exhibition and catalogue. Norton Simon's superior collection of temple sculpture from South and Southeast Asia is known the world over. And although he collected both two- and three-dimensional works of art from Europe, he was not as seduced by Indian painting as he was by sculpture. He did, however, acquire a few Indian paintings of fine quality—one Mughal and three Rajput—which are reproduced in the Introduction. The Introduction also illustrates one of three paintings from eighteenth-century Hyderabad that were donated to the Museum in 1998 by the well-known local dealer and collector Alfred E. Stendahl and his wife, for which we are thankful.

Soon after the Stendahl gifts were received, I felt that, considering the Museum's strength in sculpture, it would be nice to assemble a small collection of Indian paintings. Not only do the pictures—especially those painted for Hindu and Jain patrons—reflect the religious and aesthetic ideas expressed in stone and metal by earlier generations of Indian artists, but they also relate to the religious paintings from Nepal and Tibet, examples of which Mr. Simon did acquire. Moreover, the Museum has a large, distinguished collection of graphic arts, including Japanese prints. Therefore, examples of Indian paintings would be most useful for comparative exhibitions.

I was musing upon such matters in the company of my friend Ramesh Kapoor in New York one evening three years ago when an idea germinated: he and his wife, Urmil, would donate a selection of Indian paintings to the Museum for an exhibition. The proposal was enthusiastically supported by the Museum staff and by Executive Vice President Walter Timoshuk, and the project was launched.

Since the early 1970s, Ramesh and Urmil Kapoor have been particularly well known for their specialization in Indian paintings. This interest began early in Ramesh's life when he finished school and began working with his father, who owned a painting gallery in New Delhi, India. Apart from hands-on training, Ramesh was also fortunate to meet the many eminent collectors and scholars of Indian painting who regularly visited the gallery. Being from the Punjab, his family specialized in paintings of the princely states in the Himalayan foothills. Before 1947, when the country was partitioned into India and Pakistan, these were administratively associated with British Punjab. After Ramesh set up his own business in New York, he expanded his repertoire to Rajasthani and other painting traditions of the plains. We are greatly indebted to Ramesh and Urmil for generously providing a nuclear collection of Indian paintings to the Museum. We hope it will be augmented in the future by other collectors and donors.

Many persons inside and outside the Museum have diligently and significantly contributed to this project. Outside the Museum, I would like to acknowledge the following scholars for reading and translating the inscriptions, providing work that has considerably enhanced the value of this catalogue: Drs. Naval Krishna and V. C. Ohri, both noted scholars of Indian painting in India; Dr. Gouriswar Bhattacharya of Frei University, Berlin; Dr. Navina Haidar of the Metropolitan Museum; Richa Pauranik-Clements of Indiana University, Bloomington; Biswajeet Rath of Marg Publications, Mumbai; Dr. Gautama V. Vajracharya of the University of Wisconsin, Madison; and A. N. Walia. Dr. Asok Das, the eminent Indian scholar, has kindly read all the catalogue entries and suggested several improvements. Thanks are also due to Dr. Gursharan Sidhu for various suggestions. Susan Sayre Batton has attended to the physical and material welfare of the paintings with her usual diligence. It is a pleasure to acknowledge Antoni Dolinski for his fine photography, Jean Patterson for style editing and Lilli Colton for the attractive design of the catalogue.

Within the Museum, I would like to thank Registrar Andrea Clark and her staff and Director of Operations John Sudolcan and his staff, all of whom take care of the many logistical issues that an exhibition generates. Last but not least, my sincere thanks goes to Assistant Curator Christine Knoke, who has assumed the burden of coordinating the entire project—both the exhibition and catalogue—with her customary efficiency and dedication.

Pratapaditya Pal
Pasadena
August 2003

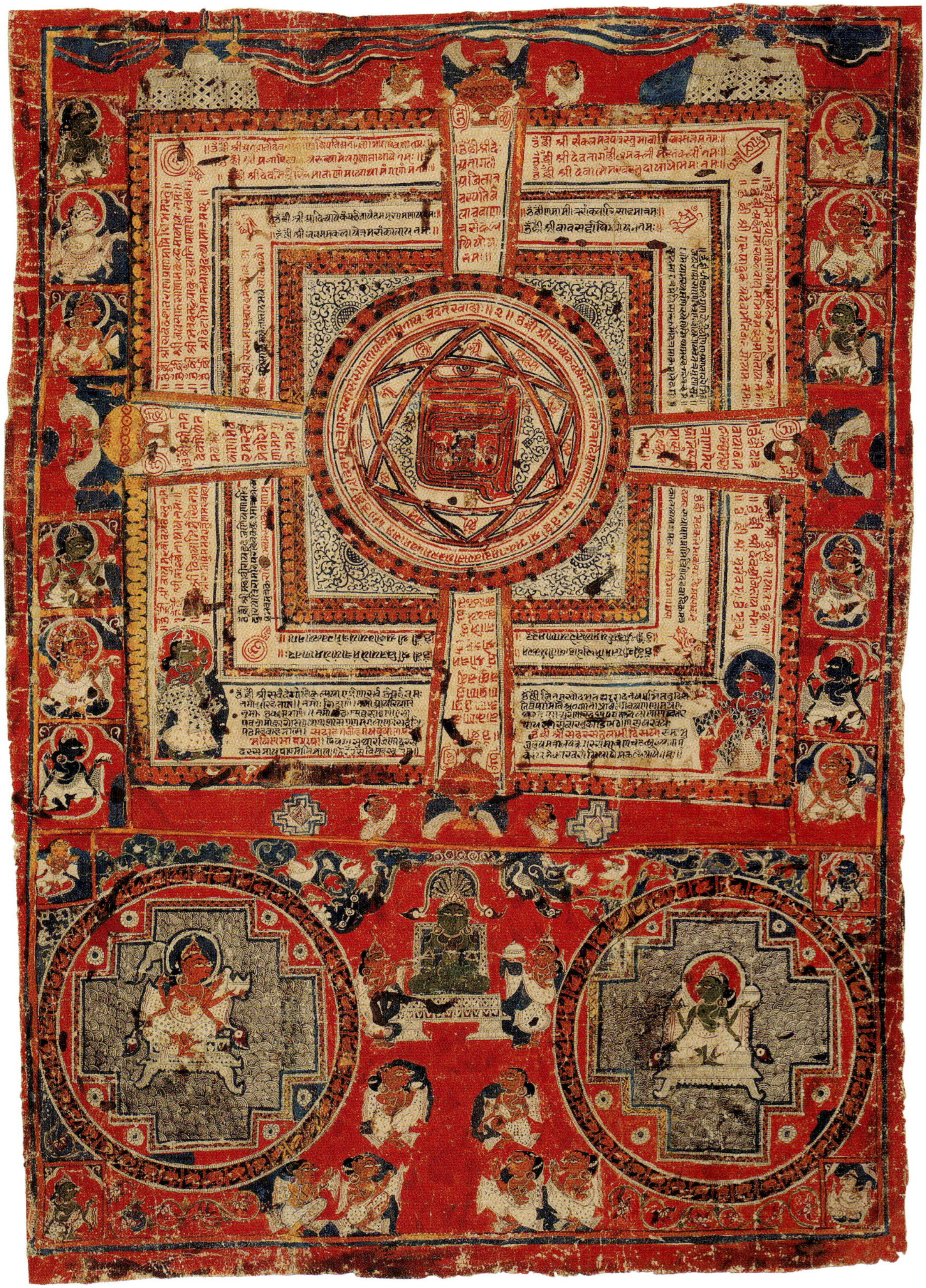

Introduction

Rajput art creates a magic world where all men are heroic, all women are beautiful, passionate and shy, beasts both wild and tame are the friends of man and trees and flowers are conscious of the footsteps of the bridegroom as he passes by. This magic world is not unreal or fanciful but a world of imagination and eternity, visible to all who do not refuse to see with the transfiguring eyes of love.

——Ananda K. Coomaraswamy [1]

With few exceptions, the majority of the paintings in this exhibition and catalogue were created for Rajput patrons. The expression "Rajput" is used loosely to describe Hindu rulers of small and large kingdoms that flourished mostly in north-central India, stretching from Jammu and Kashmir, Punjab, Himachal Pradesh and Uttaranchal in the northern Himalayan foot-hills down to the Indian state of Madhya Pradesh, parts of which were known as Malwa or Bundelkhand. In between is the state of Rajasthan, where a number of semi-independent Hindu kingdoms existed from the sixteenth century, when the entire region was part of the Mughal empire. Indeed, the Rajput tradition and patronage of painting owes much to the Muslim Mughals both aesthetically and stylistically, though the Rajputs and Mughals differed in tastes and interests.

In keeping with their ancient heritage, Rajput patrons had a penchant for religious themes, which dominate the pictures discussed here. Even ostensibly secular works are not free of religious and mythological ideas, as is the case with poetry, both in classical Sanskrit and the vernacular languages, the principal being Hindi in the plains. In addition to these two languages, various local dialects are encountered in the hill states, known collectively as Pahari (from the word *pahar/pahad*, meaning hill).

With one exception [1], in which the support is cotton, all the paintings were executed on paper. The cloth painting is a Jain religious work—a yantra or mandala used in tantric rituals—that is much larger and was painted much earlier than the average Rajput painting. The Museum's collection includes a second Jain cloth painting, also of the fifteenth century, illustrated here (Fig. 1). Although this one is of roughly the same period and belongs to the same artistic tradition, the two paintings are visually quite different in their iconographic complexities, compositions and coloring, which is far more vibrant in [1].

The typical Rajput painting was meant to be handled and not hung on the wall. It would have been passed from hand to hand among a group of connoisseurs, or admired by individuals seated in a relaxed mood. The work would have been held close to the face and observed and savored for its intimate detail. Some are illustrated pages of manuscripts, which, in the Indian tradition, were rarely bound but kept in a loose bundle. In these instances the text and pictures are usually on the same page, as

Fig. 1 Shvetambara Jain Yantras. Gujarat, fifteenth century, opaque watercolor on cotton, 23¾ x 17⅛ in. (60.3 x 43.5 cm). Norton Simon Museum, Gift of the Nathan Rubin-Ida Ladd Family Foundation under the bequest of Ester Rubin Portnow, P.2000.2

in [37]. When the painting is not an example of an illustrated manuscript, a short poem may be inscribed on the top or a longer text on the back. Some of the pictures do have historical information on the back, including dates and names of patrons, especially of rulers.

Patrons often commissioned works to observe a religious occasion, to offer as a wedding gift, or to record a special event that they thought was memorable. Some pictures were painted by artists as gifts (*nazrana*) for their patrons on celebratory occasions like a birthday [13] or a major holiday, such as the autumn festival of lights called Diwali. One painting [59], we are told, was painted "in order to entertain a minister"—an interesting admission, for it clearly shows that pictures were sometimes created purely for the patron's pleasure.

It was not common practice for artists to sign their works, but in many instances the name of the painter was added either at the bottom or on the back of the work. Apart from the name of the well-known Jodhpur painter Dana [72], three new artists' names have been retrieved from this group of paintings. One is Prag Chand, who lived and worked in the hills [47]. A second artist's name is given as Harinarayan, who was attached to the Jaipur court [54]. An inscription at the bottom of a third picture [77] is somewhat problematic. The first two words, *chitra likhatam*, clearly mean "it was painted by" and are followed by the expression *vichitra-rahi-sevaja*. The name of the artist is Vichitra and, as suggested by Navina Haidar (see Appendix), *rahi sevaja* (or *sevaka*) may indicate his court affiliation. The word *sevaka* broadly means "a devoted attendee." If the word *rahi* indicates "path," then Vichitra could be characterizing himself as a follower of the Radhavallabhi sect.

Most artists were professionals who were attached to individual courts, but some were itinerant, especially in the hills, and relied on the ruler's interest in the visual arts. For instance, the Jodhpur master Dana, who painted [72], also worked at Ghanerao. Even if the patron was not a connoisseur, the employment of court artists was often a state requirement and a matter of status. This is particularly true after the Hindu states became vassals of the imperial Mughals, whose courts they attended as generals and grandees.

The Mughals came from outside India through present-day Afghanistan. By 1605, when the third and most famous ruler of the dynasty, Akbar, died, the empire he had built included most of the territory of northern India, including Rajasthan, Madhya Pradesh and Gujarat. An avid patron of architecture and painting, Akbar had an enormous atelier that retained a large number of Indian artists and some from Persia and beyond. The solitary Mughal picture in the Kapoor collection [60] and a fine drawing in the mode known as *nim qalam*, mounted luxuriously for an album page that Norton Simon acquired (Fig. 2), provide some idea of the innovative pictorial tradition established by the imperial atelier.

Rajput rulers who were closely associated with the Mughals were quick to follow in establishing their own workshops, but their tastes differed significantly. While the Mughals preferred historical and natural veracity as well as psychologically perceptive portraiture with realistic details, Rajput patrons by and large had more of a penchant for mythological and rhetorical themes, depicted in less complex, but spirited, compositions saturated with bold and vivid colors.

Although the Rajput royalty was not as keen on recording their mundane life and achievements as their imperial Mughal overlords were, a considerable number of pictures have survived that are of enormous documentary and historical value. Several of the pictures in the collection [61–73] record both formal and informal occasions. The paintings provide glimpses of a world of pomp and ceremony, as well as the courtly pursuits and pastimes of both men and women, though through rosy, romantic lenses and glazed with a veneer of idealization.

The tradition of painting formal portraits of rulers, mostly male, began with the Mughals [60]. Typically the princes are seated, either by themselves or in conversation with visitors. The predilection is to portray the ruler as a resplendent, larger-than-life figure, often with a halo emphasizing his divine nature. Equestrian portraits were particularly popular [72–73], as they helped to emphasize the rider's heroism, especially if he was seated on a rearing horse. Though the facial features—especially the eyes—are idealized, the face does not lack individuality. The attire and carpets are rendered in great detail and with precision. Symbols are sometimes added to emphasize the sitter's personality. He may be with his pet falcon [64] to demonstrate his love for the sport, or he may hold a nosegay [67] to emphasize his cultivated nature. Pahari artists frequently showed their subjects smoking the hubble-bubble, or hookah, holding its snake elegantly [65–66]. In a rare informal picture, a prince is seen entering a mansion [71] in a realistic manner. There are also pictures of princes in the pursuit of mundane pleasures—such as watching an elephant contest [61] or a dancing girl [68]—or exhibiting piety [74–75, 79–80]. The two most perceptive and trenchant portraits, however, are not of

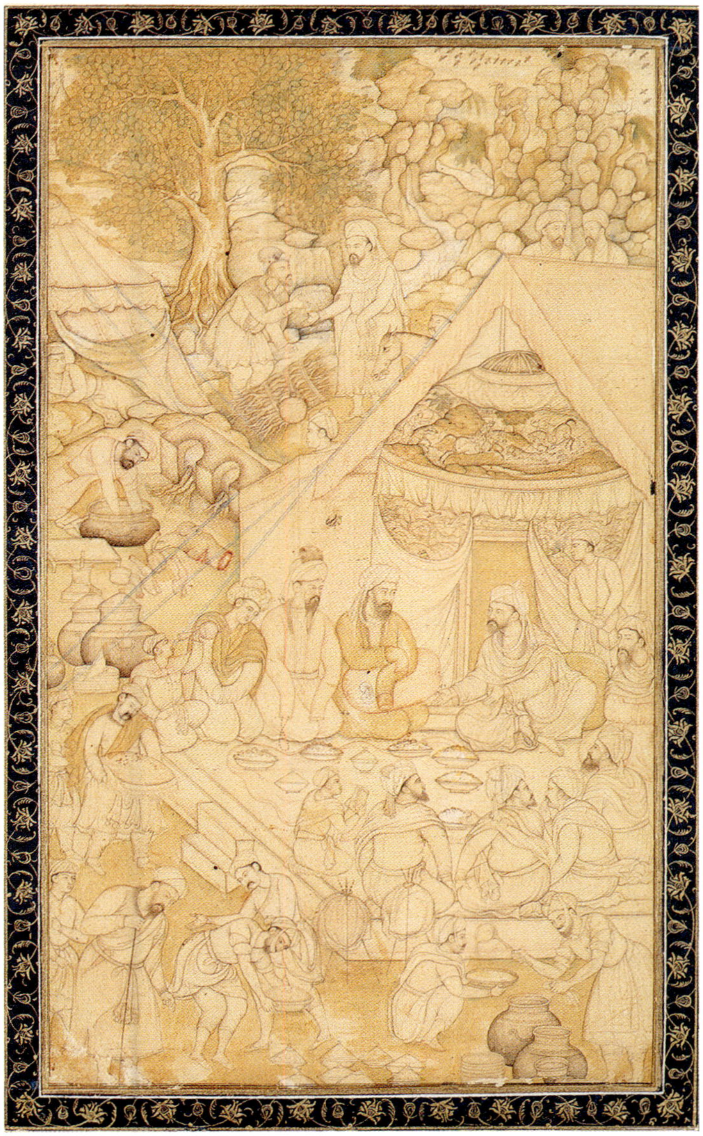

Fig. 2 Camp Scene with a Feast. Mughal, c. 1610–20, opaque watercolor on paper, sheet: 21 x 13 ¼ in. (53.3 x 33.7 cm); image: 9 x 5 ⅜ in. (22.9 x 13.7 cm). Jennifer Jones Simon Art Trust, N.1973.4.P

courtly figures but of holy men. Both were rendered in the Rajasthani state of Kishangarh [77–78]. In terms of acuity of observation and vivid visualization, these are two of the most unusual pictures in the collection.

By contrast, fewer paintings depict the activities of women. This gender inequality was inevitable in a society that kept women in seclusion and away from the prying eyes of men. Thus, whether these few pictures in the collection are the result of actual observation on the part of the artists, or just figments of their imagination, is difficult to determine. Even though the figures represent ideal types, the situations are likely credible. Listening to music [63], enjoying a dance [68], though perhaps not as openly as the men, and worshiping at a shrine, whether private [75] or public [76], were all common activities. Rarer is the scene of ladies watching a lively cockfight [62], a sport usually indulged in by men. One charming Kishangarh painting depicts a lady exposing herself after a bath in public view on a palace terrace [52], though a visualization of the short verse on top could as well be regarded as a genre picture.

Whether the subject is drawn from religio-mythological sources or from court life, poetry is usually at the heart of a Rajput painting. Most religious texts, including such classic Sanskrit epics as the *Ramayana* of Valmiki and the *Mahabharata* of Vedavyasa, both of unknown date, are in verse. So also are the texts known as *purana* (literally, old or ancient), which are vast compendia of ancient lore, mythology and history as well as social, moral and religious matter. The most popular among this class was the ninth-century *Bhagavatapurana*, a Vaishnava text narrating the life and adventures of Krishna, the popular Hindu deity. Especially appealing was the tenth book, concerned with Krishna's early life. He appears as an endearing, mischievous toddler, a supernatural terminator of titans and a precocious lover. The Kapoor collection's large number of pictures from the tenth book of the *Bhagavatapurana*, created in diverse workshops in the plains and hills, attests to the popularity of this rich narrative of adventure and romance. Here again, the small group of pictures acquired by Norton Simon includes a charming picture from a late-seventeenth-century series probably painted in the Bikaner royal atelier (Fig. 3). It is a fine specimen of the adaptation of Mughal pictorial elements to Rajput taste. Not only did such sacred books serve edifying moral purposes, but by commissioning illustrated copies, the donor derived both aesthetic pleasure and religious merit.

A subtext of a *purana* that has been of particular interest for the valorous Rajputs is the *Devimahatmya*, which glorifies the great Hindu goddess Durga. Embedded in the *Markandeyapurana*, probably by the fifth century, it lyrically describes the goddess's triumphant battles with various male titans and includes some of the finest Sanskrit eulogies written to her. Regarded as the most important liturgical text for the worship of Durga as the primary source of cosmic energy, the poem acquired an independent life of its own and proved to be popular with Rajput patrons [7–10]. Similar spinoffs occurred with many other sub-narratives that enrich the two epics and the *puranas*. Indeed, Sanskrit works of literature, both drama and poetical works known as *kavya*, often drew their narrative themes from these encyclopedic religious texts. One such popular tale of romance and chivalry was the *Rukmini-haran* (Abduction of Rukmini [by Krishna]), which proved to be particularly popular in the hills [38–40]. These recreations of ancient tales were often composed in vernacular languages such as Hindi and its dialects in the various regions of northern India.

Among the many devotional works of poetry that were composed in Sanskrit, one of the most lyrical is the *Gitagovinda* (literally, the song of the cowherd king). It was composed by Jayadeva, who lived in today's West Bengal and Orissa in the twelfth century. A long poem that extols the mystical love-play of Krishna and Radha in a very earthy manner, it is an erotically charged composition with mellifluous language [43–44]. The earlier of the two examples of the *Gitagovinda* is a double-sided folio [43] that reveals no Mughal influences and continues the more traditional mode of manuscript painting, in which the text and illustration are accommodated on the same page. In the later rendering [44],

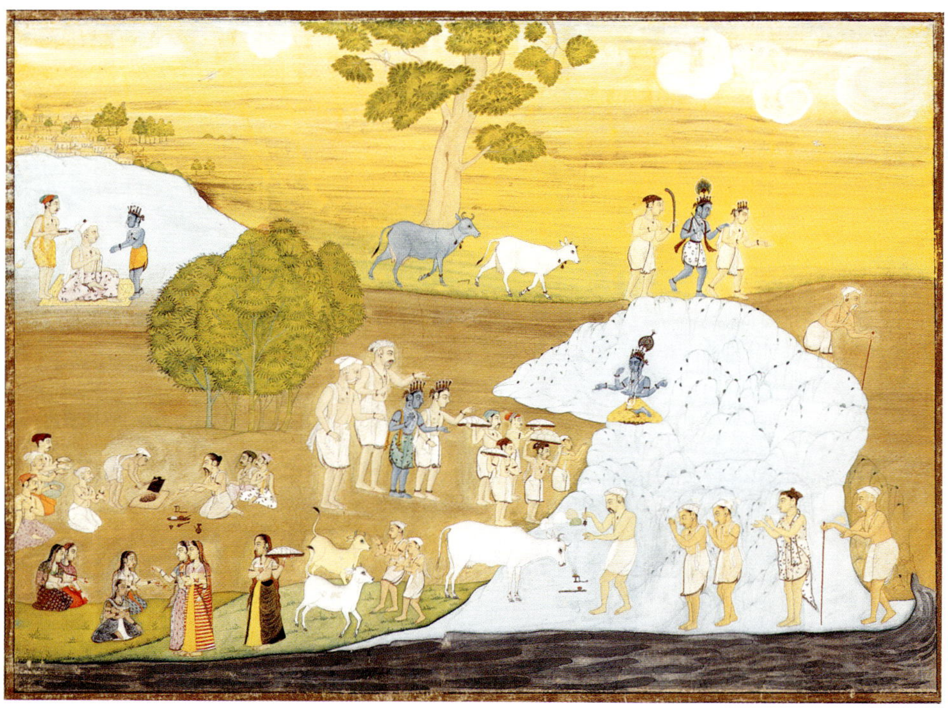

Fig. 3 Folio from the Bhagavatapurana*: Krishna, Balarama and Villagers Pay Homage to Vishnu. Rajasthan, late seventeenth century, opaque watercolor on paper, 8 ¾ x 12 in. (22.2 x 30.5 cm). Jennifer Jones Simon Art Trust, N.1974.4.3.P*

however, an unknown Pahari master has brilliantly combined compositional subtleties, landscape elements and soft, but nuanced, coloring to create a picture of delicate beauty and lyrical charm befitting the flavor of the poem. The ethereal grace and elegant eroticism of these pictures obviously made an impression on Norton Simon, for he acquired two examples from the *Gitagovinda* series (FIGS. 4–5).

In many instances, the pictures illustrate short verses composed in both Sanskrit and Hindi and included either above the pictorial composition or on the back. Sometimes a verse may be altogether unfamiliar; at other times little known. One such verse is a beautiful Sanskrit couplet involving Shiva and Parvati [5]; another depicts the return of the cows at dusk [49].

On the Shiva and Parvati painting, the first verse as translated by Gourishwar Bhattacharya is as follows: "Let Shiva be victorious, who is so absorbed with the face of Gauri (his young bride) that he is unaware of the fact that the snake forming his bracelet has drunk all the water that she pours into his hands during the performance of the evening's ritual, seeing which the [maid] Vijaya laughs." The verse is numbered one, which implies that it and the picture are the first of a series. The couplet is a variation of the first verse of an ancient anthology of Prakrit poems known as *Gatha-Saptasati*, compiled by Hala, who is usually identified with the Satavahana king of that name, belonging to perhaps the first century C.E. Following is a translation of that verse: "Salute the twilight offer of handfuls of water by Pasupati (Siva), on which remains reflected the moon-like face of Gauri, red in anger, and which (therefore) looks as if it bears the (red) lotus of adoration."[2]

The poem describing the Hour of Cowdust (see Appendix) is much longer. As far as is known, this is the first instance of a portrayal of this subject where the verses illustrated are included on the back. Apart from the Boston version of the painting, there is another in the Goenka collection in India.[3] However, the most elaborate composition that eschews the pastoral mood of the Pahari pictures is encountered in a painting of the Kishangarh school now in the National Museum, New Delhi.[4] In its sweeping and panoramic composition, it is reminiscent of a royal procession with bovines rather than a daily homecoming. What is interesting about the poem [49] is that it does not explicitly use the expression *godhuli*, meaning "hour of cowdust." Although we do not know the author of the poem, the use of the name Kesava (also a designation of Krishna) in the last line is suggestive. Significant in the Kapoor painting is the inclusion of Radha framed by the doorway; she is absent in the three other versions.

FIG. 4 Folio from the Gitagovinda*: Krishna Seated by a River Bank. Himachal Pradesh, Kangra, c. 1780, opaque watercolor on paper, 6 ½ x 10 ½ in. (16.5 x 26.7 cm). Jennifer Jones Simon Art Trust, N.1974.4.1.P*

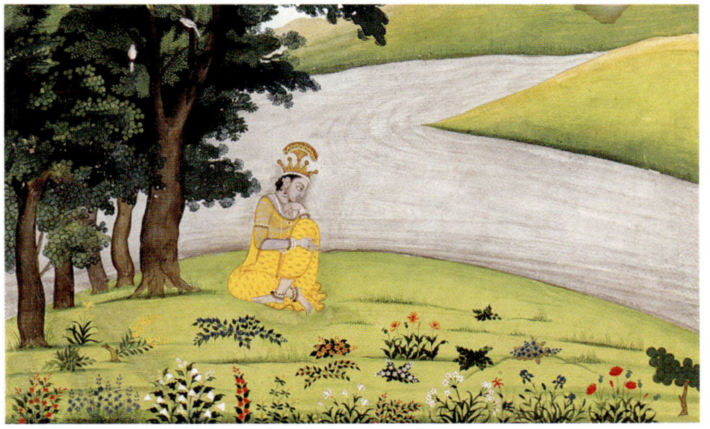

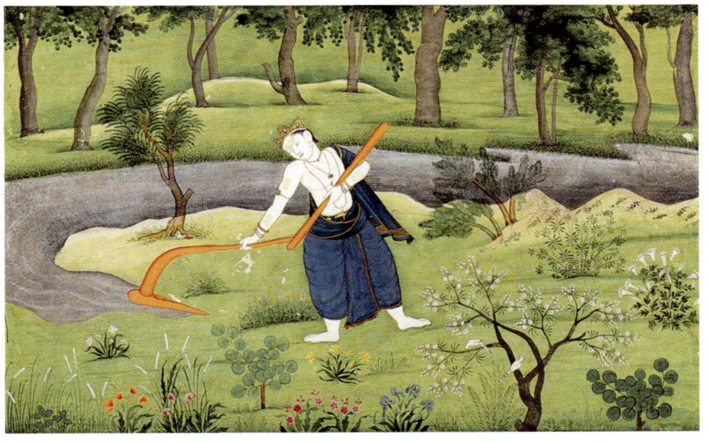

FIG. 5 Folio from the Gitagovinda*: Balarama Diverting the River Jamuna. Himachal Pradesh, Kangra, c. 1780, opaque watercolor on paper, 6 ½ x 10 ½ in. (16.5 x 26.7 cm). Jennifer Jones Simon Art Trust, N.1974.4.2.P*

The author of the Sanskrit verse in [5] is unknown, nor do we know whether a pundit or the artist of [49] selected the two verses from Keshavadas' *Rasikapriya* for the picture. Nevertheless, we can admire the very different and deft poetic expressions of the romantic and devotional moods of the same liminal moment of the day. No less graphic and poetic are the pictorial versions by the two unknown Pahari masters. We have already referred to the verses in Hala's Prakrit anthology, which probably inspired our unknown poet's effort in [5]. But Hala also includes another verse by a poet named Brahmachari of unknown date, which gives a radically different interpretation of the poignant hour of the day: "The (evening) lamp is being placed by the wife of the traveler with her neck bent, being afraid of the (inauspicious) fall of the stream of her tears rolling (over her face) at the recollection of her beloved." [5]

The most common poetical works depicted in Rajput paintings are: *Ragamala* (garland of melodies) by various authors; the *Rasikapriya*, composed in 1591 by Keshavadas (fl. 1580–1601); the *Satsai* of Biharilal Chaube (1595–1663), who is known generally as Bihari; and a genre known as Baramasa (literally, songs of the twelve months), composed by diverse poets.[6] Of these, only the texts of the *Ragamala* are composed in Sanskrit; the others are in Hindi.

Ragamala poems and their visualization in paintings are distinctive features of the Indian pictorial tradition. The genre combines three forms of artistic expression: classical music, Sanskrit poetry and painting. Indian music is based on a system of six basic *ragas*, each of which has numerous derivatives that are classified as *ragini*, or wives of *ragas*, and *ragaputra*, or sons of *ragas*. A *raga* is a specific arrangement of a progression of a minimum of five (of a total of seven) notes distributed over the octave, with a fixed prominent note, or sonant. This basic arrangement is further embellished with twenty-two micro notes or quarter-tones, known as *sruti*. The musician's improvised composition must adhere to the basic arrangement of notes (constituting the melody or mode) within the precisely delineated progressions of the *raga*.

Each *raga* is meant to evoke a certain mood or theme, such as a particular emotion, an expression of devotion, or a familiar folk melody. The very first *raga* in the northern Indian classification is known as Bhairava [55–56], a synonym for Shiva. One of its associated *raginis*, called Bhairavi [57], also has a religious association. Both are to be sung in the morning—each mode having its own specific time and appropriate season. Vasant, for instance, means spring, when it would be inappropriate to sing Meghamallar, associated with the rainy season. Early morning is of course the auspicious time for prayer and worship, but the doleful strains of Bhairavi are also considered appropriate music for parting, such as when a new bride leaves her father's home. Hence, the Bengali poet Rabindra Nath Tagore (1861–1941) begins a sad song with the lines: "With the dawn's light, Bhairavi's refrain resonates with the pain of parting." [7]

The mood and flavor of a poem was put into words by a poet, usually in couplets, which then provided the artist with the literary source for his visual renderings. The poems, however, are not always very explicit or precise, which led to a great deal of iconographic variation in the representations. Nor did musicologists adhere firmly to the classifications of the various modes and submodes, which can create confusion in identification. Moreover, different regions followed different literary and musical traditions, which resulted in diverse classifications and iconographies. For example, Bhairavi Ragini, normally associated with Bhairava Raga, in the representation in the Kapoor collection is given to the family of Hindol Raga [57]. In another picture in the Museum's collection (FIG. 6), the depiction of a lady entertaining a peacock is commonly identified as Kakubha Ragini. However, the same iconography in two other pictures from eighteenth-century Hyderabad is given to Sohni and Mallarika.[8] Commenting on *Ragamala* paintings, Coomaraswamy observed, "The burden of the music, the flavor of the poem and the theme of the picture are identical." [9] This is patently not the case, and it would perhaps be more rewarding to see how far the central mood and dominant flavor (*rasa*) converge in the music, poem and picture.

Keshavadas's *Rasikapriya* belongs to a class of treatises in verse concerned with both literary and rhetorical matters. Love is its central theme, and since the two principal characters, known as *nayaka* (hero) and *nayika* (heroine), are Krishna and Radha, the work acquires a mystical nuance, becoming symbolic of the relationship between the soul and God. In some ways the *Rasikapriya* and others of the genre continue the form and structures of the *Gitagovinda*, especially in the poetic portions. The late M. S. Randhawa, a noted scholar of Pahari painting, has provided a succinct analysis of the structure and nature of the *Rasikapriya* that is worthy of repeating here: "In an opening verse a precise definition of a particular *nayaka* or *nayika*, or an emotional situation is given, followed by one or two illustrations. Besides the speeches of the hero and heroine, the confidantes of the heroine also intervene with their advice, and other words are spoken by the poet himself, who introduces his own name in every verse." [10] Needless to say, the dominant *rasa* (flavor or mood) of such poetical works is the erotic, or *sringara*, classified further into *samyoga* (love in union) or *viyoga* (love in separation).

In the same genre, Bihari composed a work in seven hundred verses known as *Satsai*, in which love is also the principal theme. Hala's anthology of poems of the early centuries of the Christian Era is known by the same generic title, but in Sanskrit (*Gatha-Saptasati*). In the eighteenth century Bihari's *Satsai* was popular in both the plains and the hills. Two *Satsai* illustrations in the collection [50–51] are from the hills, and a third [52], from Rajasthan, relates to the text as well. In all three the compositions adhere to the texts faithfully. The charming Kishangarh picture [52] introduces us to a little-known poetical work of a Gujrati poet named Lallulala. Selected from the *Lalchandrika*, a commentary on the *Satsai*, the elegant literary concepts of the couplet are interpreted by the unknown artist in an erotically nuanced composition. Not only does the work demonstrate the painter's sensitivity to the poem's flavor (*rasa*) but also the patron's depth of interest in rhetorical literature.

One picture in the collection [53] portrays a theme from yet another poetical genre known as the Baramasa. Composed in the vernacular languages across north India from Gujarat and Maharashtra in the west to Bengal in the east, the Baramasa has no known earlier Sanskrit counterpart.[11] Its origins lie in the village and folk traditions of the subcontinent. Generally, the literature emphasizes the sentiment of love in separation, or *viraha*, often describing the feelings of the lonely heroine during her lover's or spouse's absence.

M. S. Randhawa has characterized the *Rasikapriya* poems as neat little verbal pictures limned in a few words "with the richness and sweetness of a lyrical language."[12] In fact, these observations could be applied to all Hindi poems to a greater or lesser degree, depending on the literary skill of the poets. The visual language and the syntax of the pictures may differ in the various Rajput representations, but in their laconic, colorful and vivid compositions, the mostly unknown artists were able to capture the poet's expressiveness and the flavor of the poems with equal aplomb. ❧

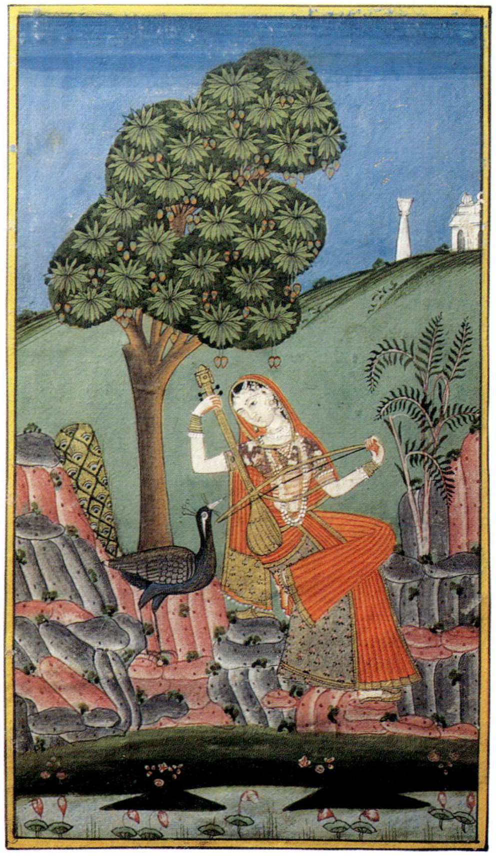

Fig. 6 Lady Entertaining a Peacock. Andhra Pradesh, Hyderabad, eighteenth century, opaque watercolor on paper, sheet: 12 ⅛ x 8 ½ in. (30.8 x 21.6 cm); image: 7 ¼ x 4 ⅛ in. (18.4 x 10.5 cm). Norton Simon Museum, Gift of Mr. and Mrs. Alfred E. Stendahl, P.1998.2.2

Footnotes

1. Coomaraswamy 1916, vol. 1, p. 7.
2. Basak 1971, p. 1.
3. Coomaraswamy 1927, pl. LXXXIX, fig. 270 for the Boston picture and Goswamy and Bhatia 1999, no. 197 for the version in the Goenka collection in India.
4. Banerjee 1978, p. 22.
5. Basak 1971, p. 50.
6. See Vaudeville 1986 for an overview of the history and development of Baramasa literature.
7. Author's translation.
8. Ragini Sohni is published in Ebeling 1973, p. 196 and the Mallarika in Gupta 1985, no. 136. It should be noted that Mallarika is not known to Ebeling. The inscription on the Mallarika identifies it as Kakubha, which Gupta says is wrong. Similarly, the label above the Museum's painting, as read by the late epigraphist Z. A. Desai, states "papa khanam," which makes little sense and cannot be translated.
9. Coomaraswamy 1926, p. 42.
10. Randhawa 1962, p. 28.
11. Randhawa 1962, chapter 10.
12. Randhawa 1962, p. 28.

Jain Paintings

1 Jain Tantric Diagram (Yantra)

Gujarat, c. 1450
Opaque watercolor and gold on cloth
27 1/8 x 26 3/4 in. (68.9 x 67.9 cm)
Lent by Ramesh and Urmil Kapoor

This striking painting represents a Jain diagram for tantric ritual. Like the Hindus, the Jains commonly refer to such a schematic configuration as a yantra, or instrument, while the Buddhists prefer the more familiar expression, mandala. In all three traditions, the two commonly employed shapes are the square and the circle, the latter being embellished with the lotus design, symbolizing the cosmos, the human heart and the citadel, as the structure further signifies the divine mansion surrounded by cosmic oceans. Limitations of space will not allow a complete description of all the rich details of this beautifully executed painting, but a few highlights may be noted.

As is usual with such diagrams, both words—in the form of sacred syllables and mantras—as well as images of deities form the constituent elements of the yantra. In the center are double triangles, familiar in the West as the Star of David. Representing both male (upward) and female (downward), the diagram symbolizes the unity of the two sexes in tantric ritual. It encloses the syllables *om* and *hrim*, also signifying the male and female respectively, as well as the complete alphabet (see Pal 1993, p. 99 for a more detailed discussion of some of these elements of the yantra). Additional syllables and incantations are written in golden letters in the innermost circle, the petals of the lotus and the alternating red and blue panels in surrounding circles. At the top and bottom of the composition are eighteen deities, three of whom are female (distinguished by the blouses they wear). Two worshiping monks wear white, which announces the yantra's association with the Shvetambara (white-clad) order of Jainism. Two mesmerizing eyes flank the *hrim* syllable, dominating the top of the yantra. In some other examples of the same yantra, either a goddess or the Jina Mahavira is represented within the combined *om* and *hrim* syllables (see Pal 1993, nos. 13 and 16 and references cited therein).

Both for its excellent condition and accomplished execution, this yantra is one of the finest to have survived from the fifteenth century. Admirable for its clean and orderly composition, precise and articulate drawing, attention to decorative detail and luminous coloring, it is clearly the work of a master artist.

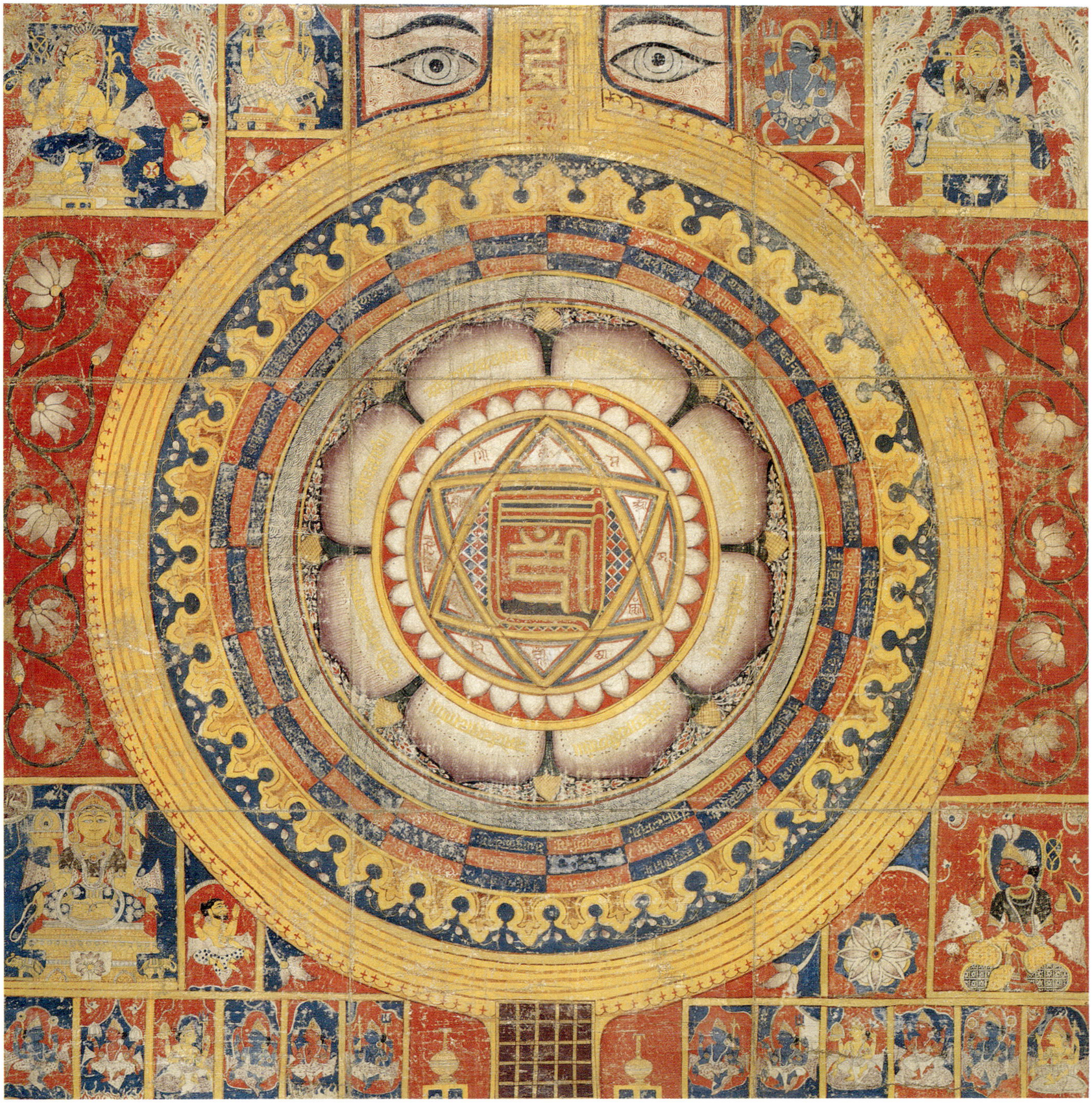

2 Folio from a *Samgrahanisutra* Manuscript: The Court of Indra

Gujarat or Rajasthan, 1575–1600
Opaque watercolor on paper
Sheet: 4 ½ x 9 ¾ in. (11.4 x 24.8 cm)
Image: 4 ⅛ x 8 ¾ in. (10.5 x 22.2 cm)
Gift of Ramesh and Urmil Kapoor; P.2003.2.7

The label in the upper-left corner identifies the subject as the celestial court of Indra. There is a long text on the back with verses numbering 102 to 111 (see Appendix); this helps to identify the manuscript as the *Samgrahanisutra* (Book of Compilations). A compendium of Jain cosmological and cosmographical ideas, the text describes the various universes and cosmic phenomena, heavens and hells and other related topics. It also includes descriptions of the denizens of the diverse universes and serves as a rich source of iconography of the deities. Although the earliest version is as old as the sixth century, only in the sixteenth did this text become popular with Jain patrons, for reasons unknown. This folio is a typical example of a *Samgrahanisutra* manuscript.

Against a ubiquitous red background, six male figures have been accommodated on a single plane. The two seated figures represent two divinities, the yellow one in front being Indra, king of the gods. The white figure may be Varuna, as he has a lasso in his upper-right hand. Both hold the elephant goad (*ankusa*) in their upper-left hands. Indra's second attribute may be a florid thunderbolt (*vajra*). The four standing figures represent other deities whose martial nature is clear from the weapons they hold.

Interestingly, while the two seated figures have bare torsos and wear the traditional dhoti, the others are all dressed in long dresses (*jama*) and pajamas, attire popularized by Muslims. Indeed, these pictures of the *Samgrahanisutra* eschew earlier figural forms and dress codes seen in the cosmographical mandala [1] for a new mode that borrowed many elements from contemporary styles that were prevalent in northern India. The facial features of the two seated figures still retain earlier traits, even with the extended further eye of Indra. The palette is more varied but lacks the deep, rich tonality as well as the gold and lapis lazuli of the earlier style. Most of the manuscripts are dated generally to the second half of the sixteenth century and later. This particular folio may well be from one of the earliest, perhaps executed between 1575 and 1600.

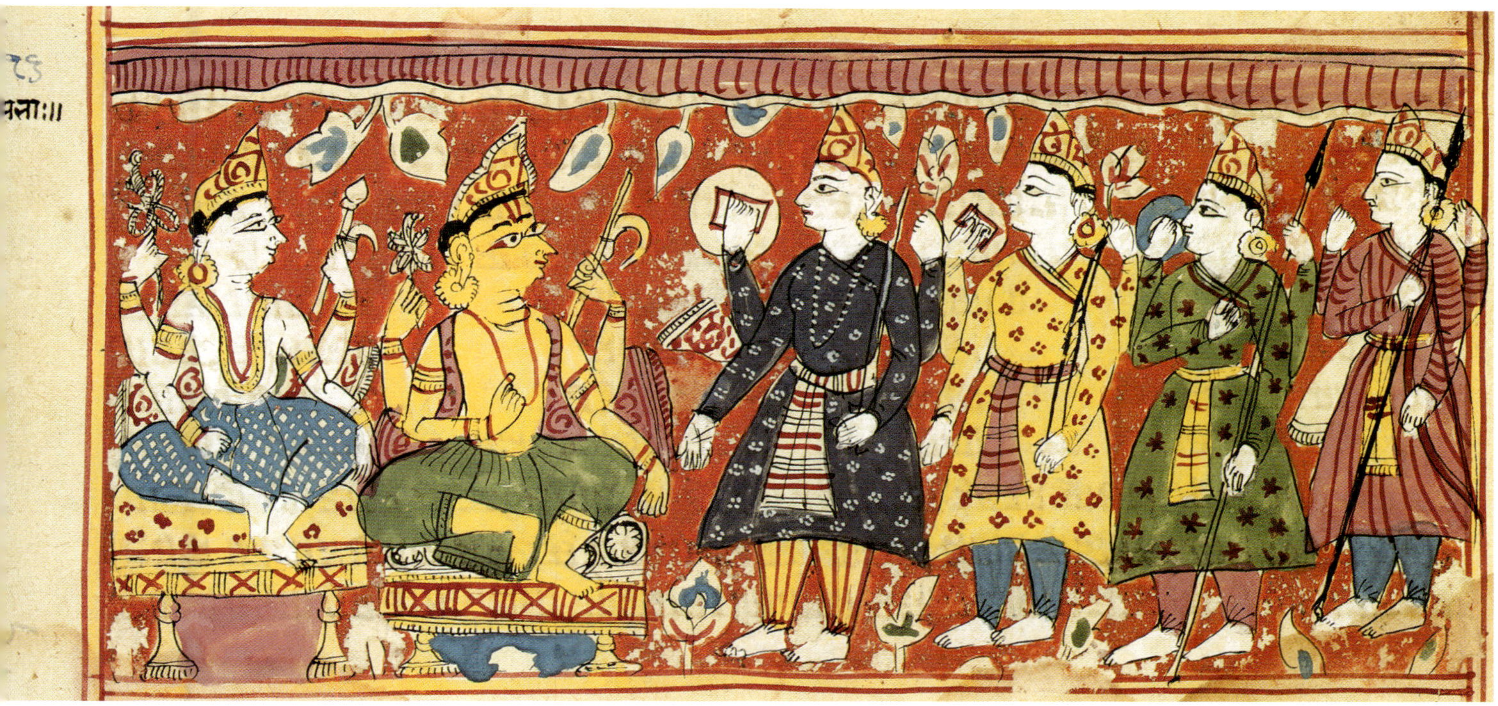

3 Greeting of a Digambara Jain Monk

Rajasthan, Amber, 1725–50
Opaque watercolor on paper
Sheet: 10 ¾ x 16 ⅝ in. (27.3 x 42.2 cm)
Image: 9 ¼ x 15 in. (23.5 x 38.1 cm)
Promised gift of Ramesh and Urmil Kapoor

Jain monks are often invited by the members of a community to come and spend the rainy season with them. In earlier times an elaborate formal letter in the form of a scroll with illustrations was dispatched; when the pontiff arrived at the outskirts, an advance party received him. That reception is the subject matter of this painting.

Against a green background interrupted by plants with leafy branches, a naked Jina of the Digambara (sky-clad) order approaches from the left. He is greeted by five noblemen standing in devotional attitude, three of them with material offerings. Behind stands a caparisoned white stallion with a groom and an elephant.

Several other leaves from the same series, distinguished by the orange border with meandering vines, are in various public collections (see Pal 1994, no. 107a and p. 241 for other citations). The series may have been painted in Amber, the old capital of the similarly named state in Rajasthan. Clearly, the series was commissioned by a follower of the Digambara order. In deference to the simplicity of the Digambara teacher, who is yellow-complected and proportionately larger than the lay figures, the representation bears an austere dignity, as both men and animals express awed reverence.

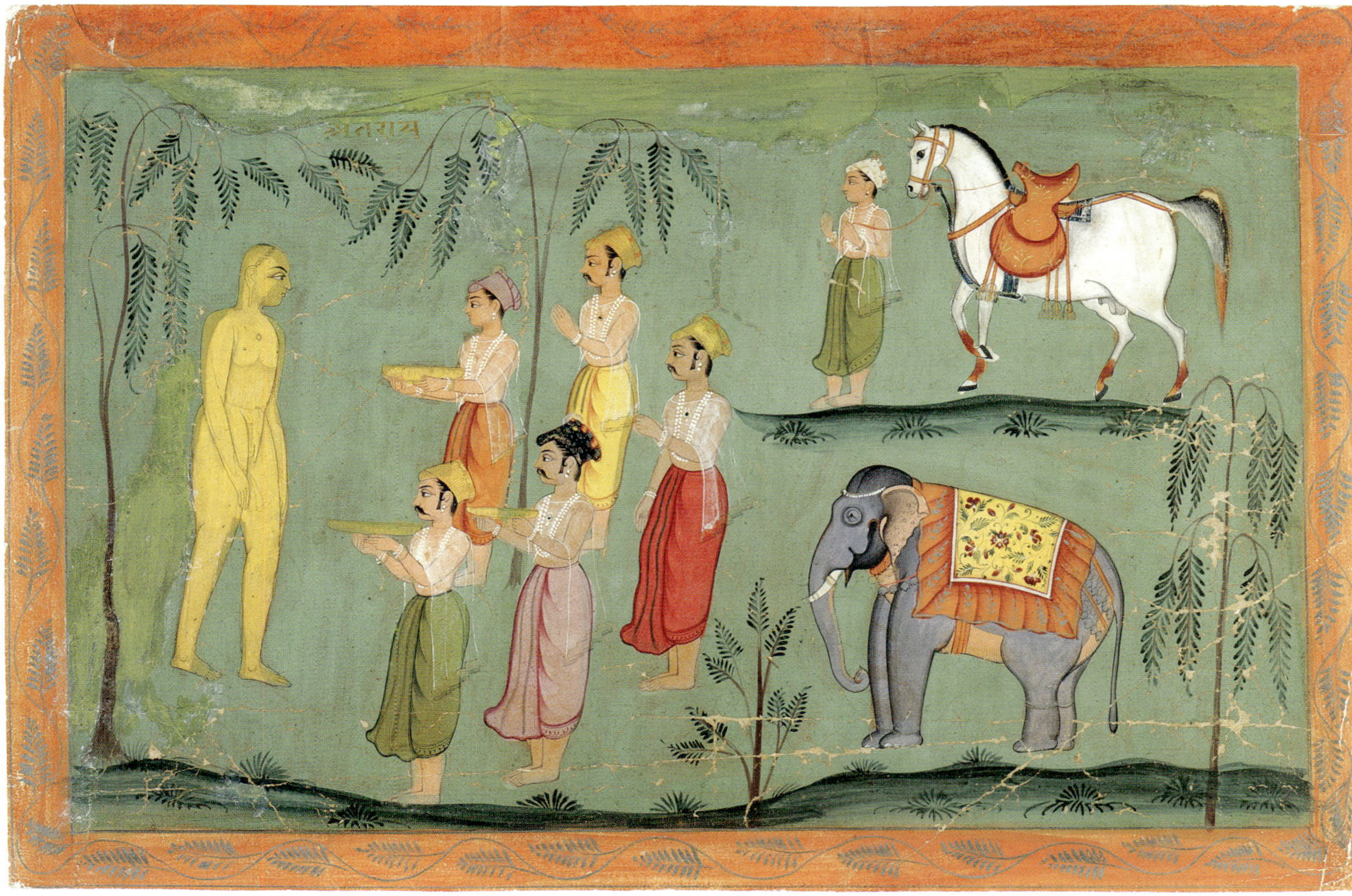

Shaiva Themes

4 Androgynous Form of Shiva and Parvati

Rajasthan, Bundi, c. 1700–1750
Opaque watercolor on paper
Sheet: 9 x 6 ¼ in. (22.9 x 15.9 cm)
Image: 8 ¼ x 5 ½ in. (21 x 14 cm)
Lent by Ramesh and Urmil Kapoor

When Shiva and his spouse Parvati are portrayed sharing one body, as in this beautiful picture, the form is known in Sanskrit as *ardhanarisvara*, or the lord whose half is woman. This form has remained popular with Indian artists and poets since the early centuries of the Common Era. One of the most graceful laudatory verses emphasizing the unity of the two deities was composed by the poet Kalidasa (c. 400 C.E.):

> *God Shiva and his mountain bride,*
> *Like word and meaning unified,*
> *The world's great parents, I beseech*
> *To join fit meaning to my speech.*
> (Ryder 1933, p. 123)

Beside a body of water with blooming lotuses, the conjoint deity sits on a tiger skin spread over mauve rock formations, which likely represent Lake Manasarovar and Mt. Kailash in Tibet, where the holy family resides. Shiva's bull sits on his right, but Parvati's mount—the lion—has been omitted. Because of Parvati's proximity, Shiva restrains his snake by grasping it in his hand and forcing it to look away at the trident, which has a small kettledrum attached to it. Both the serpent and the musical instrument are attributes of Shiva. Instead of having a white complexion, he is painted blue and bearded like an ascetic, with a cone-shaped chignon. Within the top aperture of the chignon is the head of the river goddess Ganga, who lodged in it temporarily before descending from heaven to earth. Parvati has a pink complexion and wears a short blouse (*choli*).

While the physiognomies and the slim, tall proportions of the two halves are not typical of Bundi pictures, the face of Ganga is characteristic. The shape of the rocks and the mauve color are also encountered in contemporaneous Rajasthani pictures, as is the manner of painting animals in two colors. The upper half of the bull's body is white, while the lower half is red. The painting once belonged to the Bundi court collection, as is clear from a rubber stamp on the back, the librarian's notations and the writing partially exposed below the top sheet.

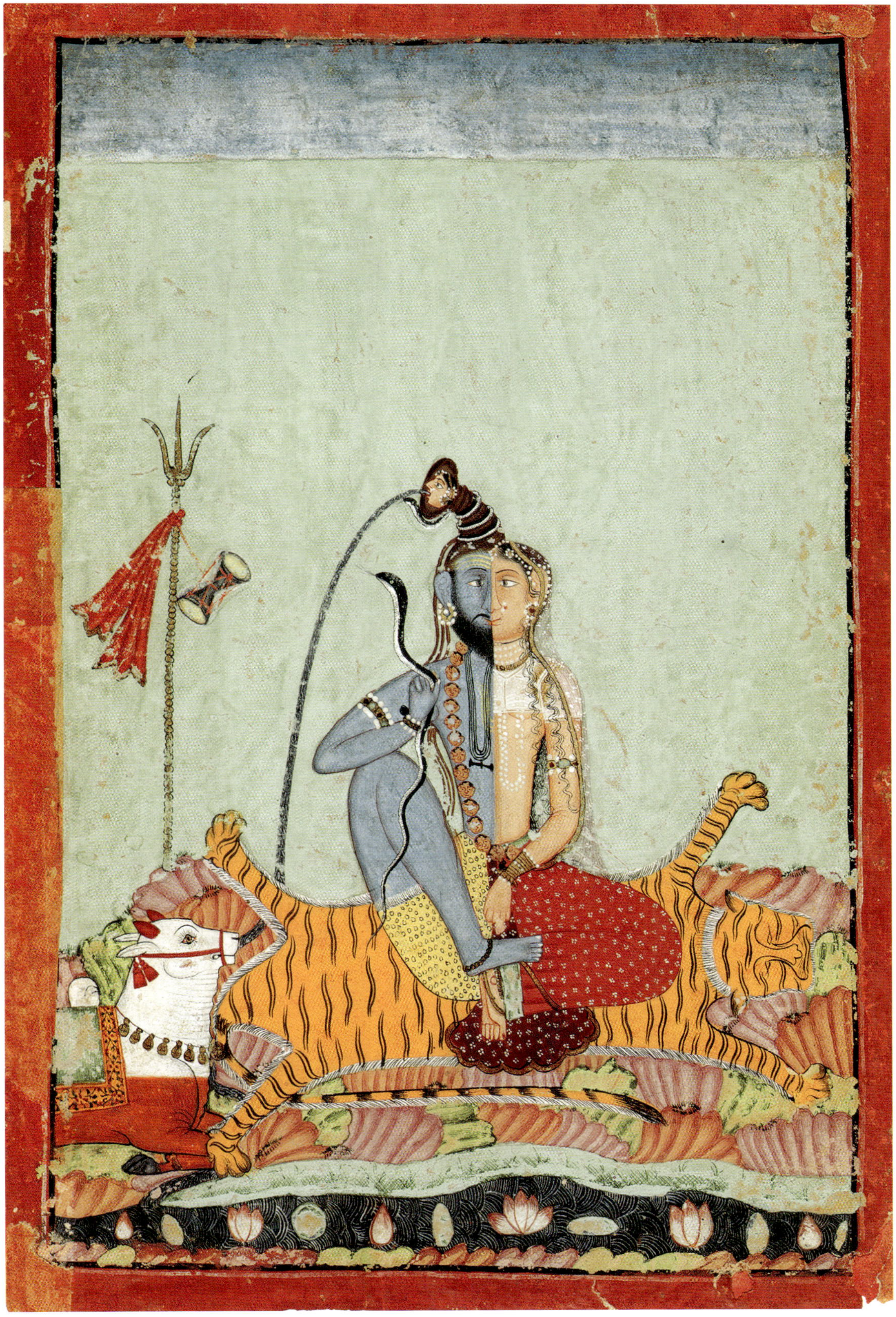

5 Shiva and Parvati with Companions

Himachal Pradesh, Kangra workshop, 1800–1825
Opaque watercolor on paper
Sheet: 11 ¾ x 9 1/16 in. (29.9 x 23 cm)
Image: 9 ¼ x 7 ¾ in. (23.5 x 19.7 cm)
Lent by Ramesh and Urmil Kapoor

A beautiful Sanskrit couplet written in the Devanagari script on the back of this picture informs us that Shiva is performing the obligatory evening rite (*sandhya*) at dusk. As Parvati pours water into his outstretched hands, Shiva is so enchanted by the beauty of her face that he doesn't realize the snake wrapped around his wrist is drinking the water. Seeing his plight, Vijaya, one of Parvati's maids, begins to laugh (see Appendix).

The unnamed artist has followed the verse only to a degree, for he has not shown Parvati pouring the water, though Shiva stands in front with proffered hands. Rather, he has portrayed her as a typical "expectant heroine" standing on higher ground and holding the branch of a tree with her right hand (see Ohri and Craven 1998, p. 120, fig. 7). The somewhat aloof Shiva seems to be engaged in adoring the goddess. However, the river, Shiva's gesture and the three conversing maids in the lower-right corner are clear allusions to the narrative intent of the verse. Why the artist took the liberty he did in changing Parvati's role remains unclear, unless the picture belonged to a rhetorical series.

Stylistically this painting is almost certainly from the workshop of Phurku of Kangra [42]. The youthful Shiva is identified here only by the sliver of a crescent moon near his forehead, seen in a picture in the Goenka collection in India ascribed to Phurku's workshop by Goswamy and Bhatia (1999, no. 219). The proportions of the figures, the decorative exuberance of the flowering plants and trees, the smooth tonality of the vivid yellows and oranges, the subtle variations of the greens and the orange glow of the setting sun on the curving horizon under the streaked blue canopy are features that can be associated with works ascribed to Phurku's workshop. While this painting is a few centimeters smaller than the Goenka picture, both have the same blue border with white flowers.

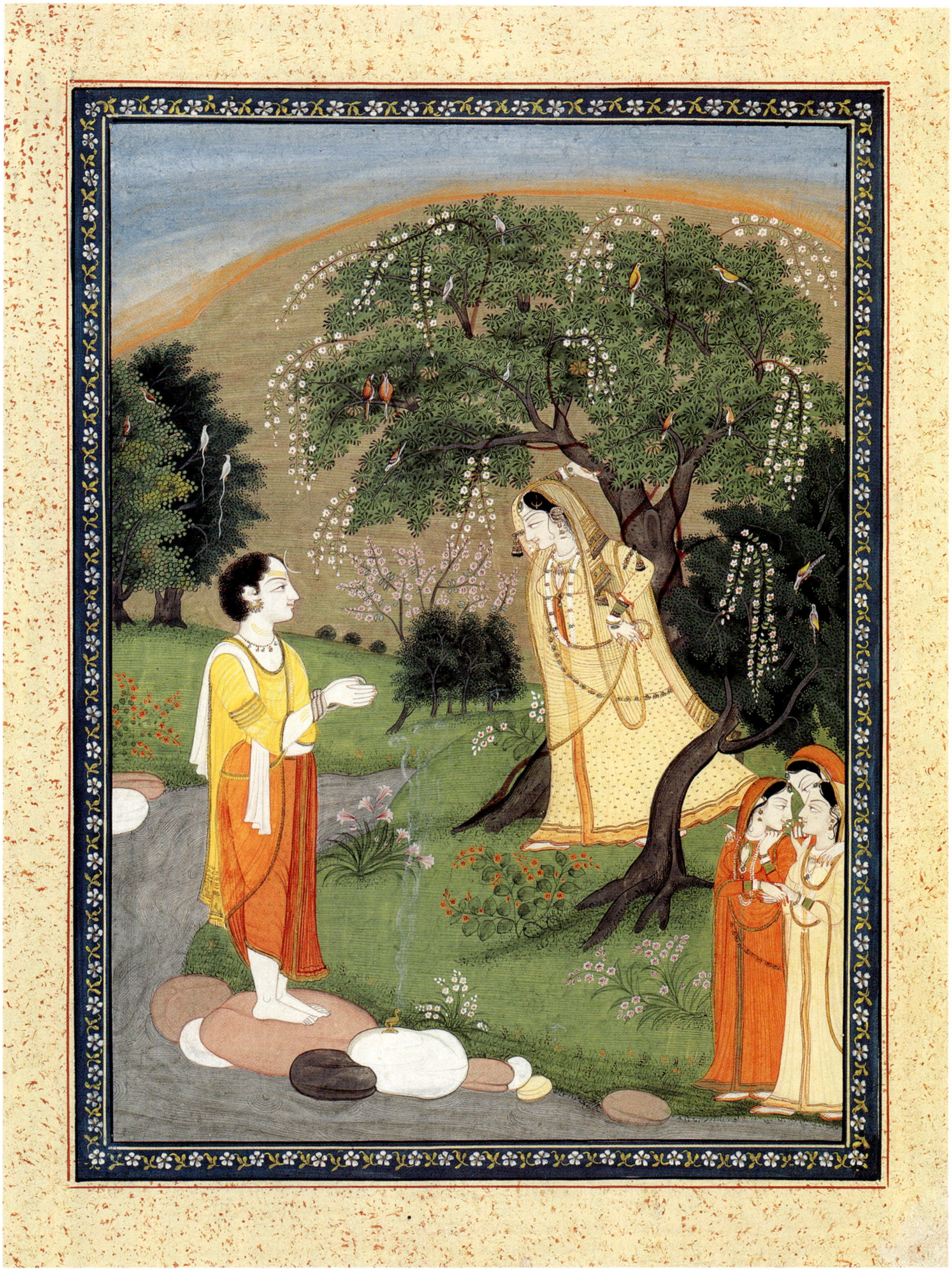

6 An Illustration from a *Kiratarjuniya* Series: Arjuna's Contest with Shiva

Himachal Pradesh, Kangra workshop, 1800–1825
Opaque watercolor on paper
Sheet: 15 ⅛ x 20 ½ in. (38.4 x 52.1 cm)
Image: 13 ⅛ x 18 ⅛ in. (33.3 x 46 cm)
Lent by Ramesh and Urmil Kapoor

Almost twice the size of an average Pahari painting, this illustration of the poem *Kiratarjuniya* belongs to a series (Archer 1973, vol. 1, pp. 304–5) that was probably commissioned by Raja Sansar Chand (r. 1775–1823) of Kangra. The series was noted by William Moorcraft, who was a guest of the ruler in 1820. Sansar Chand was a keen patron of painting who employed several artists, including Phurku (see Goswamy and Fischer 1992, pp. 368–72). However, the authors do not associate the *Kiratarjuniya* picture with Phurku, and in fact, the series has not received the attention it deserves.

Kiratarjuniya is a narrative poem by the great Sanskrit poet Bharavi (5th–6th century), who borrowed the subject from the epic *Mahabharata*. Its theme is of Arjuna's attempt through austerities to please the gods and acquire their potent weapons. He was specifically after a lethal weapon called the *pasupata*; it belonged to Shiva, who was known as Pasupati (Lord of Animals). Ultimately Arjuna was able to defeat Shiva, who appeared in the guise of a hunter (*kirata*) to claim the boar, which happened to be a demon.

The larger-than-life animal appears on the left while Arjuna, dressed as a warrior, sits in meditation, counting his beads in a bag like a pious Vaishnava. The axially placed figure behind the rocks and set off by a tree is Shiva in the attire of a *kirata*. His larger retinue includes other hunting companions, ascetics and attendants. The gods watch the scene from the clouds. The unknown master responsible for this picture was not only adept in introducing a cosmic element to the composition but was also a good animal painter (see Archer 1973, vol. 2, pl. 225, no. 61). On the same plate, Archer includes a picture of the elephant Gajendra (no. 58), which may be the work of the same artist. The soft palette and bucolic tranquility of the composition echo the aesthetic of the Manaku-Nainsukh family of artists rather than Phurku.

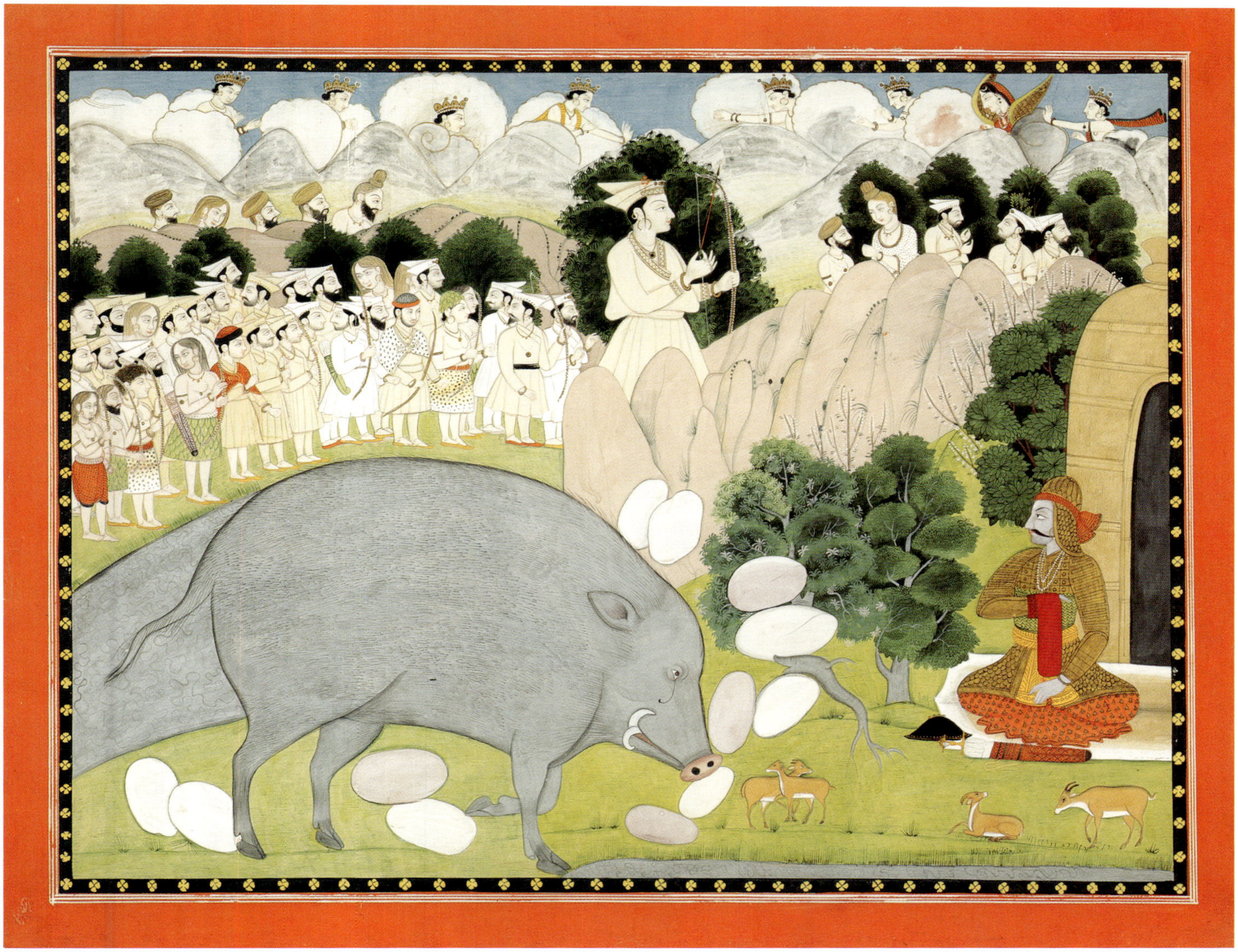

7 Folio from the *Devimahatmya*:
[a] Vishnu with Madhu and Kaitabha
[b] Vishnu Fights with Madhu or Kaitabha

Rajasthan, Bikaner, eighteenth century
Opaque watercolor on paper
Sheet: 5 x 9 in. (12.7 x 22.9 cm)
Image: 4 5/8 x 3 1/8 in. (11.8 x 7.9 cm)
Gift of Ramesh and Urmil Kapoor; P.2000.9.6

The incomplete texts on both sides of the folio are from the first chapter of the *Devimahatmya*. The verses, however, are not sequentially numbered and seem to be jumbled. Nevertheless, the illustrations do relate to the text, and their subjects are identified by cryptic labels along the margins. Both pictures depict the incident in which two titans called Madhu and Kaitabha emerged from Vishnu's ears and attempted to kill Brahma, who had just been born from Vishnu's navel.

In illustration [b], Vishnu and one of the two titans are engaged in hand-to-hand combat (*bahuyuddha*) on the edge of the ocean. Curiously, the titan uses his bare arms, though Vishnu is about to strike him with his club. Vishnu's simultaneous combat with the two titans—though only one is portrayed here—is said to have continued for five thousand years. Thereafter, the undefeated and deluded titans asked the god to kill them on a spot not covered by water (which did in fact cover the entire earth). However, when the colossal Vishnu stood above the waterline, it only reached his knees; thus, he was able to place the titans on his dry thighs and kill them. The unknown artist has given us a tame version, with a hieratic, four-armed deity seated on a lotus as the two titans sit on the water like acolytes. Neither one has a weapon, though in the other picture the titan has two sheathed daggers.

Although the artist must have been familiar with the more pictorial style that prevailed in eighteenth-century Bikaner, clearly he was bound by the well-established illuminated manuscript tradition of times past. While adhering to the horizontal format of the manuscript, he also continued to employ the older narrative strategy and conceptualization of water. What is different is the theriomorphic representation of the titans, which was the preferred mode in the Islamic tradition.

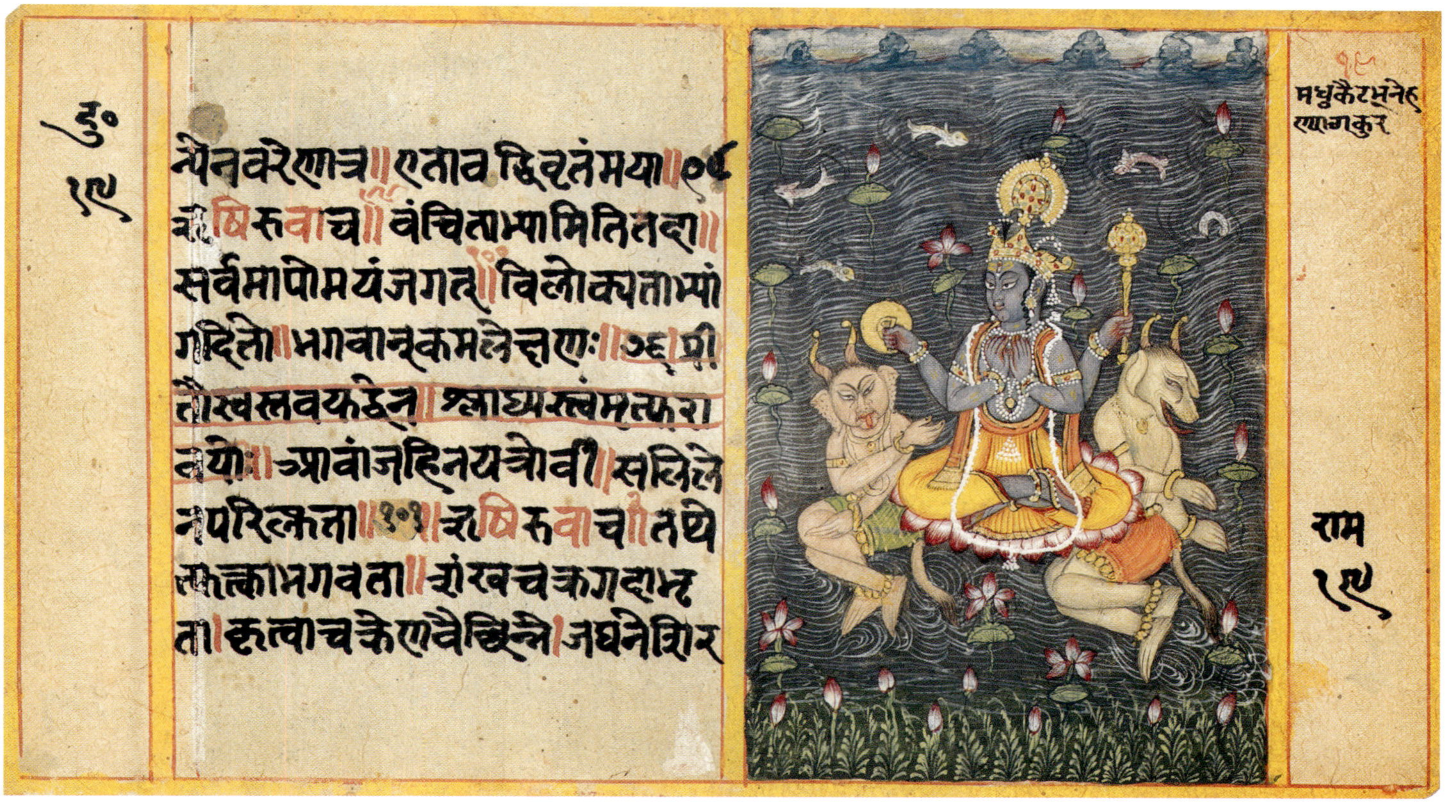

A

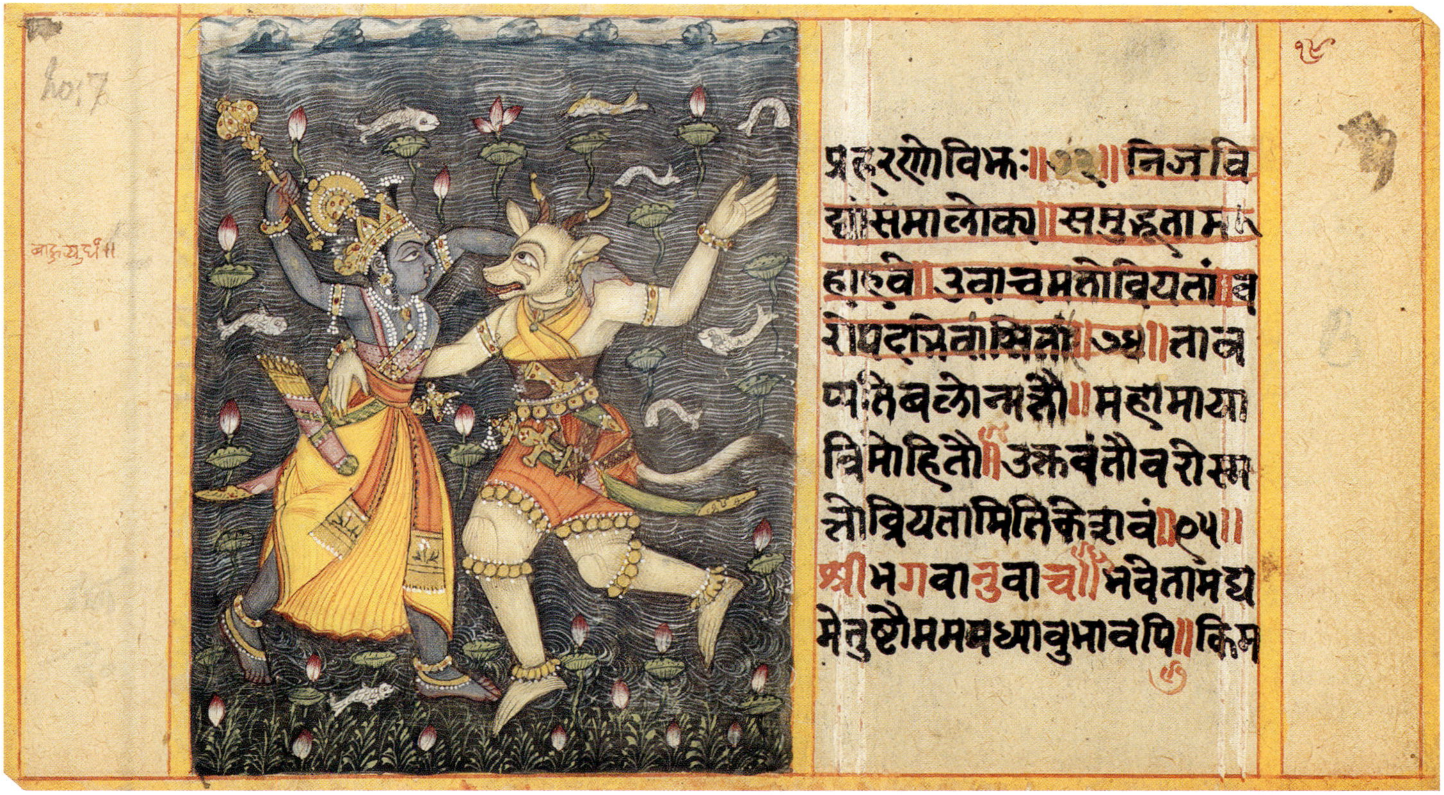

B

8 Titans Before Devi with a Proposal

Himachal Pradesh, Mandi workshop, c. 1725
Opaque watercolor on paper
Sheet: 8 ¼ x 11 ⅝ in. (21 x 29.5 cm)
Image: 6 ¾ x 10 ⅛ in. (17.1 x 25.7 cm)
Promised gift of Ramesh and Urmil Kapoor

In this scene from the *Devimahatmya*, two of the companions of the titan Mahisha espy the Devi in her human guise as a beautiful woman and offer her a proposal of marriage from their master. Demurely, she tells them that she will certainly wed the titan ruler if he can defeat her in battle. Whether the picture belonged to a series illustrating the entire *Devimahatmya* or was an isolated composition remains uncertain. The latter alternative seems more probable, as there is no text on the back.

This is a typical example of the bold but minimalist style used by Mandi workshops to produce pictures of the Devi and of her various exploits and manifestations. The background is plain and monochromatic—a peachy shade—against which the white molded mountain and the two obsequious titans are represented, equal in scale, doubtless to emphasize their colossal sizes. By contrast, the Devi is a diminutive figure clad in a bright orange sari and seated appropriately on a lotus atop the mountain. Behind her is a realistically rendered tiger that lazily turns his head to look at the strangers. In the hills, the goddess's animal mount is often the tiger, rather than the lion described in the text. The Hindustani word *sher* is often used for both animals. Mandi pictures have a folksy character and simple compositions with bold figures that add to their visual appeal. ঌ

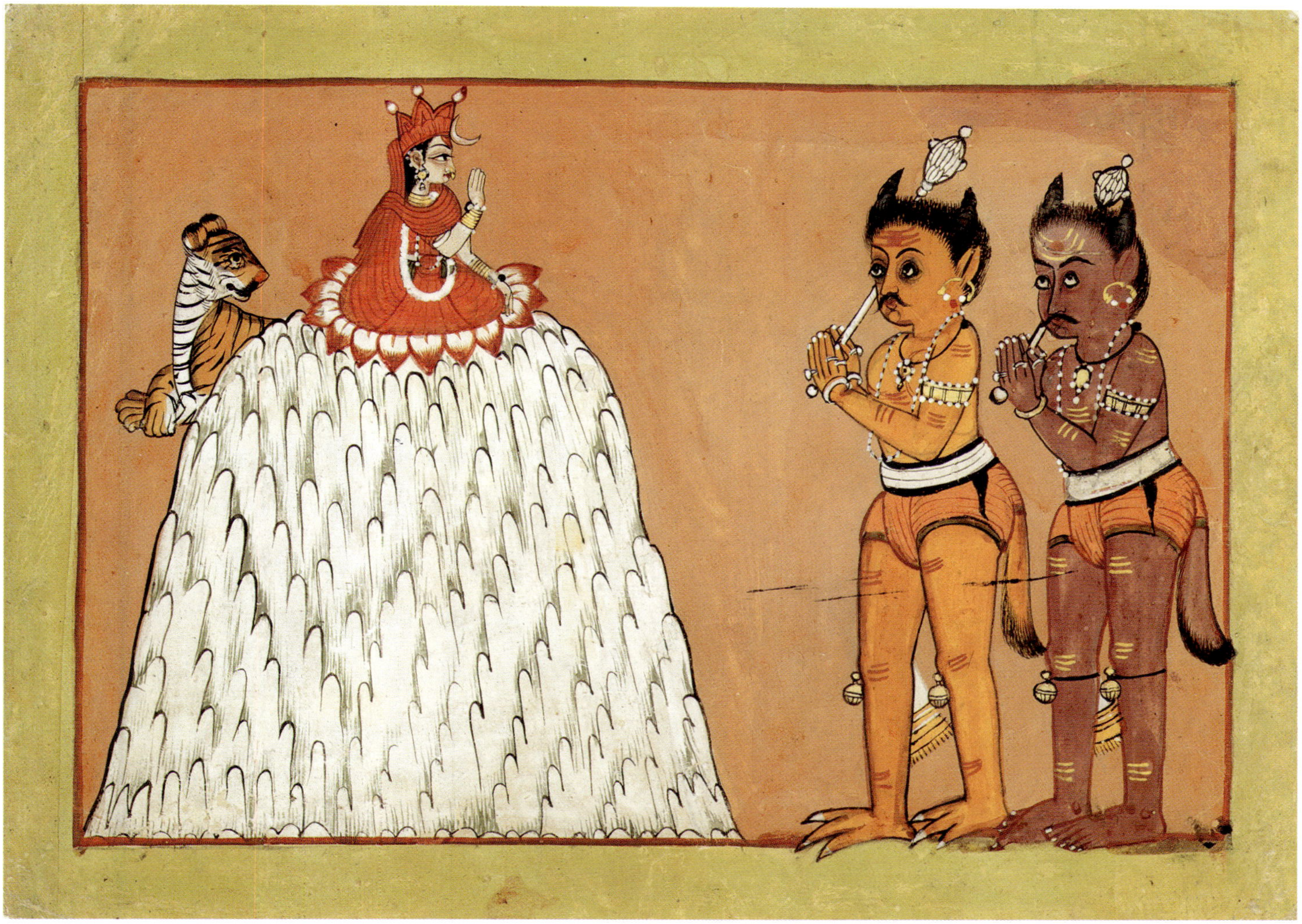

9 [A] Devi Fighting Raktavija
Himachal Pradesh, Guler workshop, 1775–1800
[B] The Cutting of Surpanakha's Nose
Uttaranchal, Garhwal workshop, c. 1800

Ink and opaque watercolor on paper
Sheet: 11 5/8 x 8 1/8 in. (29.5 x 20.6 cm)
Gift of Ramesh and Urmil Kapoor; P.2003.2.11

One of the two drawings on this double-sided folio illustrates the Devi's battle with the demon Raktavija [A]. Whether it was meant to belong to a series of pictures illustrating the *Devimahatmya* cannot be ascertained. What is certain is that the composition is a mirror image of a finished painting of the same subject rendered in 1781 in a Guler workshop (see Aijazuddin 1977, pl. 48, fig. 41 (xx)). A third example, also a drawing, is closer to the 1781 picture than to this one (see Pal 1978, no. 71). Raktavija was a very special titan, as each drop of his blood transformed into a full-grown demon when it touched the ground. The goddess recruited the help of Kali, who extended her inordinately long tongue to lap up the drops of blood. In this graphic representation of the episode, the artist has included Shiva as well as some of the Mother goddesses in Durga's train, who can be recognized by the animals they ride.

The drawing on the reverse depicts a touching story from the epic *Ramayana* [B]. During the exile in the forest, a demoness named Surpanakha came to seduce Rama. She was chastised by Rama's sibling Lakshmana, who cut her nose off and sent her packing. The incident is depicted here in three parts: in the middle ground Surpanakha approaches Rama and his wife Sita seated in a hut, in the right foreground Lakshmana cuts her nose off and in the left corner a disconsolate Surpanakha beats a hasty retreat.

There can be little doubt that the *Devimahatmya* drawing [A] is from the same Guler workshop where the 1781 series was painted. The *Ramayana* drawing [B], with some color notations, reveals stylistic features generally ascribed to Garhwal, now in Uttaranchal. The presence of a Guler drawing in Garhwal is not surprising. Pradyuman Shah (r. 1785–1804) married a Guler princess, and Guler artists could easily have moved to Garhwal. Likely, a later artist in the family was responsible for reusing the sheet with the *Devimahatmya* sketch for the *Ramayana* illustration.

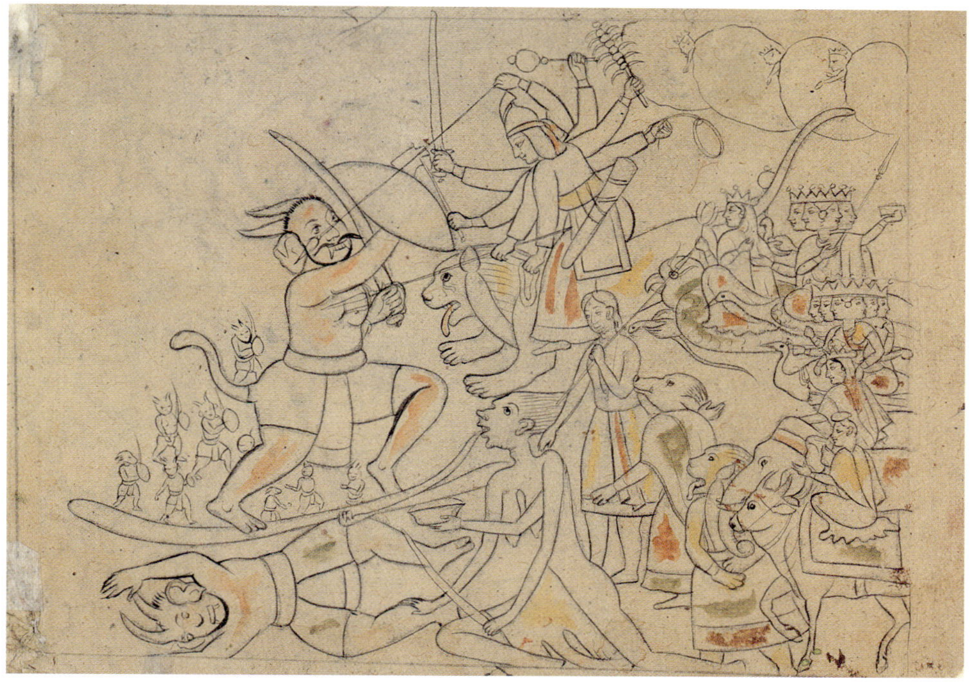
A

B
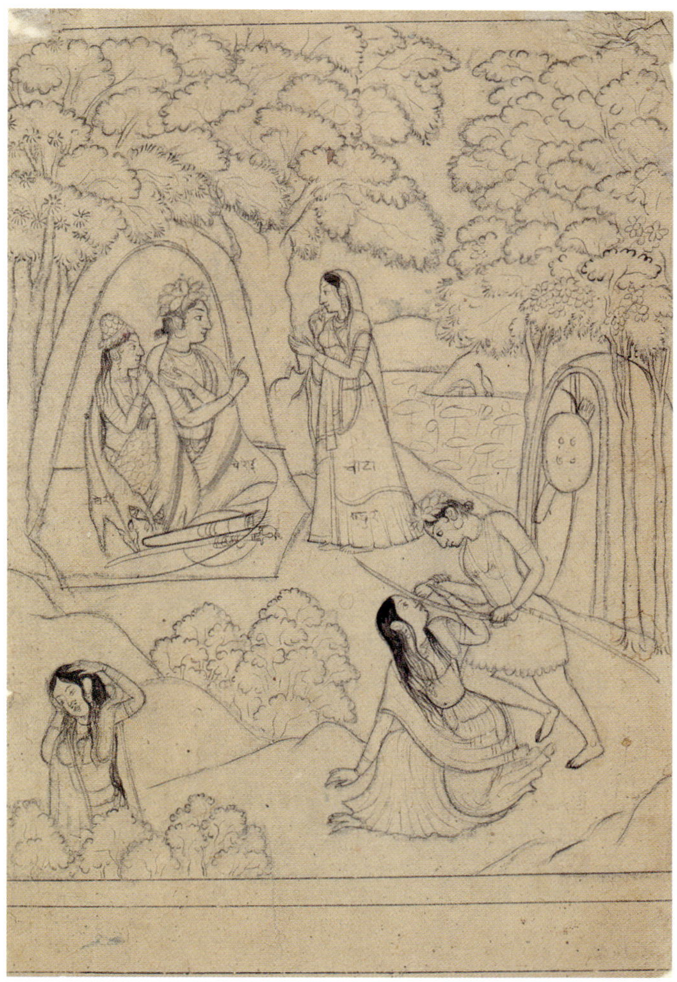

10 Illustration from a *Devimahatmya* Series: Durga Engages the Buffalo Titan

Himachal Pradesh, Guler workshop, c. 1825
Opaque watercolor on paper
Sheet: 9 7/8 x 13 in. (25.1 x 33.0 cm)
Image: 7 3/8 x 10 1/2 in. (18.7 x 26.7 cm)
Promised gift of Ramesh and Urmil Kapoor

The final combat between Durga on her lion and the titan in the form of a gigantic buffalo takes place beside a river. With his horns, the charging animal has aimed some boulders at her, but she intercepts them with arrows. Then she quaffs some mead from a golden cup and with a loud battle cry, lunges her spear and trident into the titan. Her face betrays no anger or hatred, but the swirling clouds in the sky, though decorative, contribute to the composition's menacing mood.

The picture is almost identical to the 1781 version in the Lahore Museum (Aijazuddin 1977, pl. 43, fig. 41 (viii)) and a drawing in the Museum of Fine Arts, Boston (Coomaraswamy 1926, pl. 129, no. 183). Clearly the artist responsible for the Kapoor picture had a drawing or pounce available and used it to render his own version. Pouncing is a method of transferring the outline of a drawing onto another surface. Holes are pricked along the lines of a drawing and a fine powder is forced through the holes onto another flat surface below. This series, a popular subject with devotees of the Goddess, was likely painted by either Nainsukh himself or someone in his workshop early in the eighteenth century (see Goswamy and Bhatia 1999, no. 191). To meet popular demand, pounces were probably prepared to enable successive generations of artists to continue the tradition. The Kapoor picture is one of the latest attempts known to date.

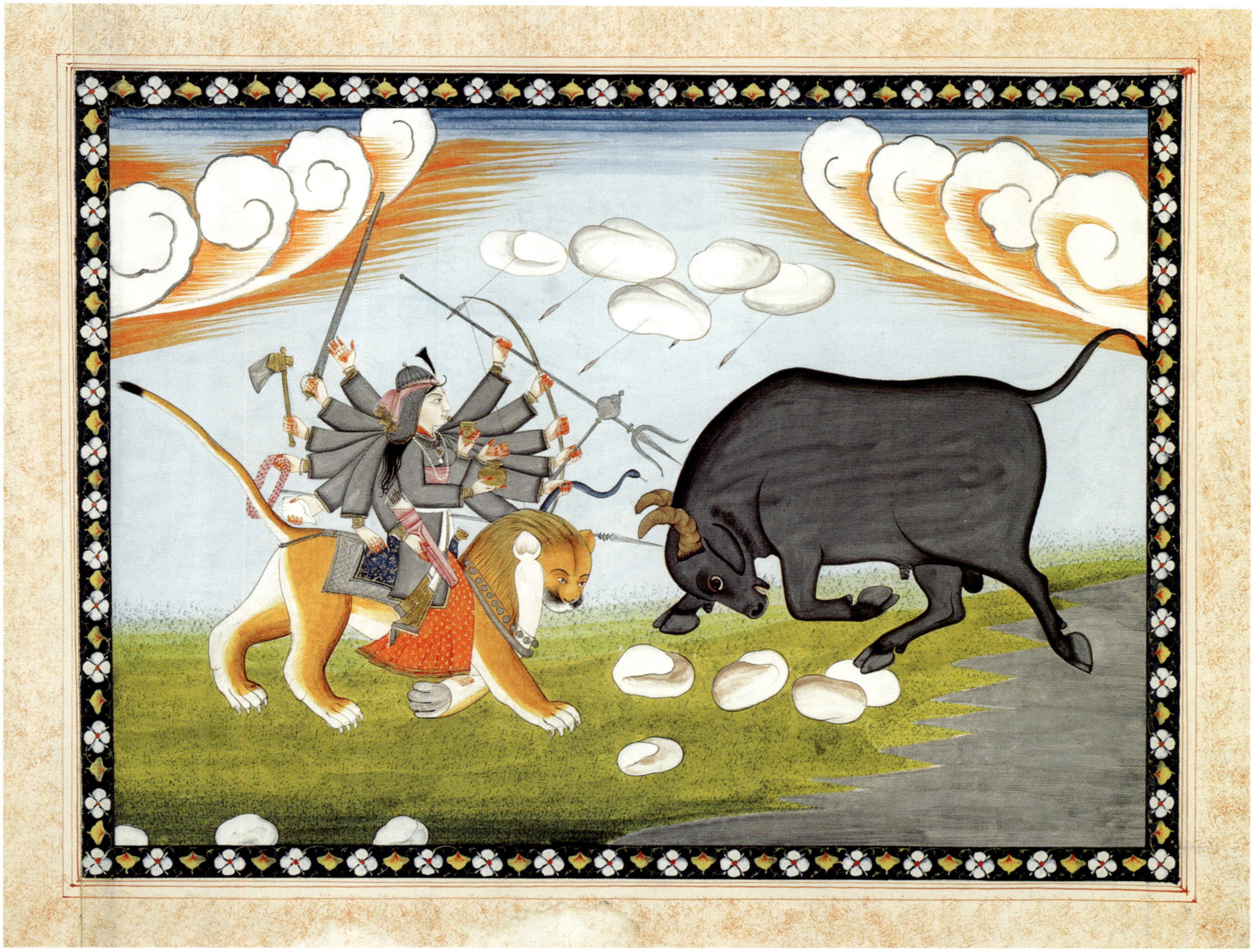

11 The Hindu Goddess Kali

Himachal Pradesh, Kangra workshop, c. 1800
Opaque watercolor on paper
Sheet: 10 5/8 x 8 3/8 in. (27 x 21.3 cm)
Image: 7 3/8 x 5 1/8 in. (18.7 x 13 cm)
Promised gift of Ramesh and Urmil Kapoor

Among the many manifestations of the great goddess Devi, a popular form in late eighteenth- and nineteenth-century Pahari paintings is that of Kali shown standing or dancing on Shiva. As she is regarded as one of the powerful Tantric divinities known collectively as the Dasamahavidya, or Ten Great or Transcendent Knowledges, it is possible that this is one of a series. Archer (1973, vol. 2, pl. 331, fig. 12) illustrates a picture in which Raja Pratap Chand of Lambagraon is worshiping this particular form of the goddess. She is extremely popular among Bengali Hindus, who worship her annually on Diwali in autumn. She is also the patron deity of Calcutta (now Kolkata).

In this beautifully rendered picture within an oval frame, the dramatic event occurs in a cremation ground beside a river. As two jackals watch, the naked Shiva stretches out on a corpse placed on burning logs. Kali, wearing a necklace of severed heads and a girdle of severed hands of the evildoers she has killed during her rampage, steps stridently on Shiva's supine form, which stops her in her tracks. With her upper hands she holds a bleeding male head and a curved sword; the lower-right arm is outstretched while the corresponding left hand forms the gesture of reassurance. A tree seems to bend down before the goddess to greet her with floral garlands.

The picture is a fine example of the lyrical style that became the norm in Kangra workshops around the turn of the nineteenth century. The overall coloring, with the pastel-like shades of the boulders, the soothing, muted gray of the water, the green and yellow ground and the wispy white clouds in a blue sky, allows the viewer to better appreciate the aesthetic effect of the central composition, with its rising orange flames and billowing smoke that forms a screen, thereby adding a sense of mystery.

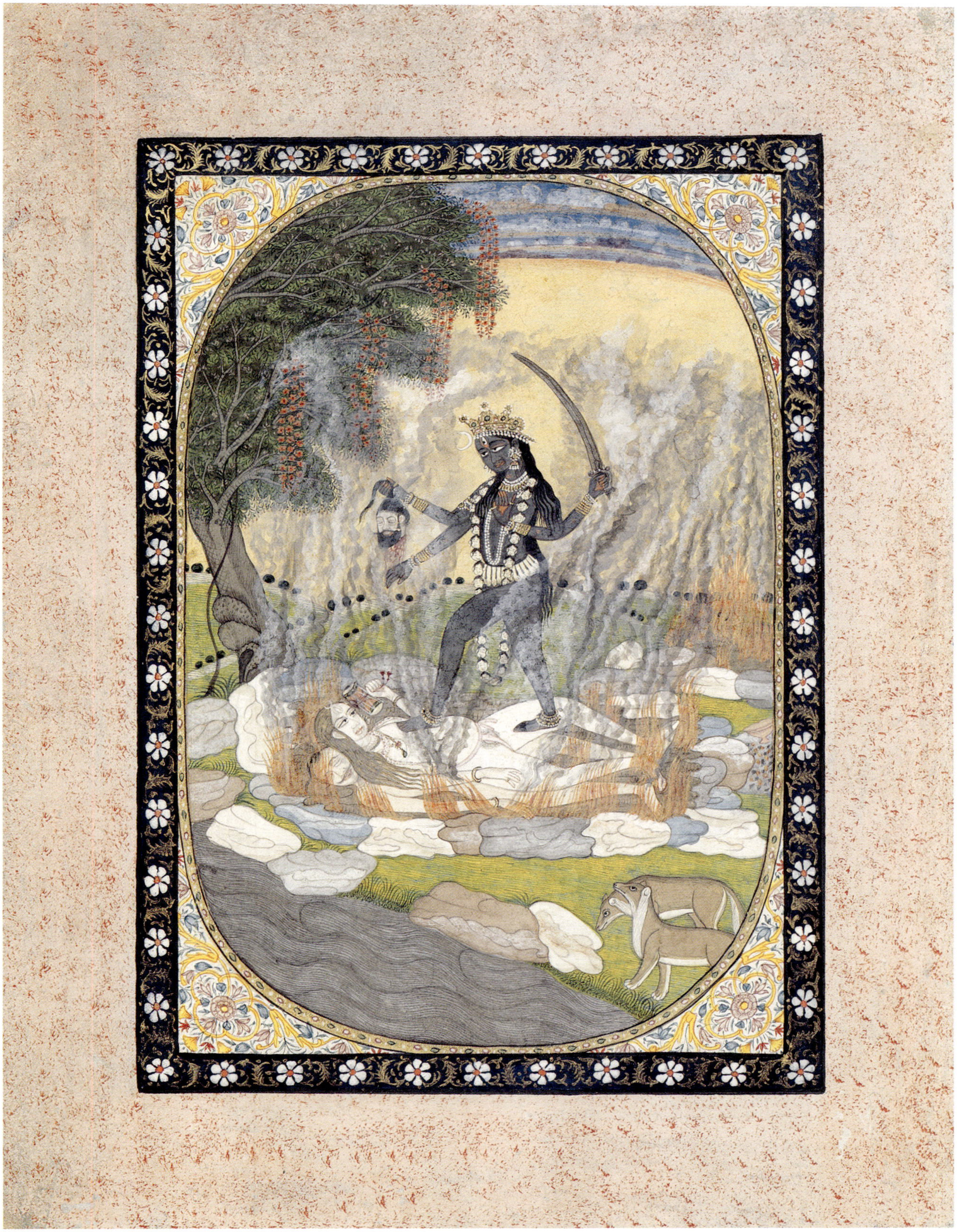

12 ADORATION OF GANESH

Himachal Pradesh, Kangra workshop, 1800–1825
Opaque watercolor on paper
Sheet: 10 ⅞ x 14 ½ in. (27.6 x 36.8 cm)
Image: 6 ¼ x 10 in. (15.9 x 25.4 cm)
Gift of Ramesh and Urmil Kapoor; P.2000.9.3

13 GANESH ENTHRONED

Rajasthan, Bikaner, dated 1854
Opaque watercolor on paper
Sheet: 8 ⅛ x 6 ¼ in. (20.6 x 15.9 cm)
Image: 6 ½ x 4 ¼ in. (16.5 x 10.8 cm)
Gift of Ramesh and Urmil Kapoor; P.1999.3.1

THE HINDU DEITY OF auspicious beginnings is represented quite differently in these two paintings, which served different purposes. The Bikaner picture [13] was a collective tribute from the guild of court artists known as Usta, and given to the ruler of the state (see Appendix). The other painting [12] may have served as a frontispiece for a narrative series, such as the story of *Rukmini-haran* [38–40], as a visual invocation (see Appendix).

In each picture the god sits on an enormous throne on a terrace. But while the frontally shown Bikaner Ganesh has an almost sad expression in his solitary existence, the Pahari painter has his deity interacting with a lady approaching with his favorite snack. His rodent mount is already nibbling away on the carpet. A second lady stands behind the throne fanning the rotund Ganesh with a standard (*morchal*), as is done with royalty. Except for his elephant head and red complexion, Ganesh could be a mortal, as he only has two arms. The left hand holds a bejeweled staff, and the right is extended toward the lady as if to accept the offerings.

There is no such narrative intent in the Bikaner painting [13], which is clearly an iconic representation, although with a touch of whimsy in the tilt of his head and the sadness of his expression. Only his elephant head is painted red; his human body is given a mauve complexion and his dhoti is yellow. Here his divinity is emphasized by the presence of four arms. With his upper-right hand he holds a golden club and in the corresponding left hand, an elephant goad. The lower-right hand grasps a rosary and the corresponding left hand supports a golden bowl with sweetmeats (*modaka*), which he scoops up with his trunk. The mouse, drawn like a bunny, looks eagerly at his *(continued on page 41)*

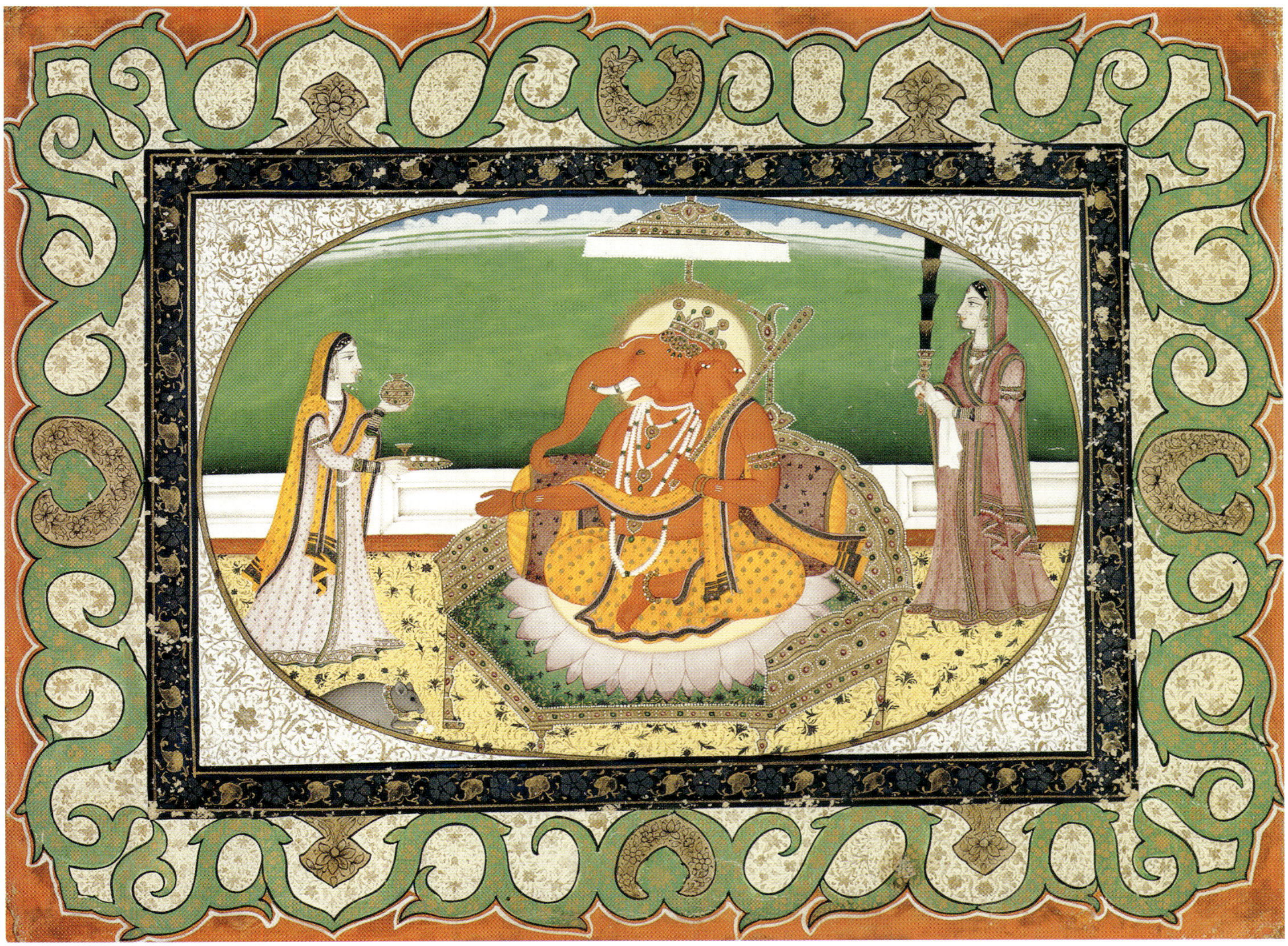

12

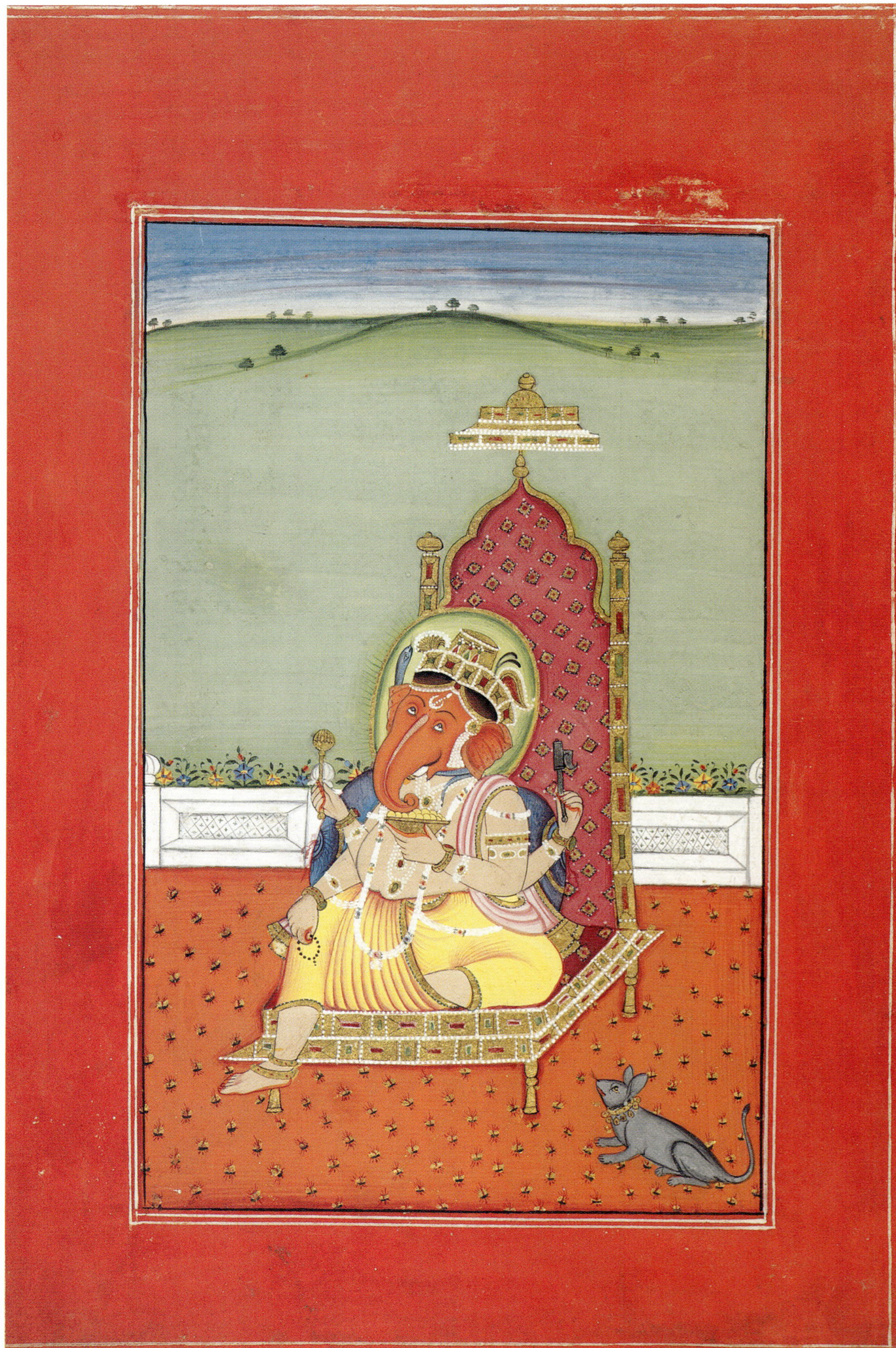

13

master, perhaps expecting a morsel. As has been observed by Naval Krishna (see Appendix), the Bikaner picture [13] reveals influences of the Jaipur school. By the mid–eighteenth century, artists from Jaipur were migrating to Bikaner and apparently overwhelming the local Usta artists.

The Pahari picture's [12] precise origin is less easy to determine. It is certainly a work of the first quarter of the nineteenth century and remarkably close to another version of the subject now in the Brooklyn Museum (Poster 1994, no. 220). The compositions are almost identical, but in the Brooklyn painting, Ganesh has four arms, a baldachin above him, trees on the sides and the background is not as verdant or well articulated. A distinct feature of the Kapoor picture is the bold green meandering vine pattern of the mount. A similarly elaborate mount, though with a different design, is visible in a picture in the Lahore Museum attributed to Mandi around 1820 (Aijazuddin 1977, pl. 84, no. 6). Another picture dated 1808 and by Sajnu (active 1790–1830) has a similar elaborate border (Goswamy and Fischer 1992, p. 316, fig. 110). Perhaps the Kapoor painting was painted at Mandi by an artist of the circle of Sajnu who was active between 1790 and 1830.

Vaishnava Themes

14 [A] The Fish (Matsya) Incarnation of Vishnu, c. 1775
[B] An Unidentified Scene, eighteenth century

Himachal Pradesh, Mandi workshop
Opaque watercolor on paper
Sheet: 8 ¾ x 11 in. (22.2 x 27.9 cm)
Image: 7 ½ x 9 ½ in. (19.1 x 24.1 cm)
Gift of Ramesh and Urmil Kapoor; P.1999.3.4

The Fish avatar, or Matsyavatara, is the first of the ten special incarnations of Vishnu. In the story he appeared as a giant fish to destroy the titan who had stolen the Hindu sacred texts known as the Vedas and then disappeared under the ocean. In this simple but dramatic composition, the fish leaps like a giant whale out of the water, disgorging Vishnu. Using his club like a magic wand, Vishnu subdues the titan, who has horns on his head, matching fangs and a lower body that seems to imitate a conch shell. The four figures in the devotional attitude likely represent the four Vedas personified.

The composition is similar to another version of the subject in Zürich (Boner et al 1994, no. 571), which is simply described as a Pahari picture of 1850/75. The Kapoor painting was, however, rendered much earlier in a manner that combines the boldness of drawing, the compositional vigor and the rustic charm of the Mandi style with the subtlety and refinement of the Guler mode of the second half of the eighteenth century. This is particularly true of the treatment of the swirling water, which in the more typical and earlier Mandi pictures is drawn in a basket pattern (see Aijazuddin 1977, pl. 82, 1 (i) and Poster 1994, no. 239). The figural forms of the Kapoor picture are based on Guler/Kangra models rather than on the earlier Mandi types.

On the reverse [B] is a folkish sketch of a scene with celestials that has yet to be identified. According to V. C. Ohri (personal communication, 2002) the inscription in Takri script is unintelligible. Ohri further notes that the subject matter of the picture seems to be based on a folk tale, most probably an episode from the story of Raja Bikramaditya. Several versions of Bikramaditya's story, differing in minor details, were popular in various areas of this hilly region until some decades ago. The picture is not related to any familiar puranic story or other work of literature.

The page is divided into two halves vertically. The right half again is divided into two unequal panels: the lower panel is adorned with columns of leaf patterns, while the upper portion is empty except for a damaged inscription on top. The composition in the other half is clearly a narrative with a temple at the head of a diagonal river. On one side are three winged males—two of them riding a ram and a horse and one walking. They are receiving directions from a wingless male figure standing near the temple. A human couple stands at the lower corner and watches a male dive into the river as a winged female floats on the surface and turns her head to look at the approaching riders. On the other bank, human heads and two snakes seem to emerge from the uneven ground amidst tufts of grass. Stylistically close pictures in fragmentary condition have been ascribed to an early-eighteenth-century Mandi workshop (Archer 1973, vol. 2, pl. 265, figs. 11–12).

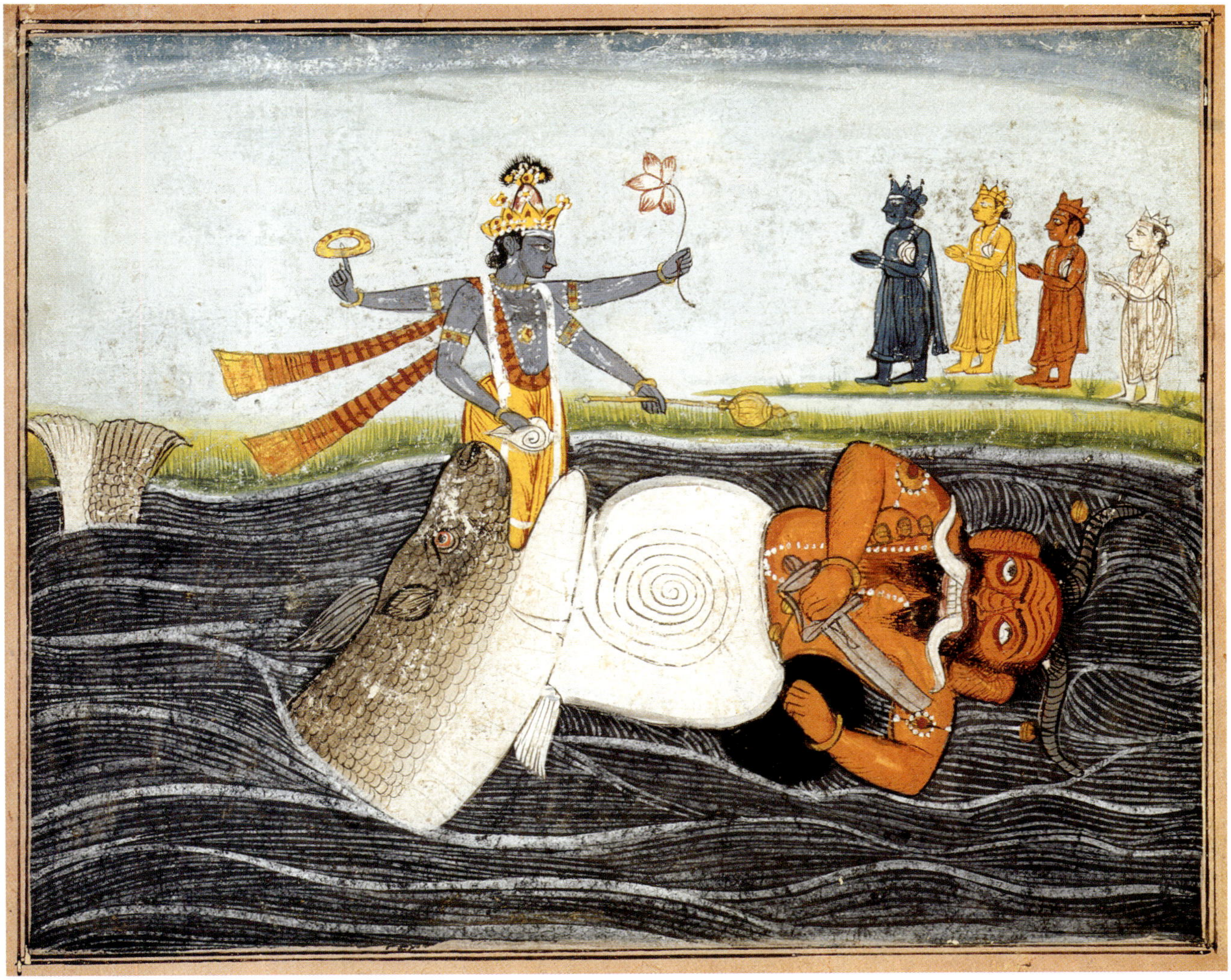

A

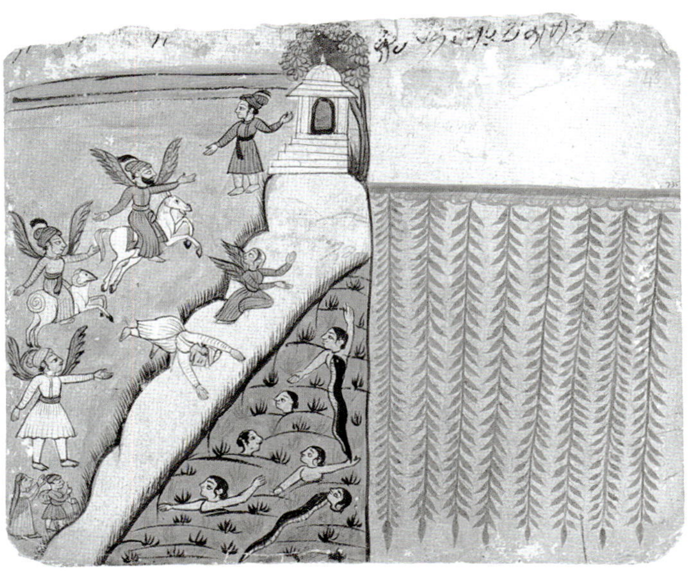

B

15 MAN-LION INCARNATION OF VISHNU

Rajasthan, Mewar, c. 1650
Opaque watercolor on paper
Sheet: 7 ½ x 9 ½ in. (19.1 x 24.1 cm)
Image: 6 ⅝ x 8 ⅝ in. (16.8 x 21.9 cm)
Promised gift of Ramesh and Urmil Kapoor

16 MAN-LION INCARNATION OF VISHNU

Jammu and Kashmir, Mankot or Bahu, c. 1700
Opaque watercolor on paper
Sheet: 7 ⅜ x 6 ½ in. (18.7 x 16.5 cm)
Image: 6 ⅛ x 5 ½ in. (15.6 x 14 cm)
Gift of Ramesh and Urmil Kapoor; P.2000.9.7

ALTHOUGH SEPARATED IN BOTH TIME and space, these two representations of the Narasimha avatar, or Man-lion incarnation of the god Vishnu, are interesting to compare. While the same basic iconography and compositional formula for the conflict are used in both, the two pictures are dramatically different.

Of the ten classic avatars of Vishnu, the Narasimha avatar is one of the most gruesome in expressing violence. In the story, Prahlada, the son of Hiranyakasipu, became a devotee of Vishnu despite his father's objections. One day, Prahlada claimed that Vishnu was everywhere, including the pillar beside them. Hiranyakasipu kicked the column, which split asunder and revealed Vishnu in the guise of half-man, half-lion. The god then threw Hiranyakasipu across his lap and killed him by tearing open his belly and pulling out his entrails. This is the moment portrayed in both pictures.

In [16], the unknown Pahari artist has provided an architectural setting for the drama by depicting a pavilion. The only witness is Prahlada, who stands in the devotional attitude. A significant variation is that Vishnu appears as a tiger instead of a lion; moreover, only his feet betray any human characteristics. In the Pahari tradition the tiger often substitutes for a lion, especially in Devi paintings [8]. The iconic centrality of the deity is emphasized by the radiating halo within the doorframe, reminiscent of the design of a mandala. A Devanagari inscription on the red border above reads "*narasigha avatar.*"

In the earlier Mewar picture [15], the theriomorphic form is portrayed with more subtlety. Except for his head and the long claw-like nails of his hands, nothing betrays his leonine form. Here Narasimha's divinity is indicated by the two additional arms that pull out entrails as the other two dig into the bloodied belly. Another significant variation is the animal head—perhaps a jackal—of Hiranyakasipu, following the Mughal mode of giving demons and titans animal heads. The mortal ruler's crown lays on the ground at Prahlada's feet, as he and a lady—perhaps his mother or Lakshmi, Vishnu's spouse—watch the gory scene. Two other crowned figures watch on the other *(continued on page 47)*

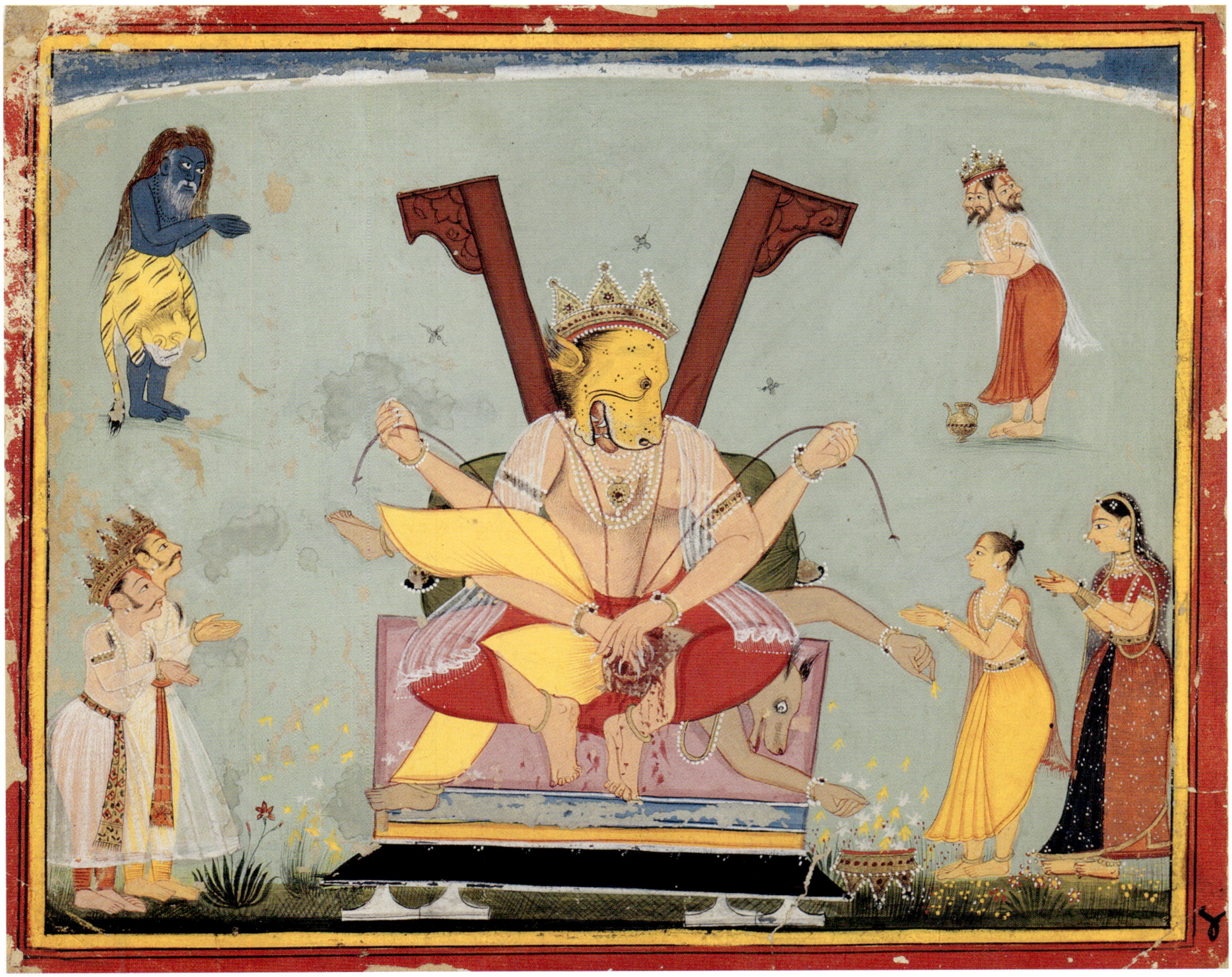

15

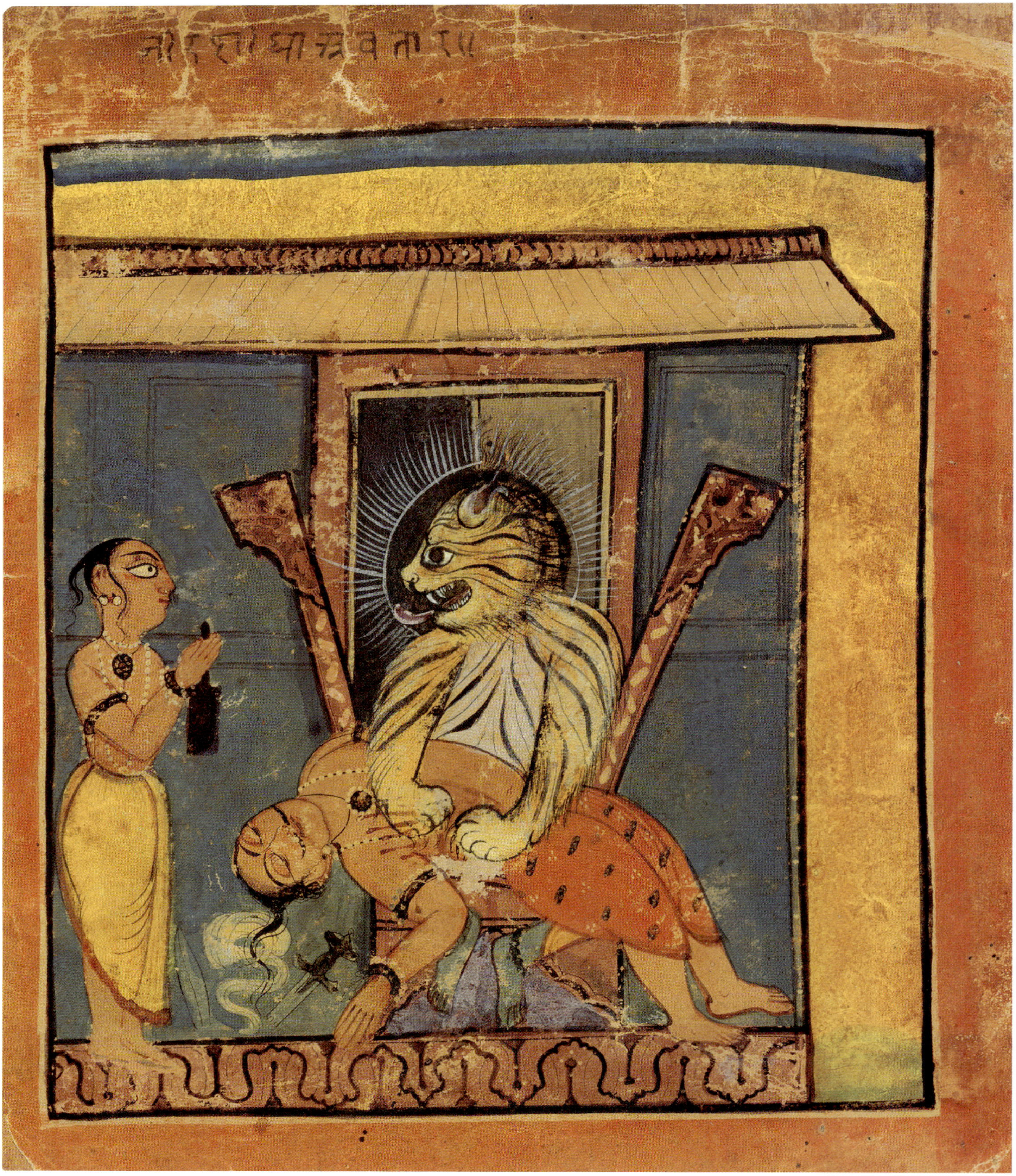

16

side. Sitting above are Brahma with his four heads and water pot, and the ascetic, vagabond Shiva with his tiger-skin garment.

On stylistic considerations, the Mewar picture can with some confidence be assigned to the workshop of the master Sahibdin (c. 1625–1660), who was the court artist certainly of Maharana Jagat Singh (r. 1628–52). In 1629 Sahibdin's workshop produced an illustrated *Gitagovinda*, a text that requires pictures of the ten avatars (see Topsfield 1981). However, the Narasimha in that manuscript is iconic and uninteresting compared to this dramatic depiction (Topsfield 1981, fig. 505).

The Pahari picture [16] is certainly rendered in the early Basohli style, but its exact place of origin remains uncertain. The closest work both compositionally and iconographically is another version in the Alice Boner collection in Zürich attributed to Mankot around 1700/25 (Boner et al 1994, tafel 14). There, too, Narasimha is a tiger rather than a lion; he has two arms and is actually seated within the split column. Likewise, Prahlada is the only witness. While the Kapoor painting is not as refined as the Boner example, it has a folkish spontaneity and unaffected charm. A noteworthy detail is the artist's manner of rendering Prahlada's individual eyelashes, which is generally not encountered in such pictures. An exception is a *Ragamala* painting attributed to a master of Bahu (Goswamy and Fischer 1992, no. 35), in which the lady's eyelashes are similarly delineated. Indeed, the figure of Prahlada is of the same type as seen in this *Ragamala.* Thus, either a Mankot or Bahu workshop could have produced this picture for an avatar series.

17 Parasurama Slaughters Kartyavirya

Himachal Pradesh, Chamba or Bilaspur workshop, 1775–1800
Opaque watercolor on paper
Sheet: 6 3⁄8 x 8 3⁄4 in. (16.2 x 22.2 cm)
Image: 5 7⁄8 x 8 1⁄4 in. (14.9 x 21 cm)
Promised gift of Ramesh and Urmil Kapoor

The greater part of the composition is occupied by the figures of the battle axe–wielding Parasurama and the multi-armed Kartyavirya. Parasurama was the son of the ascetic Jamadagni and his wife Renuka. Once when Renuka was alone in the hermitage, King Kartyavirya paid a visit and was suitably entertained by her. Upon his departure the king took away Surabhi, the cow of plenty. Parasurama gave chase and killed the king, as is portrayed here. Disturbed by the violence, the winged cow runs away in the upper-left corner of the picture while Renuka and Jamadagni sit and watch their heroic son. In other representations of the subject, Renuka is usually shown seated with Jamadagni's corpse. He was killed in revenge by the sons of Kartyavirya, who were in turn slaughtered by Parasurama. The unknown artist who painted this picture seems to have been particularly concerned about the proper chronological sequence of the story.

The picture probably belonged to an avatar series, for Parasurama is the sixth incarnation of Vishnu. Noteworthy is the fact that here, as in most Pahari paintings, he is invariably modeled on Krishna in terms of his skin color and dhoti. The basic composition of the two antagonists is first encountered in a picture from a Chamba workshop of around 1700 (Boner et al 1994, no. 278). There, too, the cow runs in the upper-left corner, but without wings. Wings do appear in two later pictures, one of which is ascribed to Chamba (Boner et al 1994, no. 309). The Kapoor picture was certainly painted by an artist who was familiar with earlier works attributed to Chamba, where avatar series were particularly popular in the eighteenth century.

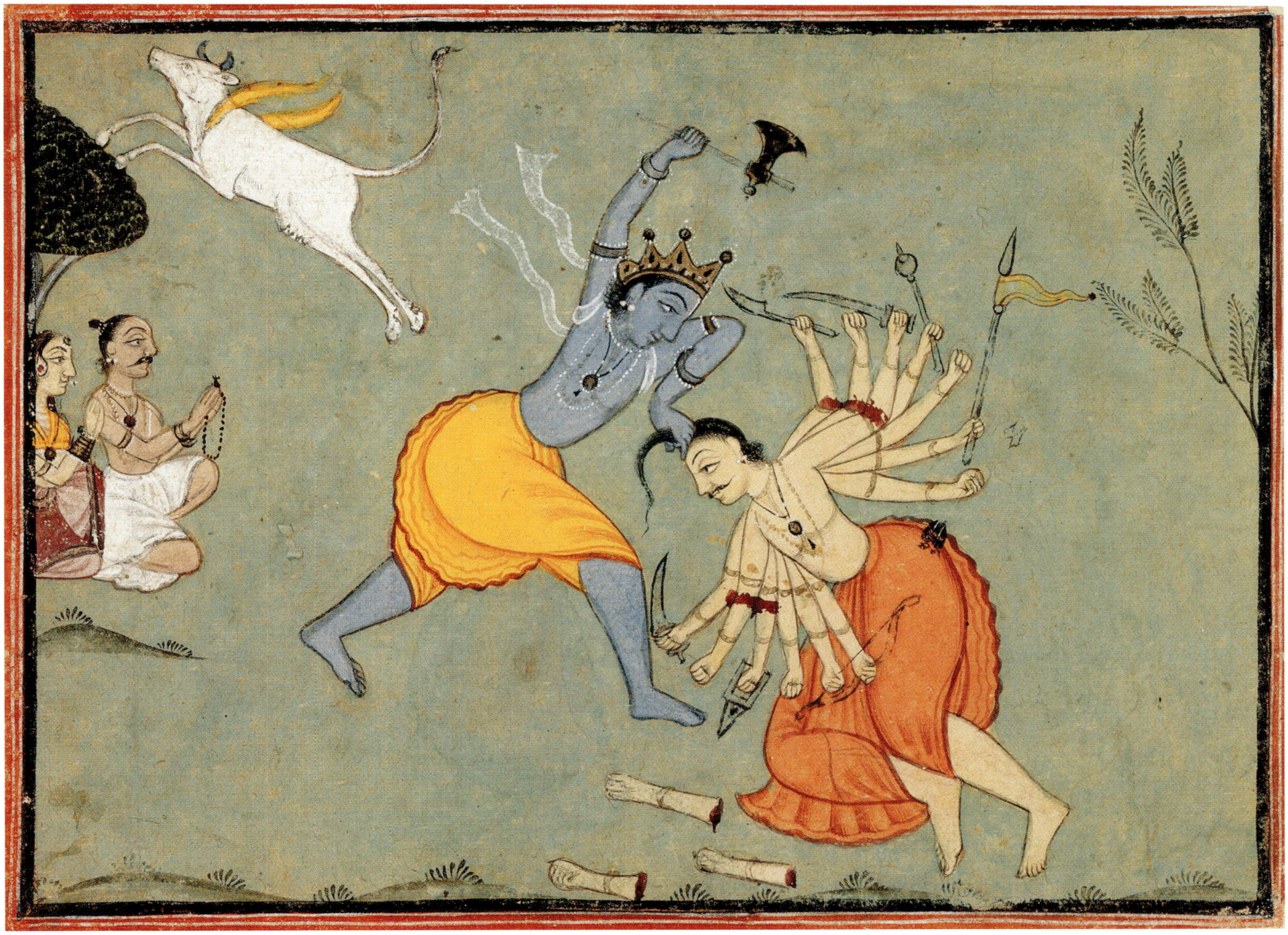

Themes from the Epics

Two Illustrations from the "Shangri" *Ramayana*

18 Rama and Lakshmana Arriving at the Rishyamukha Hill

Himachal Pradesh, c. 1750–75
Opaque watercolor on paper
Sheet: 8 5/8 x 13 3/8 in. (21.9 x 34 cm)
Image: 7 x 11 5/8 in. (17.8 x 29.5 cm)
Lent by Ramesh and Urmil Kapoor

19 Rama, Sita and Lakshmana Arriving at the Hermitage of Sage Agastya

Himachal Pradesh, c. 1750–75
Opaque watercolor on paper
Sheet: 8 5/8 x 12 3/4 in. (21.9 x 32.4 cm)
Image: 7 3/8 x 11 3/4 in. (18.7 x 29.8 cm)
Lent by Ramesh and Urmil Kapoor

Rama, the hero of the Sanskrit epic *Ramayana*, follows the Parasurama incarnation of Vishnu. He appeared on earth to destroy the titan king Ravana, whose transgression was coveting Rama's wife Sita. These two illustrations are from a large *Ramayana* series commonly known as the "Shangri" *Ramayana* because of the discovery of a significant group in the family of Shangri rulers. They were the subject of an intense study by Archer (1973), who divided them into four stylistic groups and dated them to between 1690 and 1710. Karl Khandalavala, however, gave them a wider span of dates stretching from 1700 to 1760–65 (1958), with which V. C. Ohri agrees (personal communication, 2002). Archer had assigned all four styles to Kulu, but Goswamy and Fischer (1992) have made a case for a Bahu origin for style I and II pictures and have said nothing about the other two styles. These two pictures in the Kapoor collection belong to what Archer characterized as style IV, and, as Ohri has suggested, they were likely painted in a Mandi workshop or perhaps by an artist familiar with the distinct Mandi idiom. This is a complex art historical issue and cannot be addressed here.

What is clear is that the two paintings, similar in style, represent two episodes from two different books of the *Ramayana*. The subject of [18] is taken from the book of Kishkindha (Kishkindhakanda), where we see only the two siblings arriving at Rishyamukha Hill. Interestingly, an inscription on the back of the painting in Devanagari script reads "113 Kishkindha" (V. C. Ohri, personal communication, 2002), which would imply that it was part of a large series. In [19], Rama, Sita and Lakshmana are being welcomed to an ashram by the sage Agastya, as described in the book of the forest (Aranyakanda). An inscription in Takri script in the red border on the front of the painting reads, "The illustrious Maharaj [Rama] is paying obeisance to Agastya" (V. C. Ohri, personal communication, 2002).

V. C. Ohri, an authority on Pahari painting, attributes both pictures to a Mandi workshop and gives them the same date of c. 1760–65 (personal communication, 2002). *(continued on page 53)*

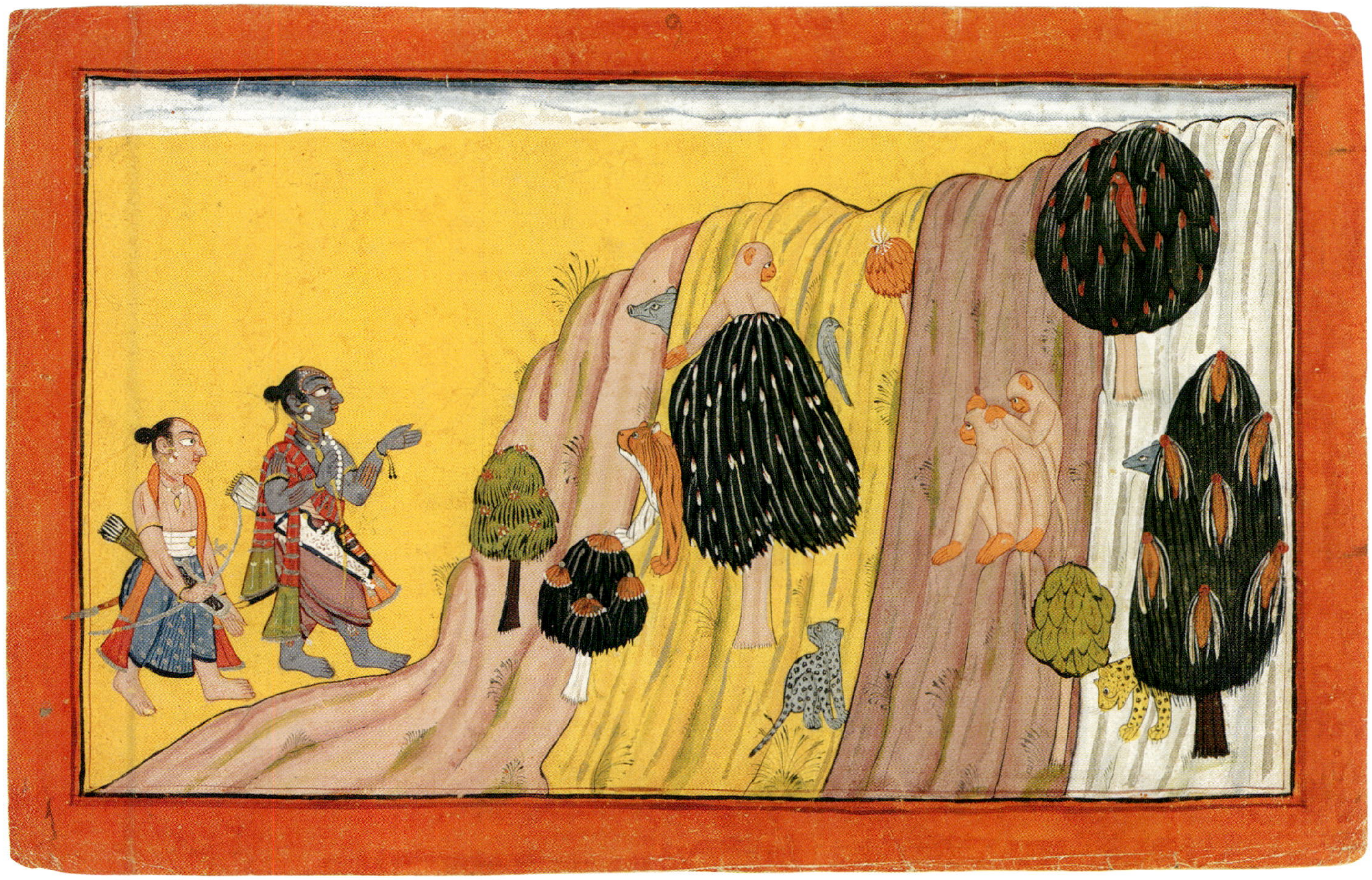

18

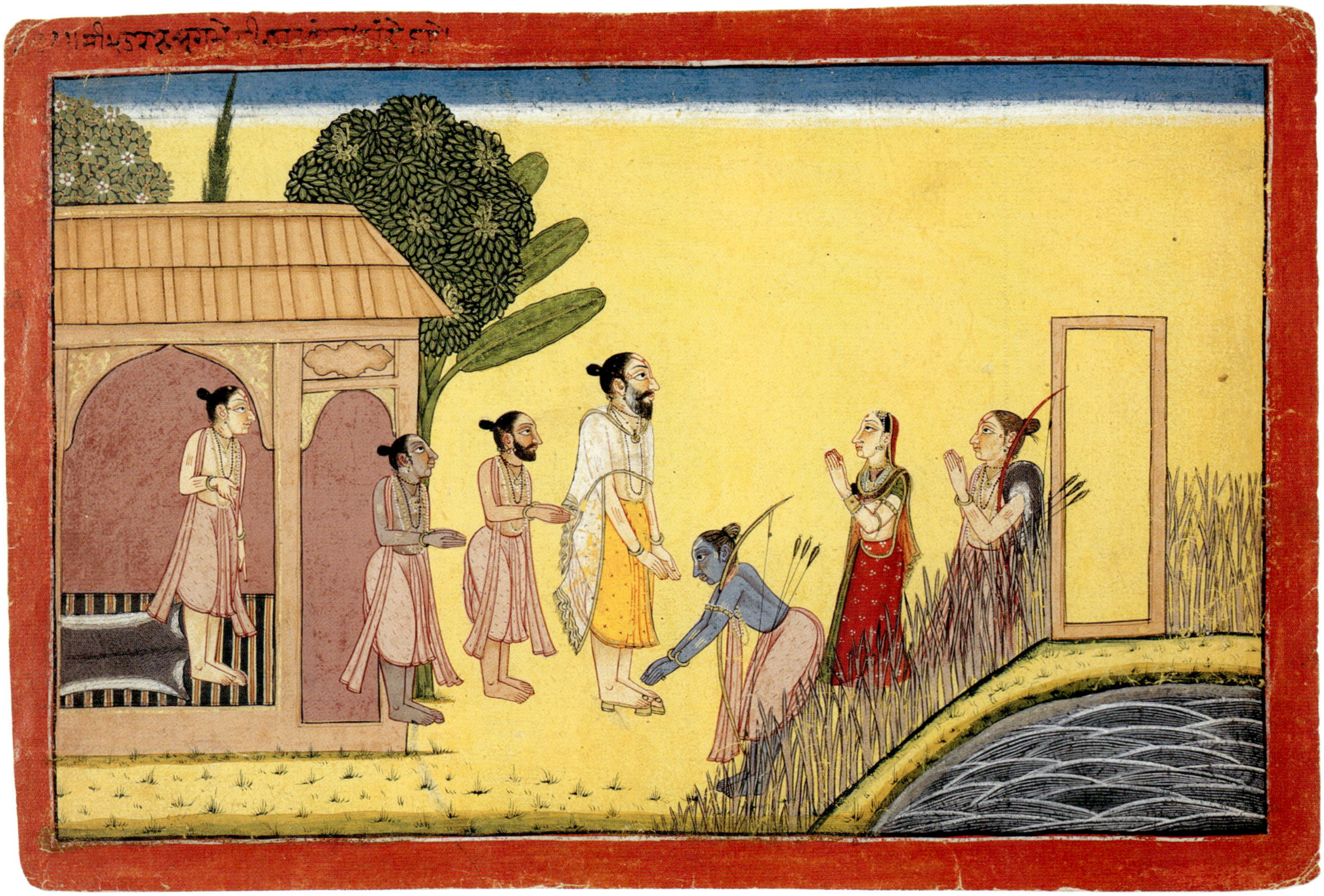

19

However, there are distinct stylistic differences between the two pictures, especially in the proportions and morphological characteristics of the human figures. The figures in the painting with Agastya are clearly like others of style IV (Archer 1973, vol. 2, pl. 243). Those pictures have even more marginal texts on the front. However, the other painting has figures with quite different lineation and proportions, including larger eyes, as in pictures of Archer's style III (Archer 1973, vol. 2, pl. 242 and Poster 1994, no. 212). The representation of the lively animals and rocks are also discrete characteristics of style III paintings.

Of course, these two paintings could have been done by two different artists of the same period. Or, more likely, the style III paintings were done earlier, especially in view of their closer relationship with style I and II pictures. Whatever their exact date and provenance, the two pictures differ in mood and flavor. In the scene of Agastya's ashram the mood is tranquil, as the three forest wanderers approach the sage with devotion, having walked along a narrow path on the bank of the river and entered through a door-like rectangular opening in a rustic fence made of staves. Noteworthy are the slim proportions of the figures and the heavy shading of the faces—a feature that, according to Ohri, is seen in contemporary Mandi pictures. The composition is much livelier in the other painting: Rama and Lakshmana approach the escarpment with decorative trees, birds and a variety of curious animals, including a tiger, cheetahs, bears and the monkeys who will later help Rama recover his abducted wife Sita. The seated simian pair, one of whom picks bugs out of the fur of the other, seems unconcerned about the alarm raised by a third monkey, clearly announcing the arrival of the two humans.

20 Illustration from a *Ramayana* Series: The Episode with the Tribal Chief Guha

Rajasthan, Mewar, Udaipur, 1700–1725
Opaque watercolor on paper
Sheet: 10 ⅛ x 16 in. (25.7 x 40.6 cm)
Image: 8 ⅞ x 14 ½ in. (22.5 x 36.8 cm)
Promised gift of Ramesh and Urmil Kapoor

The inscription along the top of the painting identifies the scene as the meeting of Rama and Guha Bhil, as described in verse 73 of the book of Ayodhya (Ayodhyakanda) of the *Ramayana* (Naval Krishna, personal communication, 2002). After being exiled from Ayodhya, Rama, along with his devoted sibling Lakshmana and spouse Sita, headed south to the river Ganga. They crossed the river with the help of Guha, who is described in the inscription as a Bhil, one of the tribes that are still prominent in Rajasthan and Madhya Pradesh.

The foreground shows the river and a boat. On the far bank we see Guha, dressed not in tribal attire but like a Rajput prince. He receives the distinguished visitors: the blue Rama, followed by the fair Lakshmana and petite Sita. Behind Guha stands a pair of tethered steeds—their lower bodies painted red—along with a groom and a chariot. In the middle ground, while Rama and Sita take a nap below a tree, Lakshmana whiles away the time by chatting with Guha and three of his followers. Here the companions are less elaborately dressed but not as Bhils.

The picture is clearly a work of the first quarter of the eighteenth century and more precisely during the reign of Sangram Singh II (r. 1710–34). In particular, it is related in style to the 1712 Balakanda (of the *Ramayana*) that is now in the British Library (see Topsfield 2002, pp. 142–44 for other contemporaneous works). Since the Ayodhyakanda follows the Balakanda, one wonders if the two illustrated series were not sequential (see also Goswamy and Bhatia 1999, no. 107 for a *Bhagavatapurana* series from the same workshop).

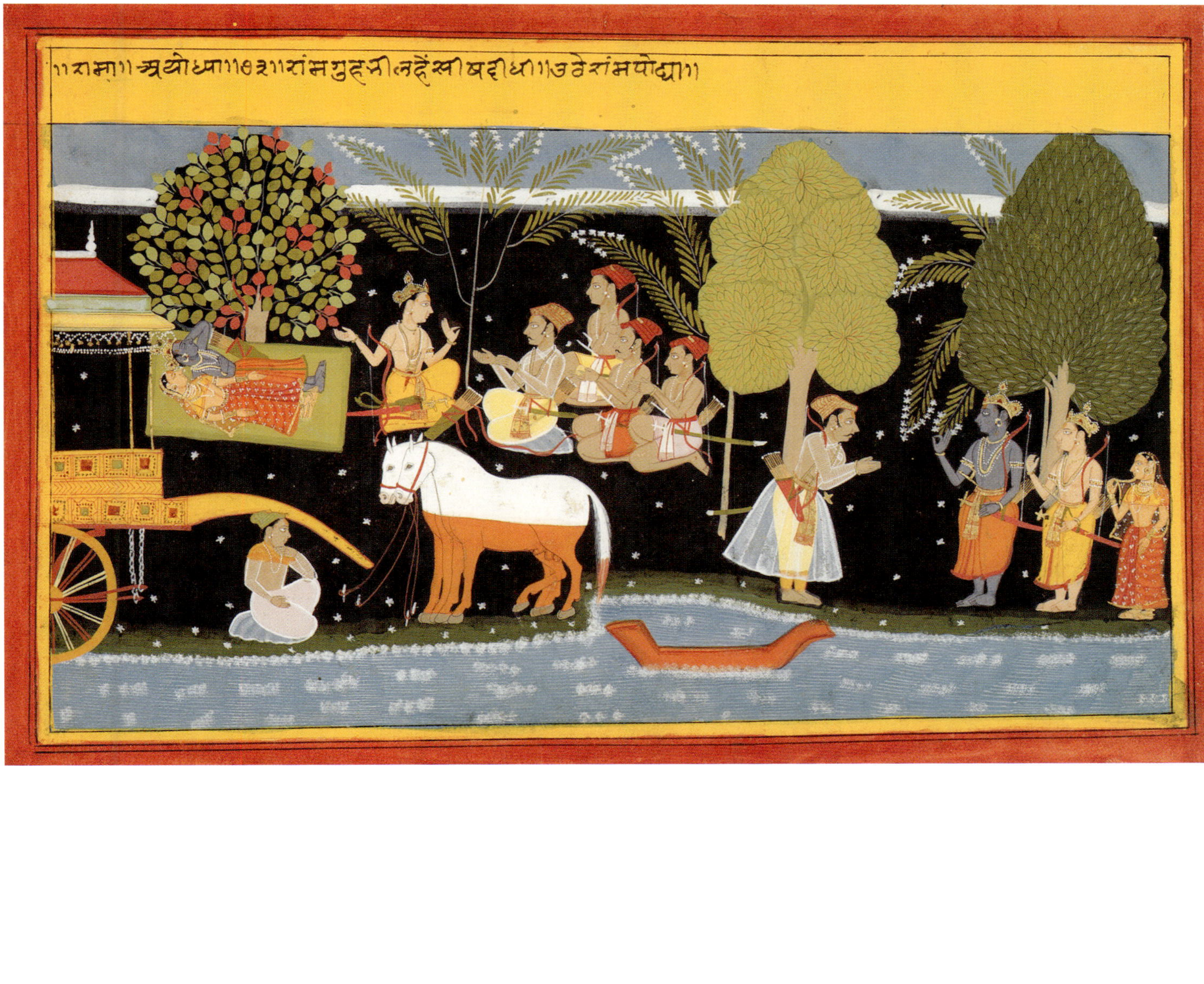

21 Illustration from a *Ramayana* Series: Rama, Sita and Lakshmana in the Forest

Himachal Pradesh, Guler style at Kangra, c. 1775
Opaque watercolor on paper
Sheet: 9 ¾ x 14 1/16 in. (24.8 x 35.7 cm)
Image: 7 ⅞ x 12 in. (20 x 30.5 cm)
Lent by Ramesh and Urmil Kapoor

This lyrical picture is from a large *Ramayana* series now dispersed in many public and private collections. The original patron of the series was probably Sansar Chand of Kangra, who had at his court a number of artists belonging to the family of the master of Nainsukh of Guler. While Goswamy and Fischer (1992, nos. 144–45) ascribe the series to "a Master of the First Generation after Nainsukh," V. C. Ohri (personal communication, 2002) has suggested that the most likely candidate is Nainsukh's second son, Gaudhu (c. 1740–1820). Unfortunately, not much is known about the opus of Gaudhu. Obviously, he was a chip off the old block, even if he did not reach the aesthetic heights of his father.

In soft muted shades of green, gray and mauve, Gaudhu has given us a subtle and delicate version of an important occasion described in the book of the forest (Aranyakanda). Outside their hut on the bank of the river, the exiled Rama and his wife Sita seem to be enjoying an intimate moment, as he anoints her. Dressed in leaves, they have abandoned their royal attire to don that of the forest dweller. They seem to be unaware of the approaching army on the other bank, which accompanies Bharata, a younger sibling who has come to escort Rama back to the kingdom. Lakshmana, who joined the couple in their exile, keeps his distance, but it is not clear if he is watching Rama and Sita or the approaching army. In any event, Bharata was unsuccessful in his attempt. He returned to Ayodhya with Rama's slippers, which were placed on the throne as a symbolic presence until Rama returned from exile.

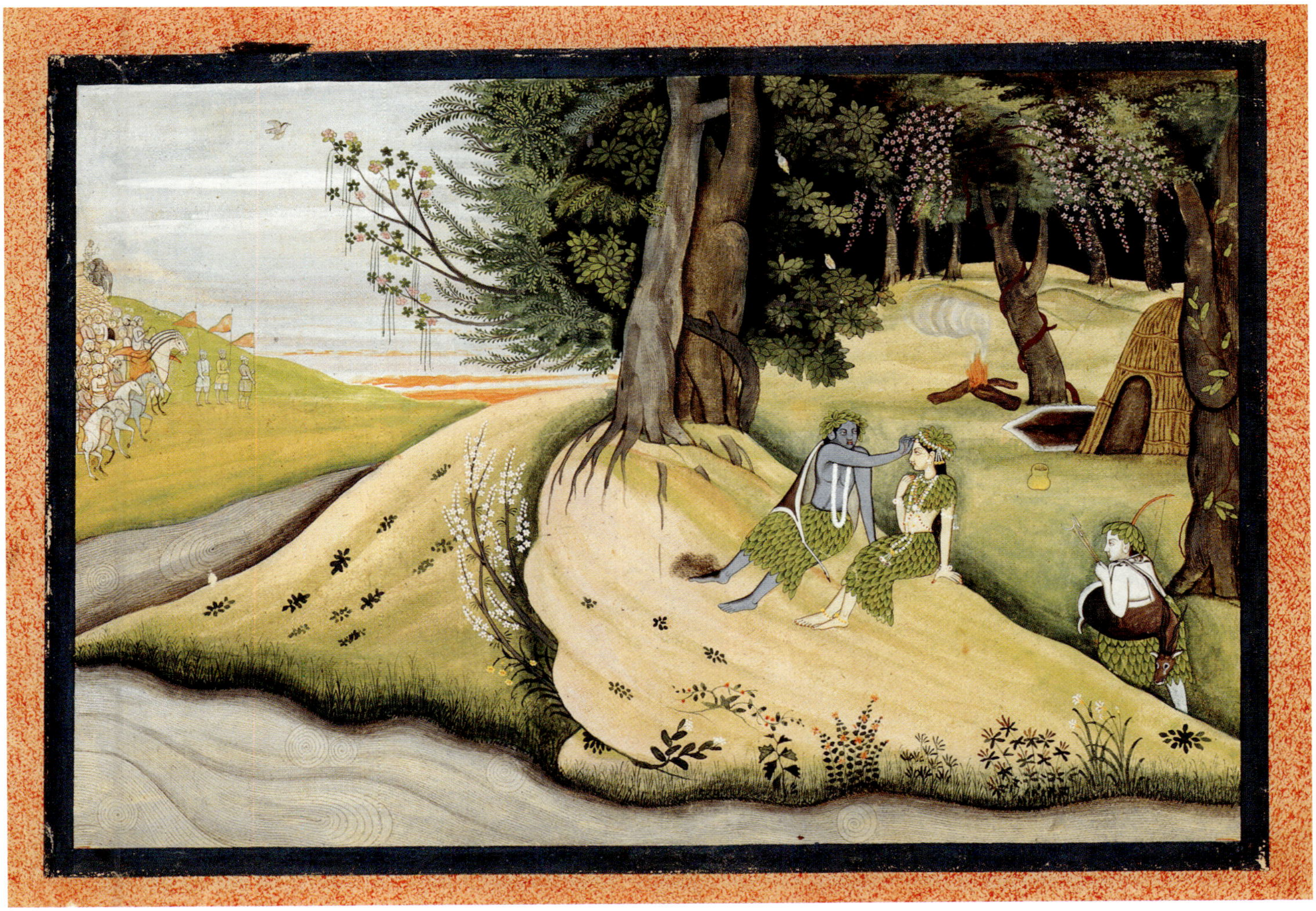

22 Folio from a *Ramayana* Manuscript: Marriage Festivities

Himachal Pradesh, Kangra workshop or Uttaranchal, Garhwal workshop, c. 1825
Opaque watercolor on paper
Sheet: 11 x 15 ¼ in. (27.9 x 38.7 cm)
Image: 9 ⅜ x 13 ½ in. (23.8 x 34.3 cm)
Gift of Ramesh and Urmil Kapoor; P.2000.9.4

A short inscription on the back identifies the painting as a scene from the book of childhood (Balakanda) of the *Ramayana*. Small inscriptions within the painted area identify the various figures. The three figures in the courtyard on the viewer's left are identified as Janaka, king of Mithila and the father of the bride Sita, in conversation with the sage Visvamitra, who sits in front of Satanand. On the other side in the upper corner is Sita with companions, with Samji in the enclosure below. Beneath the baldachin is Rama's father, Dasaratha, who converses with his family priest, the sage Vasishta. Immediately below, Dasaratha offers cows to brahmans. Dasaratha is seen a third time in the tent, seated in court. Loads of wedding gifts arrive along the bottom left of the picture, with musicians playing in the opposite corner.

The picture conforms generally to the Guler/Kangra manner of the first quarter of the nineteenth century, especially with works that have been ascribed to artists of the second generation after Nainsukh. Specifically, one finds similarities with another wedding picture signed by Sultanu, the son of Gaudhu, one of Nainsukh's sons (see Goswamy and Fischer 1992, p. 317, fig. 111). There is no certainty of Sultanu's dates or of where the picture was done. The painting may also be compared with others attributed to both Garhwal (Archer 1973, vol. 2, pl. 87, fig. 24) and Kangra (Pal 1978, no. 78; Poster 1994, no. 228; Pal 2001, nos. 60–62), the last two belonging to two different series depicting *Ramayana* themes. Thus, for the present, a Kangra attribution seems the safest, with a strong probability of its association with Sultanu.

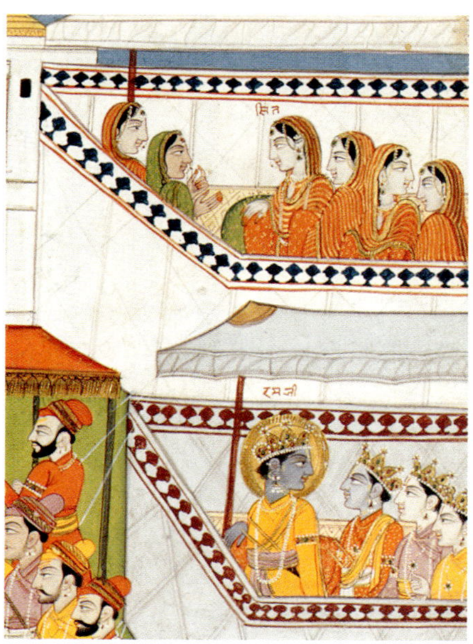

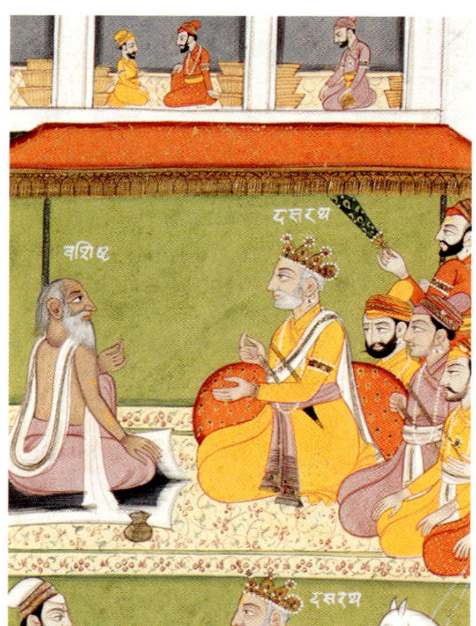

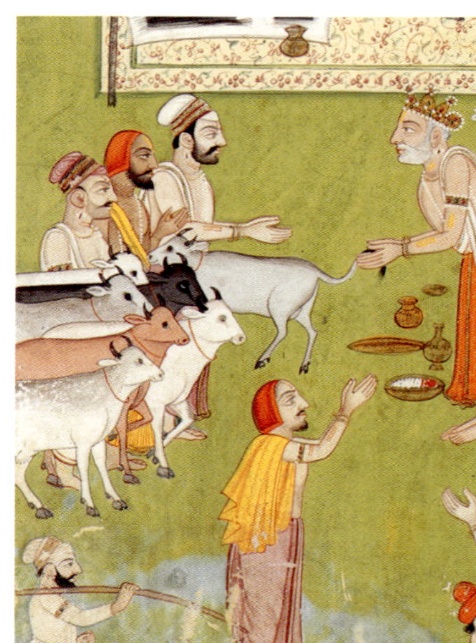

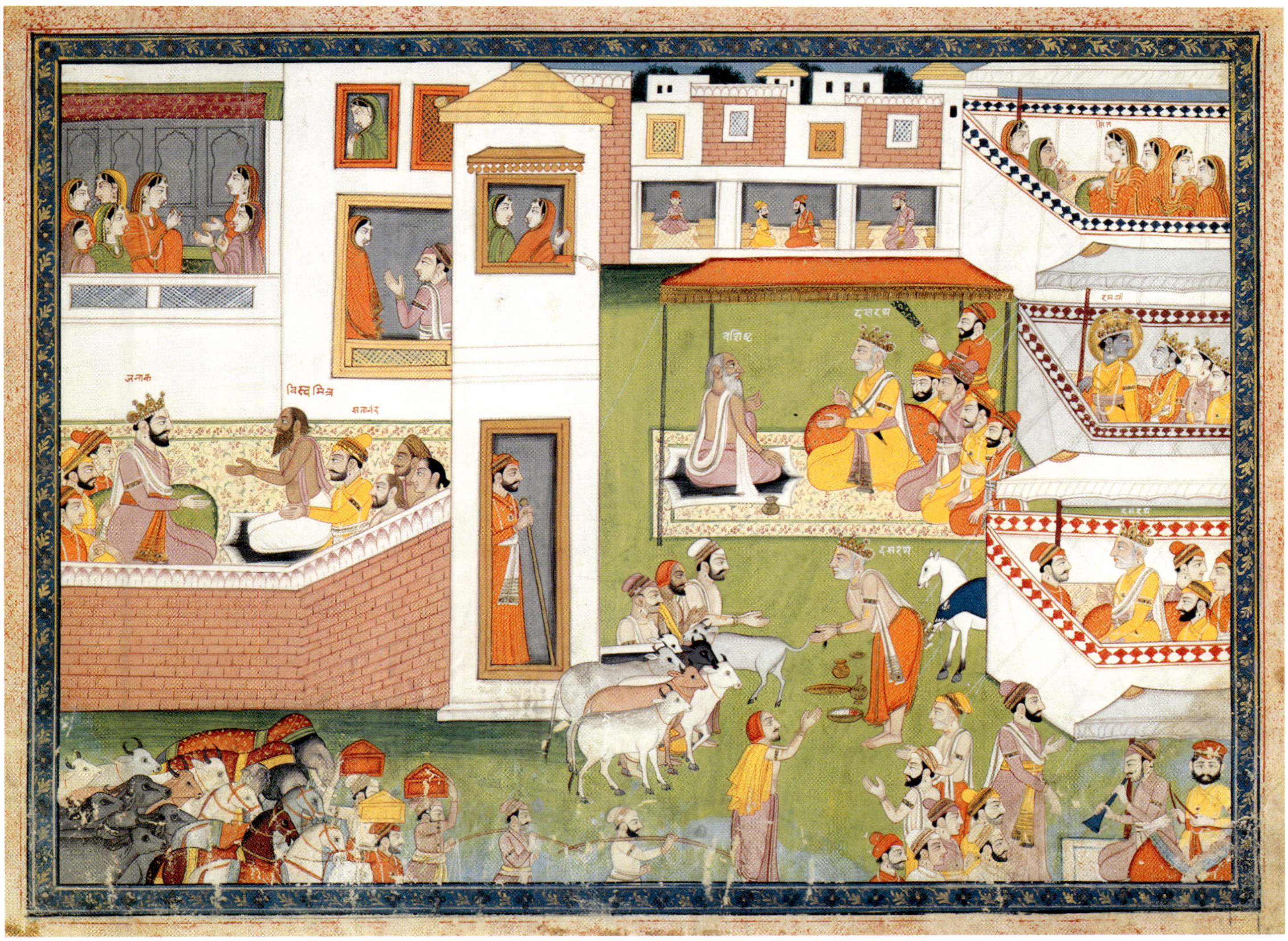
जनक
विस्वमित्र
वशिष्ठ
दसरथ

23 Folio Illustrating Episodes from the Jarasandha Story

Rajasthan, Bikaner, 1625–50
Opaque watercolor on paper
Sheet: 6 x 11 3/8 in. (15.2 x 28.9 cm)
Image: 3 3/4 x 10 5/8 in. (9.5 x 27 cm)
Gift of Ramesh and Urmil Kapoor; P.2001.13.3

Krishna and Balarama's protracted struggle with Jarasandha, the king of Magadha (modern-day Bihar), forms an important saga in epic and puranic literature. The tyrannical ruler of Mathura, Kamsa, who was slain by Krishna, was the son-in-law of Jarasandha. Although an important component of the epic *Mahabharata*, the text and the illustrations on this folio recount a version of the story that is probably from one of the puranic texts (see Appendix). Side [A] depicts the flight of the two brothers before the advancing army of Jarasandha. The scene on side [B] shows the two brothers seated atop a mountain called Pravarsana. In most texts the mountain is called Gomantaka, and in fact, Krishna and Balarama are said to have taken refuge in a cave. Unable to find them, Jarasandha sets the mountain on fire, which may have been represented in the following folio.

Clearly, the artist has depicted the essential elements of the story. In [A] the two brothers, with the dark Krishna leading, climb up a rocky escarpment as they are chased by two foot soldiers and three others on horses. In [B] Krishna and Balarama watch Jarasandha arrive on a horse. Curiously here, Balarama is dressed in a dhoti and shawl, while in the other picture, he wears a long stitched dress and pajamas like his pursuers. Although the events are represented on a single plane, the composition in [A] graphically conveys the drama of the chase through the movement of the figures and the treatment of the background with mauve and splashes of gray. The mood is calmer in the other composition, with a monochromatic yellow ground. Both illustrations are a riot of bright hues, seem in the attire, the horses and the candy-shaped rocks. Rather curious are the frame-like rectangular objects along the left margin of the chase scene.

The representation continues the illustrated manuscript tradition of the late sixteenth century, with the text written in four lines along the top of each side. Closely related is an isolated folio from a *Bhagavatapurana* manuscript attributed to early-seventeenth-century Gujarat (Vajracharya 2002, no. 27).

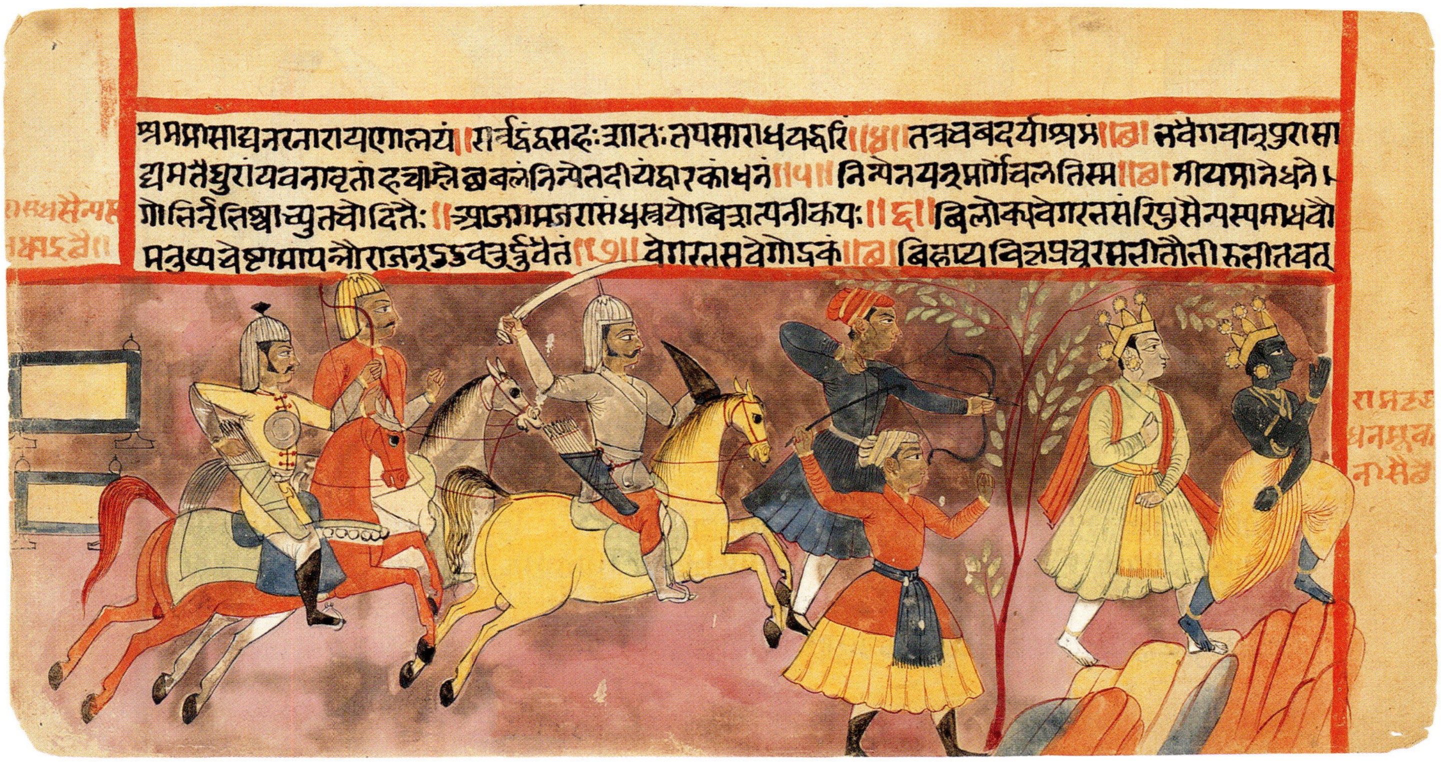

A

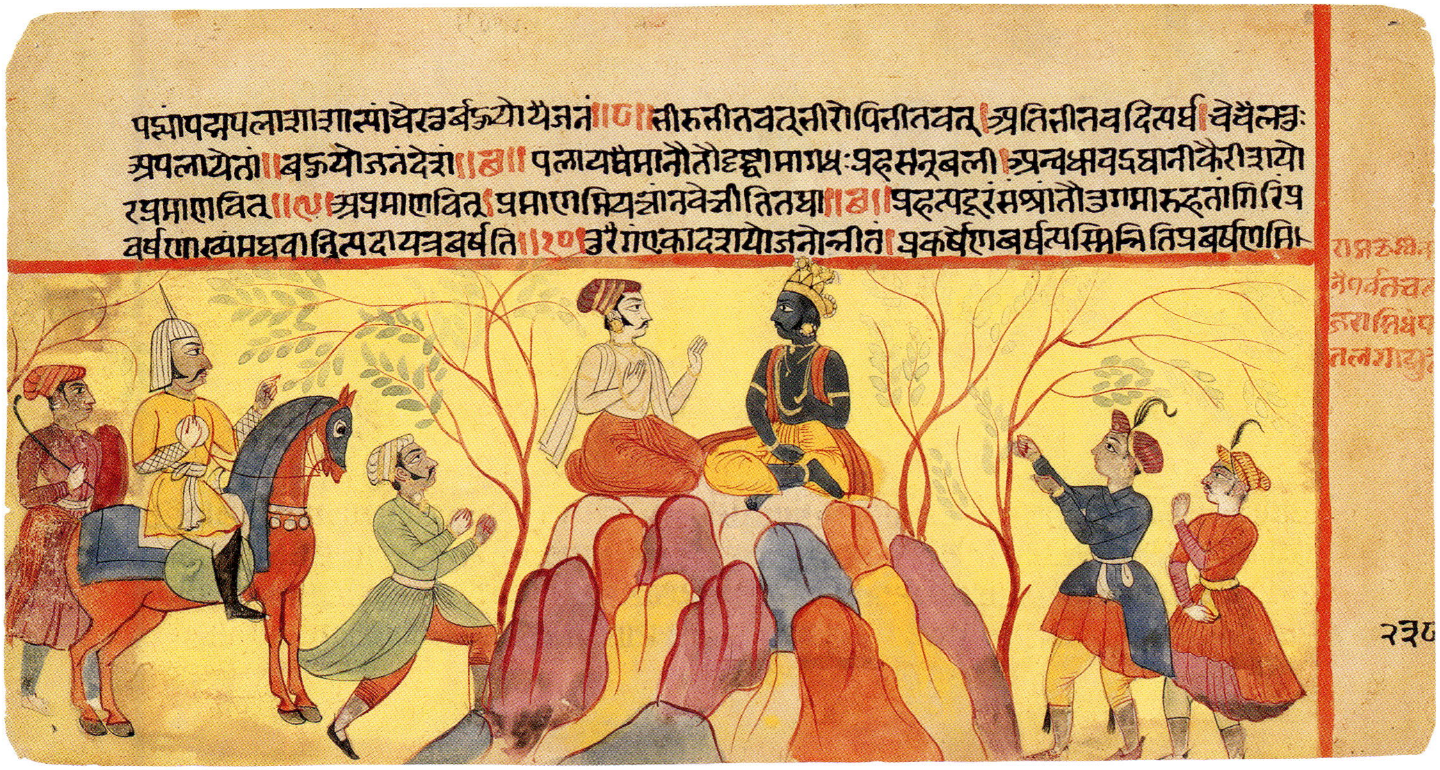

B

24 The Cosmic Form of Krishna

Himachal Pradesh, Chamba (?) workshop, 1750–75
Opaque watercolor on paper
Sheet: 11 7/8 x 9 3/8 in. (30.2 x 23.8 cm)
Image: 11 x 8 in. (27.9 x 20.3 cm)
Lent by Ramesh and Urmil Kapoor

Small Devanagari inscriptions above the two standing attendant figures identify the female as Lakshmi and the male as Arjuna (V. C. Ohri, personal communication, 2002). The presence of Arjuna clearly indicates that the painting was inspired by the account of his vision in the *Bhagavadgita*, in which Krishna expands himself to cosmic proportions to convince Arjuna that it is he who pervades and contains the entire universe. A popular subject in Vaishnava temple sculpture, it continues to be prevalent in Rajput painting, especially with Pahari artists.

With multiple limbs and heads, Krishna is an awesome and awe-inspiring figure who stands like a giant column. His head and torso probably signify the heavens, for the dress he wears, though pink, is dotted with tufts of grass. The legs, arms and heads are painted in a variety of bright colors, while his long brown tresses cover his torso like a finely knitted wool sweater, with several human heads emerging from within. The artist has rendered with remarkable accuracy all of the hand attributes of the cosmic deity, most of which are weapons.

V. C. Ohri (personal communication, 2002) has suggested that the painting was likely rendered in a Chamba workshop in the third quarter of the eighteenth century, in which case it could be the work of a master artist called Mahesh (active c. 1730–c. 1770) [see Goswamy and Fischer 1992, pp. 166–87], some of whose representations of divinities are both powerful and idiosyncratic. A slightly earlier version in the Edwin Binney 3rd Collection at the San Diego Museum of Art has been ascribed to Bilaspur (Okada and Hurel 2002, no. 65). Noteworthy also is a depiction of Shiva Bhairava in the Museum Reitberg, Zürich (Fischer 1998, fig. 9), in which the hand attributes, especially the noose, have the same precision as those in this picture. The two pictures, as well as a Narasimha avatar (Fischer 1998, fig. 8), have a similar tonality of pigments. It should be noted, however, that a later version of the cosmic Krishna has been given an 1875–1900 date and ascribed to Kashmir (Boner et al 1994, no. 641). If these various attributions are correct, then a master sketch must have moved about from one region to another.

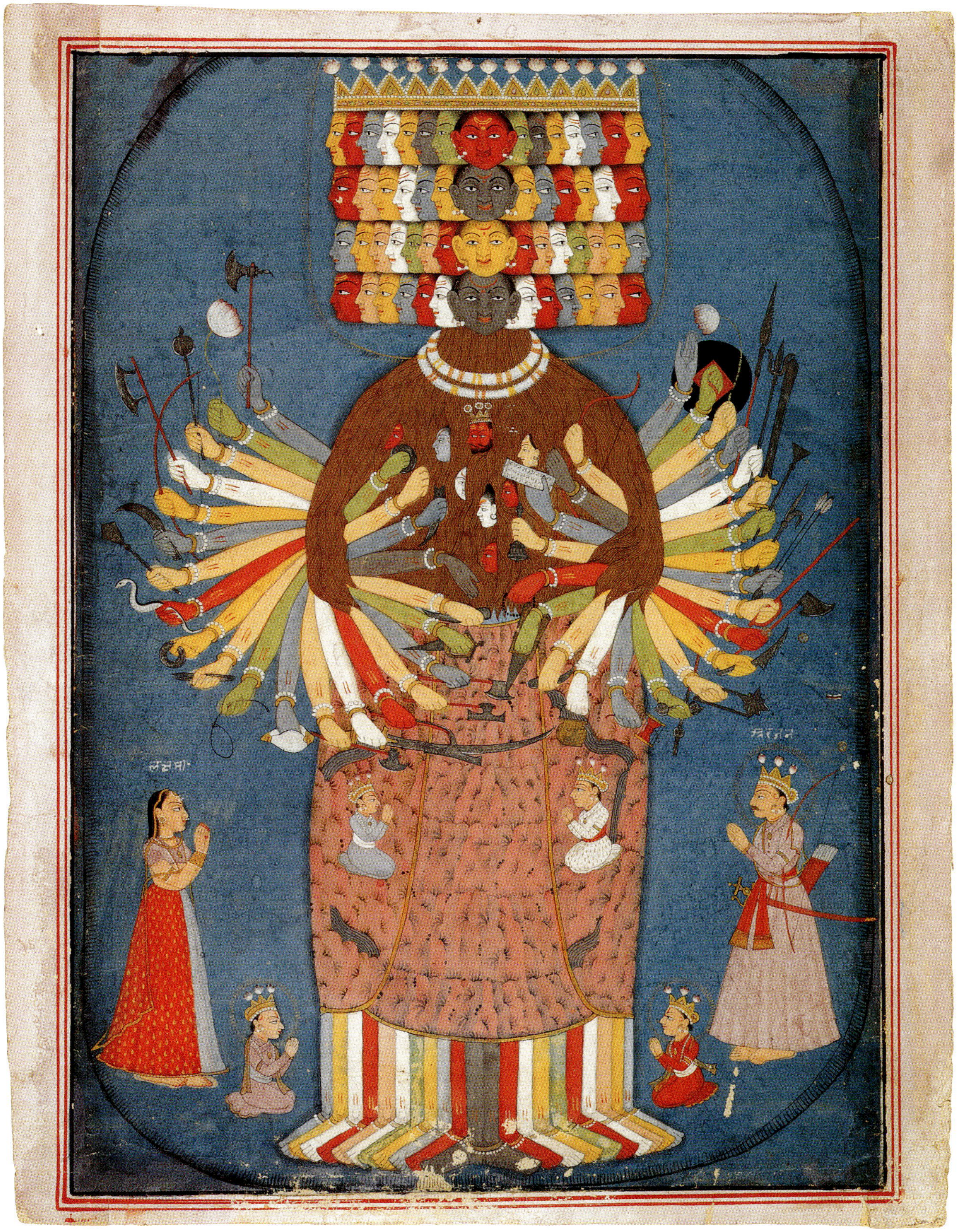

The World of Krishna

25 Illustration from a *Bhagavatapurana* Series: Krishna Upturns the Cart and Destroys Crows

Rajasthan, Bikaner, c. 1600
Opaque watercolor on paper
Sheet: 9 ¾ x 12 in. (24.8 x 30.5 cm)
Image: 6 ¾ x 9 ¾ in. (17.1 x 24.8 cm)
Lent by Ramesh and Urmil Kapoor

The brief inscriptions on the back of this painting identify the scene as both the destruction of crows (*kagavadha*) and the destruction of Sakatasura, or cart demon (*sakatasuravadha*). Both inscriptions are preceded by the number 25. The Bikaner state library's inventory stamp has been marked out, as is the case with most such pictures of this large series, now dispersed in many private and public collections.

In the picture we see the naked, but tiara-wearing Krishna on his back in a swing, kicking the horizontal pole of the furniture, on which two crows or ravens are perched. He also grasps two birds with his hands. Other birds hover above the swing, while a horrified Yasoda runs toward Krishna, a precursor scenario to Hitchcock's film *The Birds*. In the *Bhagavatapurana* narration of upturning the cart, there is no mention of an attack by ravens, though such attacks are not unknown when an infant is left out in the open. In fact, Yasoda had placed the child in a small swing below the cart, obviously to shade him. A few minutes later, Krishna became hungry and kicked the heavy cart, which then toppled over. However, the tradition of Krishna holding a crow with his right hand is encountered as early as the fifth century in a carved panel from the Deogarh temple (see Banerjee 1978, p. 72 and fig. 36). Generally in other representations of the subject, the bird is not included (Banerjee 1978, fig. 38).

This series of *Bhagavatapurana* pictures represents perhaps the earliest efforts of the court artists of Bikaner. Paintings in a similar style are often confused with popular Mughal pictures, and there seems no doubt that artists trained in the Mughal style were attached to the Bikaner court as early as around 1600, when this series was undertaken. However, the basic aesthetic elements—the flat red background, the yellow wall of the pavilion, the arrangement of figures in a single plane and the overall simplicity of the composition—reveal continued influences of the manuscript illuminations. The mode of attire and the drama of the situation expressed by Yasoda's reaction are Mughal nuances.

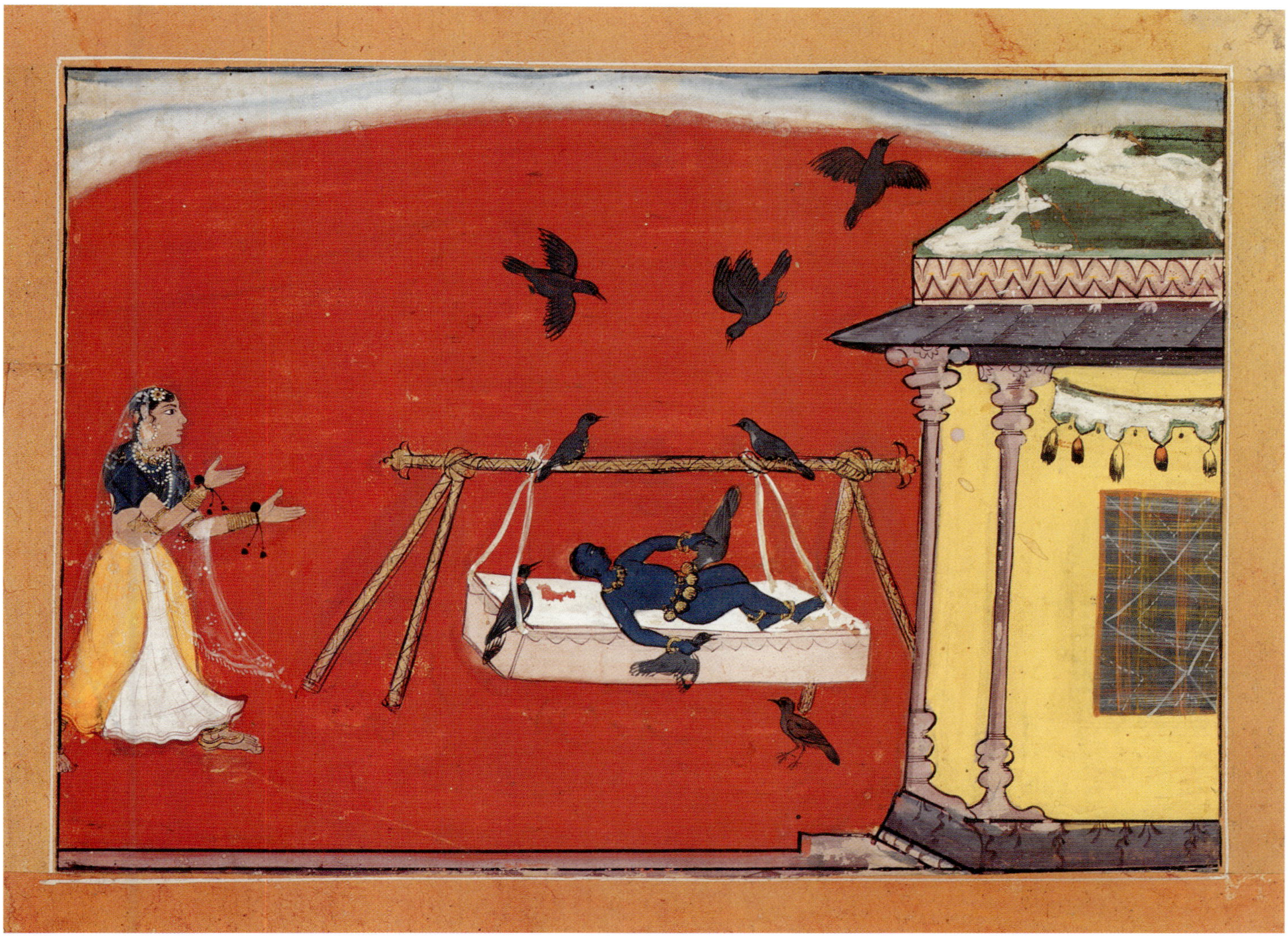

26 Emancipation of the Ogress Putana

Madhya Pradesh, Malwa, 1675–1700
Opaque watercolor on paper
Sheet: 9 ½ x 14 in. (24.1 x 35.6 cm)
Image: 8 ½ x 13 in. (21.6 x 33 cm)
Gift of Ramesh and Urmil Kapoor; P.2001.13.4

The text on the back (see Appendix) is a Hindi translation of passages from the episodes entitled "Emancipation of Putana" in book ten (chapter seven) of the Sanskrit *Bhagavatapurana.* According to the story, the wicked king Kamsa of Mathura dispatched the ogress Putana to kill the infant Krishna. In the guise of a beautiful damsel, Putana arrived at Vraja while Nanda, the child's foster father, was away. With his divine powers, Krishna saw through the deception. As she took the infant in her arms to suckle him with her poisonous milk, he tore her breasts out and killed her. However, because she died at his hand, she was liberated from the chain of rebirth.

The rectangular format of the picture and the horizontal division into two registers clearly indicates the adoption of the visual strategy of narrative scrolls on cloth. In the bottom register, the ogress has assumed her original hideous form upon death. Krishna appears as an older child hovering over her right breast, while other teenage cowherds watch the event. Above, Nanda is seen returning on a cart and then within a pavilion, holding Krishna, who is represented here as an infant, true to his tender age. As the text says:

> *Taking up the child (in his arms), as if he had returned from the jaws of death, the noble-minded Nanda smelt him on the crown of his head [a common way of blessing a child] and was overwhelmed with joy.*
> (Tagare 1976, pt. IV, p. 1293)

In each register the figures, trees and props are presented in a single plane. The gray monochromatic background and the flat, sparse composition with red and green predominating are characteristic of a distinct style of pictures whose exact provenance is not known, but assigned to a region of Madhya Pradesh known as Malwa. ❧

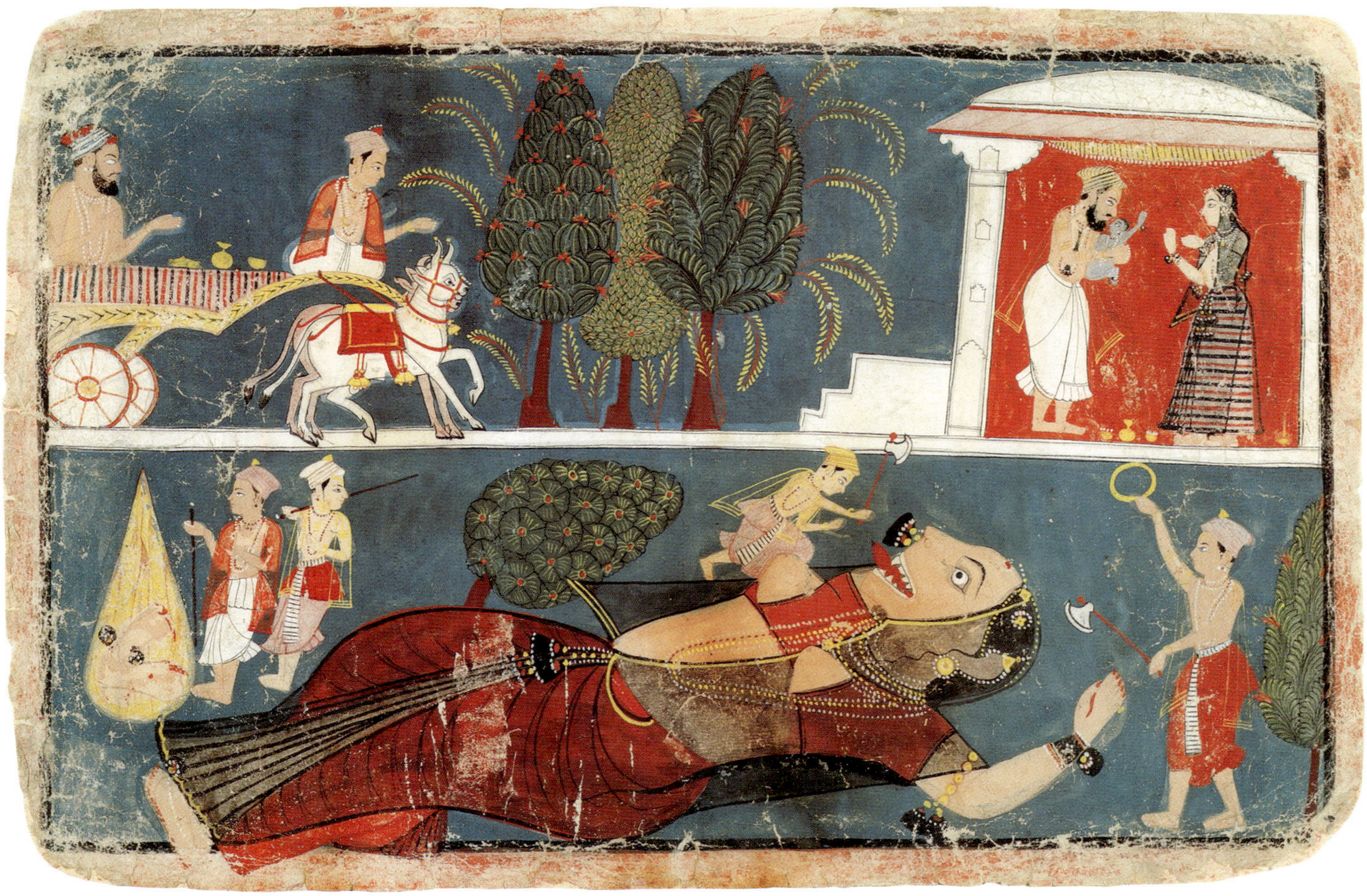

27 Krishna the Butter Thief

Himachal Pradesh, Bilaspur workshop, 1725–50
Opaque watercolor on paper
Sheet and image: 8 x 5⅝ in. (20.3 x 14.3 cm)
Gift of Ramesh and Urmil Kapoor
in honor of Ramesh Kapoor's late mother,
Shashi Kanta Kapoor; P.2003.2.8

The infant Krishna was inordinately fond of milk products—especially butter—just as the child-god Ganesh [12–13] was fond of sweets. When his mother was absent, Krishna would frequently raid the larder. Hence, he is known endearingly as the "butter thief" (*makkhan chor*) or Nanigopal (*nani* meaning "butter" and *gopal*, a common epithet of Krishna meaning "cowherd"). Usually in sculpture, especially in the south, he is seen as a naked child crawling or dancing with a butter ball in one hand.

In this narrative picture, however, an unknown Pahari artist has portrayed him as a bold but greedy child who dips his right hand into the pot even as he is about to put some butter in his mouth with his left. He looks back at his mother, who seems unconcerned as she continues to churn the butter. Krishna's foster brother Balarama is less audacious; wearing a see-through dress, he stretches his arm out in the hope of getting some. A maid stands behind and watches the goings-on.

That the picture is from a Bilaspur workshop is clear from its style and in its comparison with other works of the second quarter of the eighteenth century (see Boner et al 1994, nos. 375–79). The women in Bilaspur paintings are distinguished by their strong, assertive features, sometimes emphasized with shading. The forms are strongly delineated against a single flat plane, but the style of attire for both men and women, and here especially of Balarama, echoes that seen in earlier Mughal pictures of the mid–seventeenth century. Bilaspur artists' palettes also reveal a distinct tonality of colors, particularly in the use of brown, brownish-red and green.

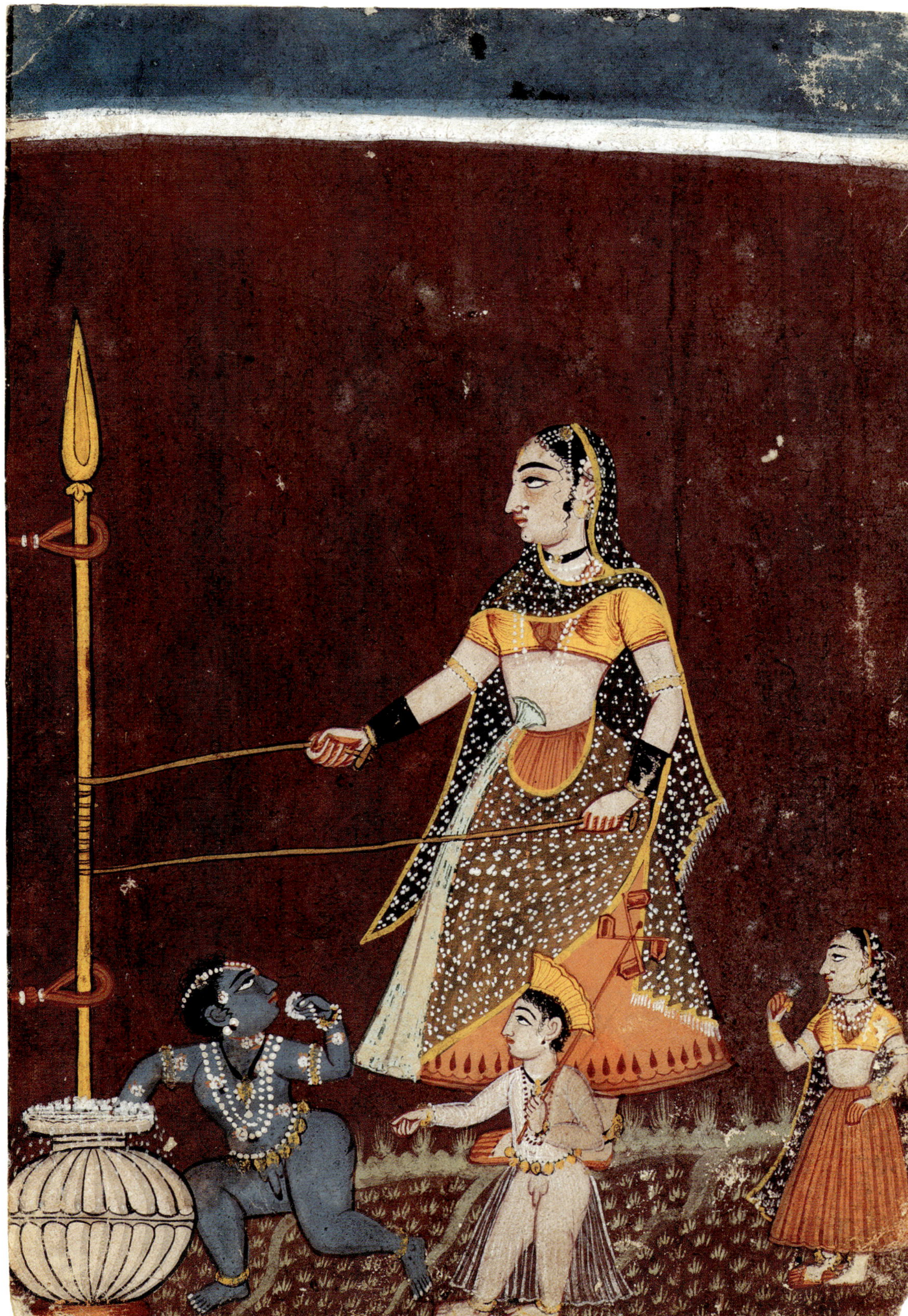

28 Infant Krishna Destroys the Demon Trinavarta

Himachal Pradesh, Kangra workshop,
c. 1775–1800
Ink and opaque watercolor on paper
Sheet: 10 x 13 ¾ in. (25.4 x 34.9 cm)
Image: 8 ⅛ x 12 ¼ in. (20.6 x 31.1 cm)
Gift of Ramesh and Urmil Kapoor; P.2003.2.10

The unfinished work was probably intended for a series depicting Krishna's childhood adventures in the tenth book of the *Bhagavatapurana*, as is clear from the number 24 inscribed above. Kamsa, Krishna's maternal uncle and nemesis, sent the demon Trinavarta to slay the divine infant. Assuming the form of a tornado, Trinavarta abducted the infant and went up into the sky. However, Krishna increased his body weight and strangled the demon. When the demon's body fell to the ground, the child was reunited with his mother.

In the sketch, the artist has followed the mode of continuous narration to first depict Krishna playing with his mother on the terrace. The funnel-shaped whirlwind or tornado is a dramatic motif that rises diagonally above Krishna to divide the composition into two halves. At the top end of the funnel is the demon carrying the infant. Directly below on the ground lies the dead demon on the mat-like boulder, with Krishna on his chest being eagerly greeted by his mother, Yasoda, and companions. The trees beside the buildings sway to the right from the gusty wind generated by the tornado.

A finished picture of the subject, probably from the same pounce, or *charba*, is in the Bharat Kala Bhavan in Varanasi (Dallapiccola 1982, fig. 156). The drawing here seems to be more freehand, and the tornado and trees more articulated, with bolder brushwork.

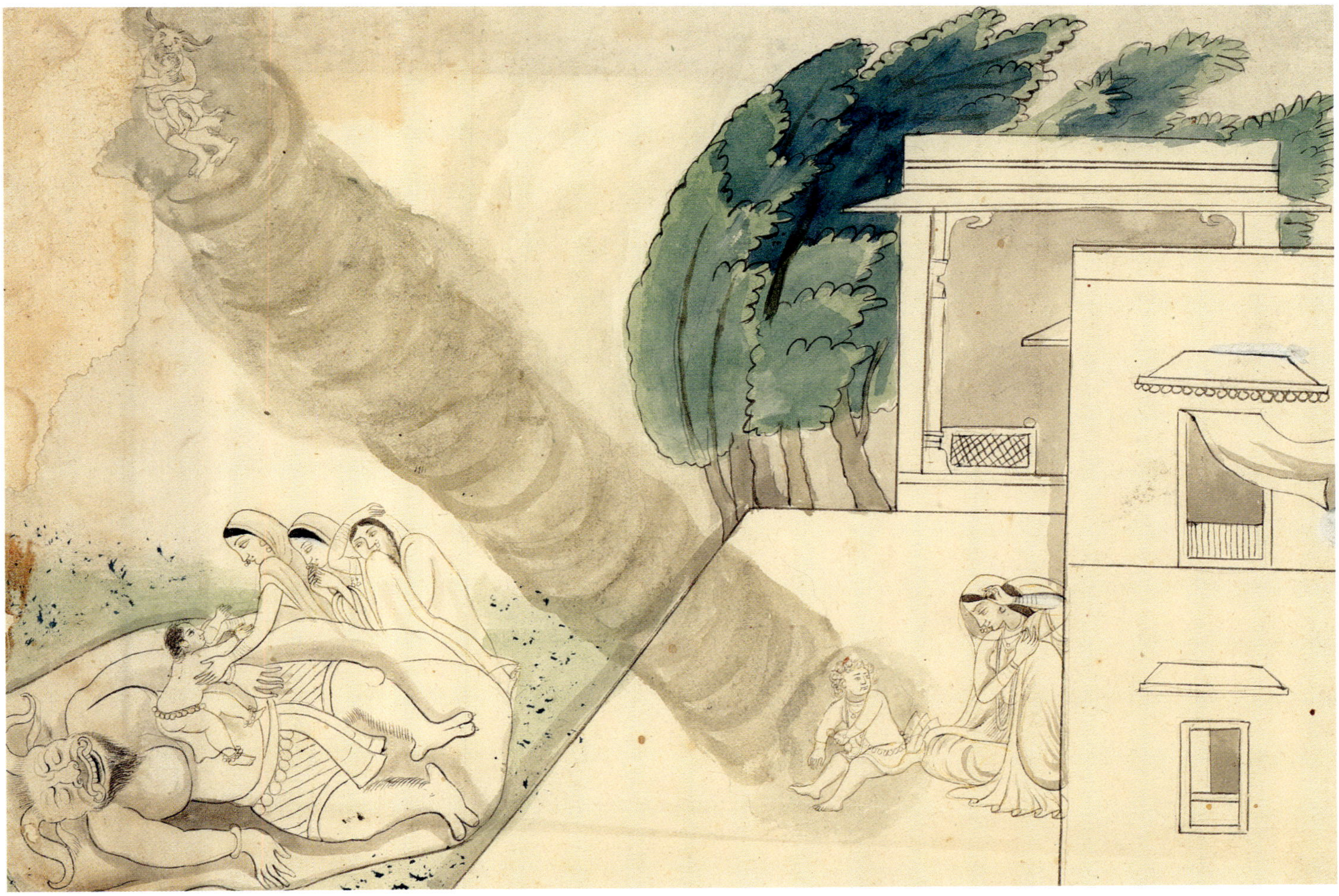

29 Victorious Krishna Dances on Kaliya

Rajasthan, Kishangarh workshop, c. 1775
Opaque watercolor on paper
Sheet: 15 x 10⅝ in. (38.1 x 27 cm)
Image: 11⅝ x 7⅜ in. (29.5 x 18.7 cm)
Gift of Suneet and Alka Kapoor; P.2001.14

One of the most popular myths of the young Krishna, revealing both his power and compassion, is that of the subduing of the snake king Kaliya. The mighty serpent with multiple hoods was poisoning the river Jamuna, where he had taken refuge to escape the mythical bird Garuda, an enemy of the snakes. After an initial struggle, Krishna succeeded in taming Kaliya by dancing on his hood. After Kaliya and his ladies pleaded for mercy, Krishna spared him but confined him to his aquatic habitat.

The unknown Kishangarh master has given us a lyrical version of the subject without the slightest hint of violence. As the four mermaids with their delicate beauty plead for their reptilian master, his elegant form serves as a pedestal for the blue god dancing and playing upon the flute. The clarity of the water is deftly conveyed, as if the defeat of the snake monster instantly rid the river of pollution. Typical of the Kishangarh manner, the landscape beyond the four decorative banana trees spreads out generously to gently rolling pastureland with herds of grazing cows, a walled garden typical of Rajasthan and a cluster of buildings, perhaps representing the settlement of Vraja, the paradisiacal habitat of Krishna. All these structures and the animals in white sparkle against the soft green ground and are rendered with incredible detail. However, in this serene composition of muted greens and grays and luminous white, there is no ambiguity about the focal point, which is certainly the blue god attired in bright yellow garments.

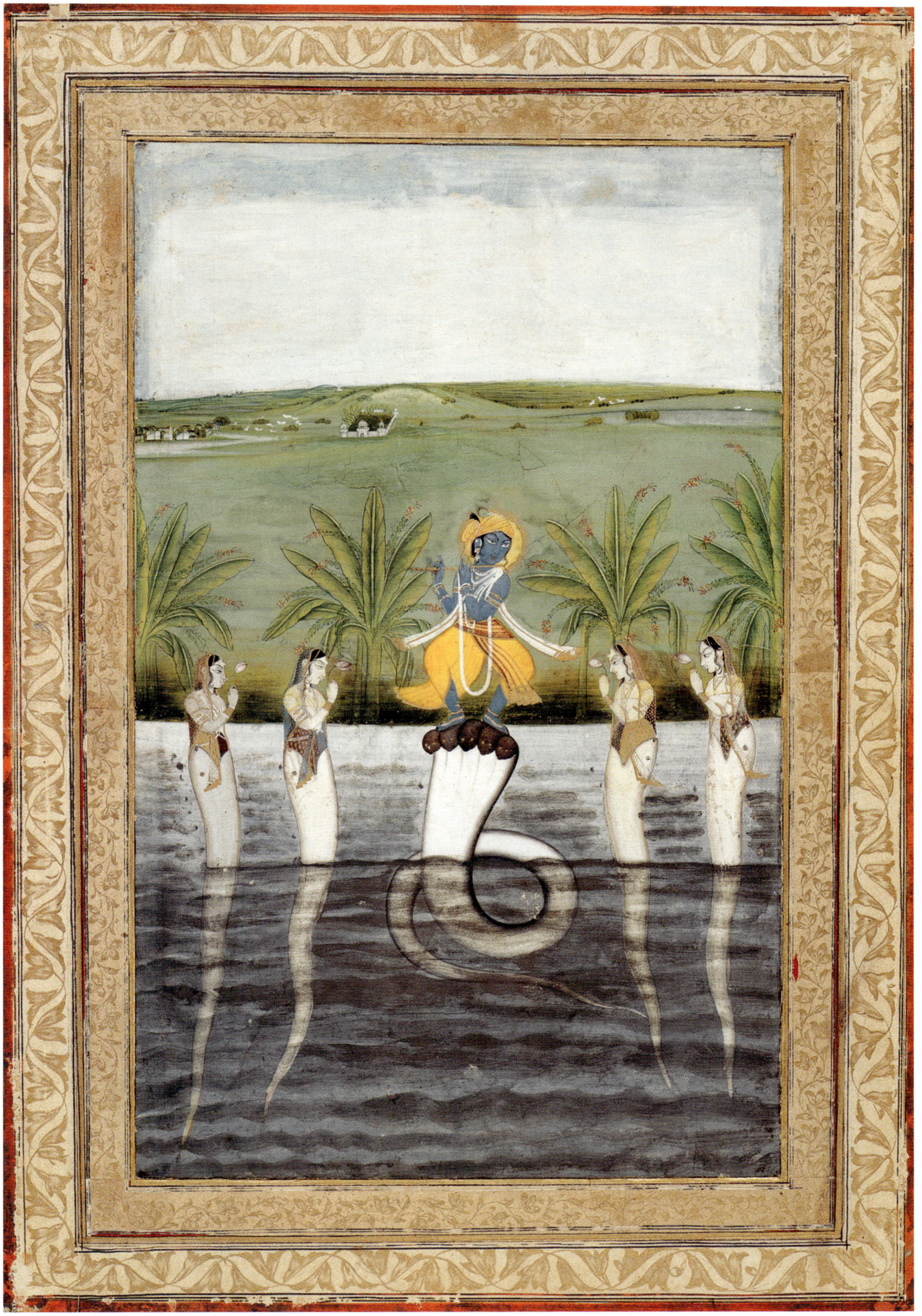

30 Krishna Upholds Mt. Govardhana

Rajasthan, Kota workshop, 1750–75
Opaque watercolor on paper
Sheet and image: 14 x 10 in. (35.6 x 25.4 cm)
Lent by Ramesh and Urmil Kapoor

The story of Krishna's conflict with the Vedic deity Indra takes up three chapters of the tenth book of the *Bhagavatapurana*. It was also popular as an independent subject, partly because the image of Sri Nathji at Nathadvara is the narrative's iconic form. This shrine has remained extremely popular, and Brijnathji is the family deity of the Kota royalty. In a nutshell, the story relates how Indra, enraged by the seven-year-old Krishna's claim of superiority, unleashed a major storm. However, Krishna successfully protected the citizens of Vraja by holding up the nearby Mt. Govardhana to serve as a giant umbrella. As soon as the storm began raging, all the humans and cattle entrusted themselves to the mercy of Krishna, who "though a child uprooted with ease the mount Govardhana with one of his hands and held it up sportively as if it were a mushroom" (Tagare 1976, pt. IV, p. 1418).

In this dramatic representation, an unknown Kota master has added a few interesting visual touches to the verbal narrative. Krishna, who is certainly older than seven, is calm and self-assured in contrast to the agitated Indra, who rides his elephant Airavata in the stormy sky above. Beside the mountain, Brahma, Shiva and a third deity watch the marvelous event. Standing firm as a cosmic pillar, Krishna effortlessly and "sportively" raises the mushroom-like mountain covered with vegetation and animals with one finger of his left hand. Colorfully clad residents of Vraja gather around him without anxiety, and one lady fans him with a flywhisk. A few cowherds and some animals scurry to the shelter, thereby expressing the intensity of the storm. Perhaps the most intriguing addition is the elephant seemingly leaping out of the river. He is likely Airavata, who has abandoned his master Indra to seek shelter with the savior god; if so, this is an extra-textual episode rarely encountered in other painted versions of the subject.

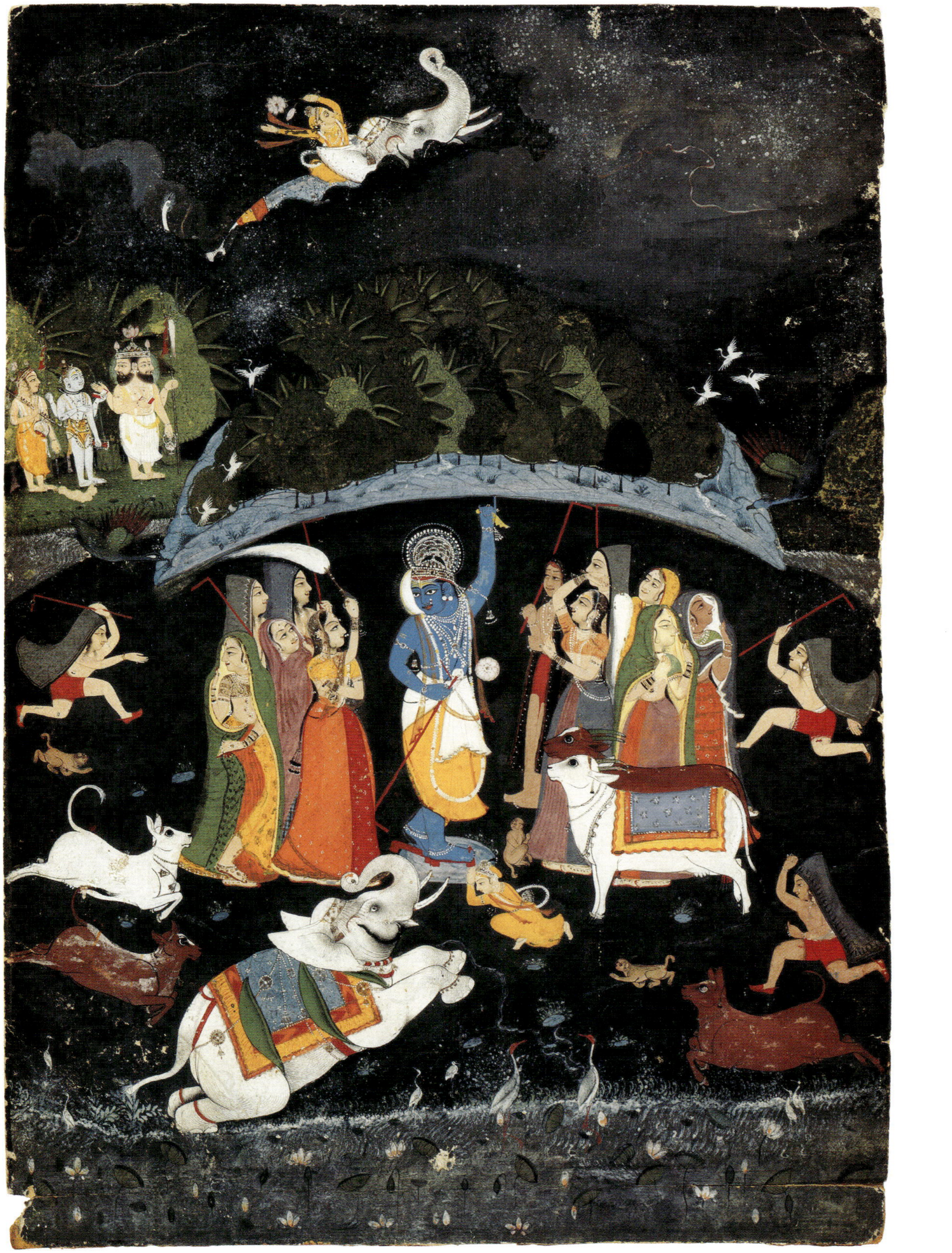

31 Illustration to the *Bhagavatapurana*: The Building of the Fort

Himachal Pradesh, Kangra workshop, c. 1825
Opaque watercolor on paper
Sheet: 15 3/8 x 21 in. (39.1 x 53.3 cm)
Image: 14 x 19 7/8 in. (35.6 x 50.5 cm)
Gift of Ramesh and Urmil Kapoor; P.2000.9.5

The interest of this lively picture lies in its subject matter: the beginning of an architectural project, with a large number of masons, artisans and foremen involved in various tasks. Indeed, so engaged are some of them, it appears as if they are about to come to blows, using their spades and axes as weapons. The composition is divided by a row of formal trees, beyond which are tents surrounded by a cloth wall (*qanat*). In the middle high ground, to the right, some masons have already built the stone wall, while others prepare the stone blocks. On the other side, Krishna, identified by a small inscription in Devanagari characters above his head (V. C. Ohri, personal communication, 2002), is obviously engaged in discussing the project with a group of architects (*sutradhara*) while his kinsmen stand behind him. Krishna's eminence is emphasized not only by his dress (all the others are attired in the Mughal-Rajput manner) but also by the space that separates him from the two groups.

The picture probably illustrates chapter 50 of the tenth book of the *Bhagavatapurana*, in which Krishna ordered the building of a fort in the sea at Dvaraka in Gujarat to protect his tribe from the dual assault of Jarasandha and Kalayavana. "Therefore let us construct today a fortress," he said, "inaccessible to human beings and keeping our kinsmen safe in that fort, we shall arrange for the killing of this Kalayavana" (Tagare 1976, pt. IV, pp. 1569–70). In the picture, the unknown artist has taken some liberties. The fort is not in the sea, though a narrow strip of water is delineated along the foreground. Secondly, the tent city makes it seem as if Krishna has already moved his kinsmen rather than waiting for the fort to be constructed.

In any event, the unknown artist has captured the bustle of a construction site with verve and humor by exaggerating the movements of the laborers and engaging them in what appear to be heated discussions. This picture likely belonged to a series illustrating the tenth book of the *Bhagavatapurana*, painted around 1825.

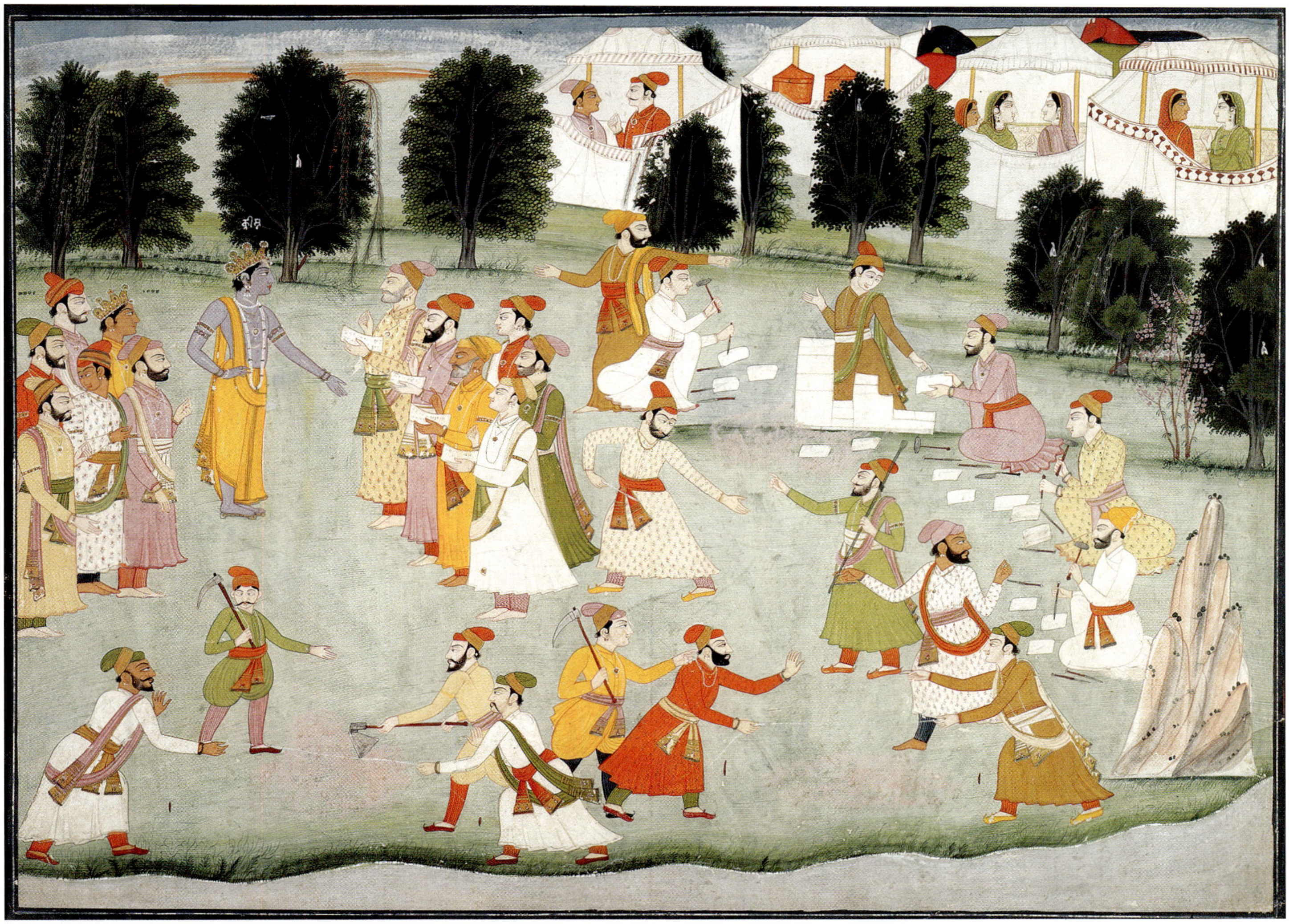

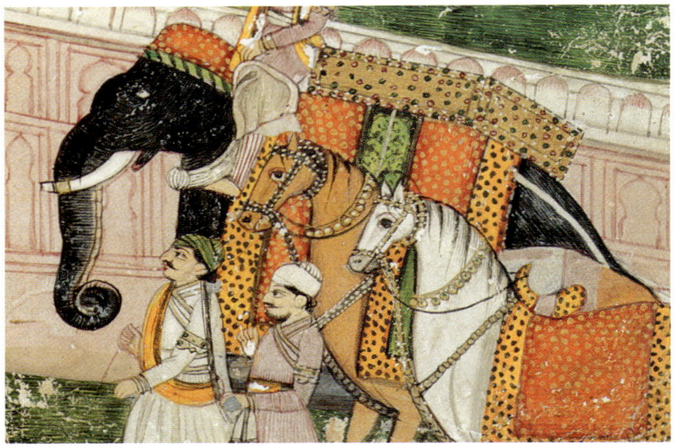

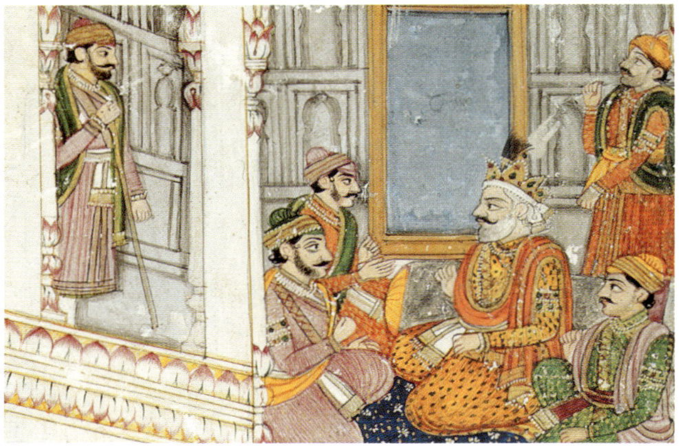

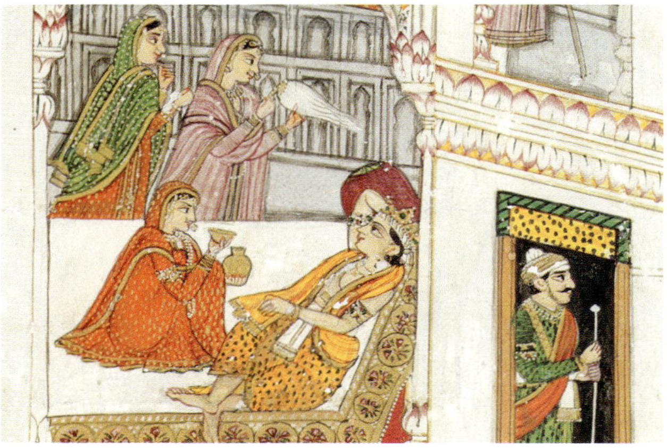

32 Krishna's Palace in Dvaraka

Himachal Pradesh, Kangra workshop, c. 1850
Opaque watercolor on paper
Sheet: 15 ⅞ x 18 ⅝ in. (40.3 x 47.3 cm)
Image: 15 ⅛ x 17 ⅞ in. (38.4 x 45.4 cm)
Gift of Ramesh and Urmil Kapoor; P.2001.13.2

Both thematically and compositionally, this is an unusual picture. Without any text, it is difficult to identify the subject or determine whether it belonged to a series. However, since the principal figure is Krishna, there can be little doubt that it portrays an incident from his life, such as one of his visits to a palace, or the arrival of visitors to see Krishna in Dvaraka, his capital in Gujarat (see [31]). In the foreground are various forms of transportation: a chariot on one side of the entrance and horses and elephants on the other. In the two pavilions along the right side of the painting are two different princes in conversation. Could the one in the upper story be Duryodhana and the other Arjuna, both of whom arrived simultaneously to seek Krishna's support for the imminent war in the epic *Mahabharata*? Interestingly, in the four other pavilions, Krishna (dark) and his foster brother Balarama (fair) are shown twice each. In the central composition, Balarama, who was fond of liquor, is being offered a drink by a lady, presumably his wife.

Framed by a floral border, the composition is dominated by the palace architecture, which has been cleverly depicted with multiple frames to give us a doll's-house view of the interior. Within the courtyard, the walls of the palace are arranged almost like a five-fold screen to provide a continuous visual narrative. Spatial depth is indicated by the three planes of the outer wall, the domestic shrine flanked by two trees on a grass-carpeted courtyard, and the gleaming white palace itself. With its emphasis on architecture, the picture is typical of those produced in the Pahari region around the mid–nineteenth century (see Archer 1973, vol. 2, pl. 233, figs. 71–72 and pl. 334–35, figs. 3–4). ❦

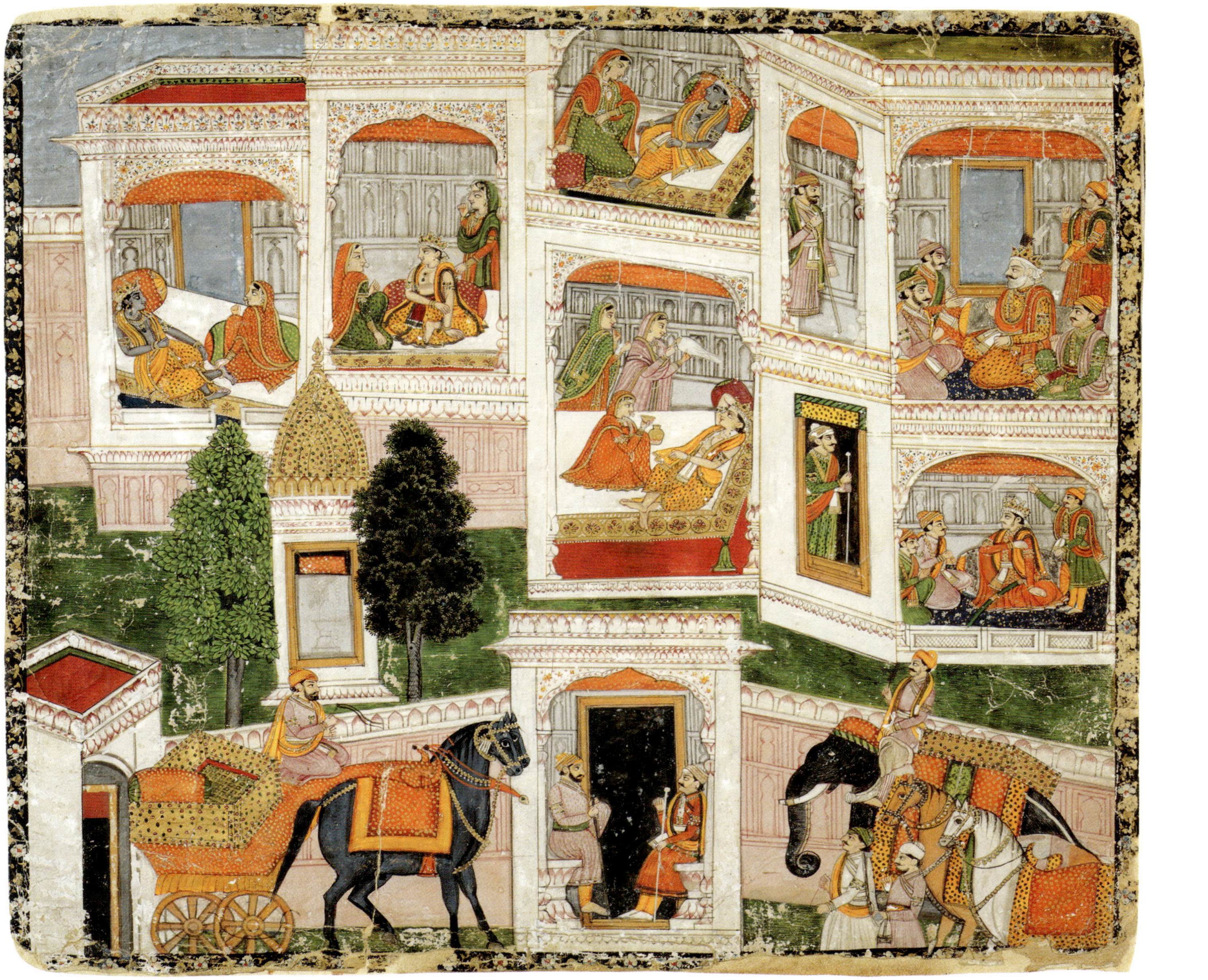

33 Illustration from a *Bhagavatapurana* Series: Story of the Syamantaka Gem

Madhya Pradesh, Malwa, c. 1700
Opaque watercolor on paper
Sheet: 7¾ x 14½ in. (19.7 x 36.8 cm)
Image: 6⅝ x 14 in. (16.8 x 35.6 cm)
Gift of Ramesh and Urmil Kapoor; P.2003.2.6

A long text in the Hindi dialect of Vrajabhasha, written on the back (see Appendix), helps to identify the subject as being from two chapters (56–57) of the tenth book of the *Bhagavatapurana* (Tagare 1976, pt. IV, pp. 1604–19). It is a tale of theft, misunderstanding, murder, revenge and two marriages of Krishna, for whom the stone proved to be romantic. Changing hands, the stone finally fell into the hands of a bear chief, Jambavan. When Krishna went to his cave to recover it, Jambavan recognized his divinity, and apart from returning the stone, gave him his daughter in marriage. Krishna then returned the gem to its rightful owner, Satyaki, who offered Krishna his sister Satyabhama as well as the stone. Krishna declined the stone but accepted the girl.

In the left half of the composition, the wedding takes place under a tent and brahmans perform the fire ceremony (*homa*). On the right, Krishna is the dark figure in the middle register holding the stone, which is also in the hands of the figure facing him and again in the maid's hand in the lower register. The text on the back, however, does not directly relate to the illustration. At least three other sequential illustrations of the same story are in the National Museum, New Delhi (Banerjee 1978, figs. 192–93, 195). There can be little doubt that the vernacular version is more embroidered than the Sanskrit original.

The representation is simple, direct and graphic. Although rendered a century after the Bikaner *Bhagavatapurana* [25], the narrative strategy has changed little. Like the clusters of grass that dot the ground like starbursts, the gesture of the right hand is repeatedly used to animate the figures, except for the priests offering oblations. For other examples from the same series, see Pal 1978, no. 26 and Dye 2001, no. 134, in which a discussion (p. 323) of the text by Richard J. Cohen is given.

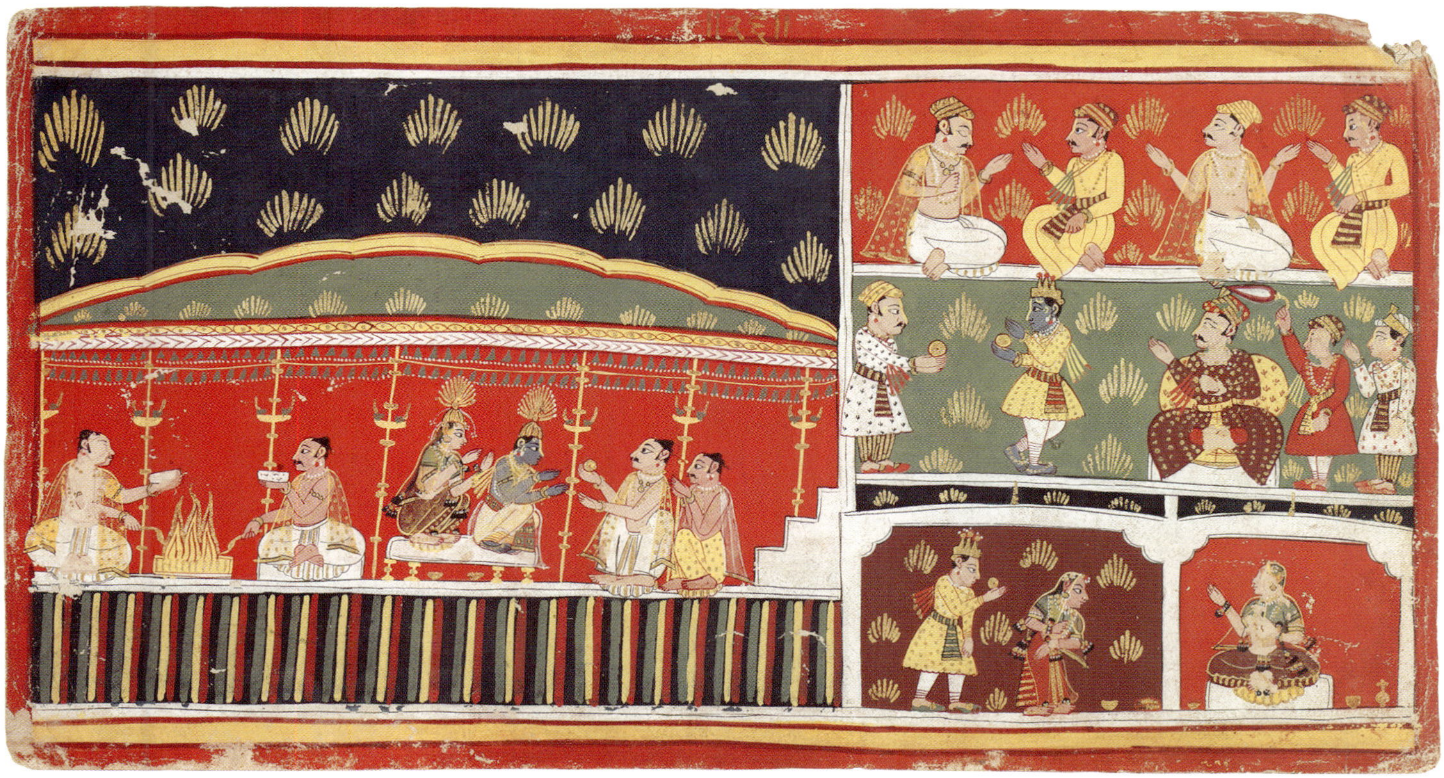

Two Illustrations to the *Bhagavatapurana*

34 A King in a Pavilion

Himachal Pradesh, Guler workshop, c. 1750
Opaque watercolor on paper
Sheet: 7 3/8 x 11 5/8 in. (18.7 x 29.5 cm)
Image: 6 7/8 x 11 3/8 in. (17.5 x 28.9 cm)
Lent by Ramesh and Urmil Kapoor

35 Sage Sukdeva and King Parikshit

Himachal Pradesh, Guler workshop, c. 1775–1800
Opaque watercolor on paper
Sheet: 8 1/2 x 11 1/4 in. (21.6 x 28.6 cm)
Image: 7 1/4 x 10 1/16 in. (18.4 x 25.6 cm)
Gift of Ramesh and Urmil Kapoor; P.2002.2.7

As there are no inscriptions on the front or back of the picture with the solitary figure [34], it is difficult to identify him precisely. However, there is no doubt that he represents a mythical elderly ruler. Almost certainly the picture is from the *Bhagavatapurana* series published by William Archer and attributed by him to Basohli, c. 1760–65 (1973, vol. 2, pl. 37–39). Goswamy has reattributed the series to Manaku of Guler, who apparently began working on it around 1740. His sons may have continued to do so into the 1760s (Goswamy and Fischer 1992, pp. 244–45). This painting could conceivably be by Manaku himself, or by Fattu (d. c. 1785), one of his sons. Fattu was particularly fond of juxtaposing architecture and landscape elements in an unrealistic manner, as is done here (see Jain-Neubauer 1998). The rendering of the rich vegetation, sky and spatial depth also indicate an artist from the first generation after Manaku. A master's sure hand is further evident in the dignified, portrait-like treatment of the royal face.

In the second picture [35], small inscriptions above the figure's heads identify them as the sage Sukdeva and King Parikshit (see Appendix). They are two important characters in the *Bhagavatapurana* and in fact, the former is the narrator of the text. He recited it in the course of a week to Parikshit so that the latter would gain salvation by listening to the tale of Krishna. Parikshit had only a week to live due to a curse laid on him by another sage, who he had offended.

In the text, the scene takes place on the bank of the holy river Ganga, where the sage and the monarch meet. In the picture, however, the two are seated within a pavilion that improbably sits or floats on the water, which swirls around the structure. Clearly the same mode of composition has been used in both paintings: the central pavilion bears little realistic relationship to its surroundings—the structure being used as a frame, especially in the second picture. The water is depicted with greater tranquility than is seen in Manaku's paintings but is comparable to the river in a picture of the 1781 *Devimahatmya*, probably from the same family workshop, now in the Lahore Museum (Aijazuddin 1977, pl. 41 (iii)).

There can be little doubt that the two paintings were rendered by artists of the same family. During the second half of the eighteenth century, the members of the talented Guler family were working for various patrons in the hills. Fattu, for instance, moved to Kangra to work for Sansar Chand. If this simple but bold composition is not by him, it could have been created by one of his three sons—Madho, Molak or Kanshiram—whose dates are unknown but who were active toward the end of the century.

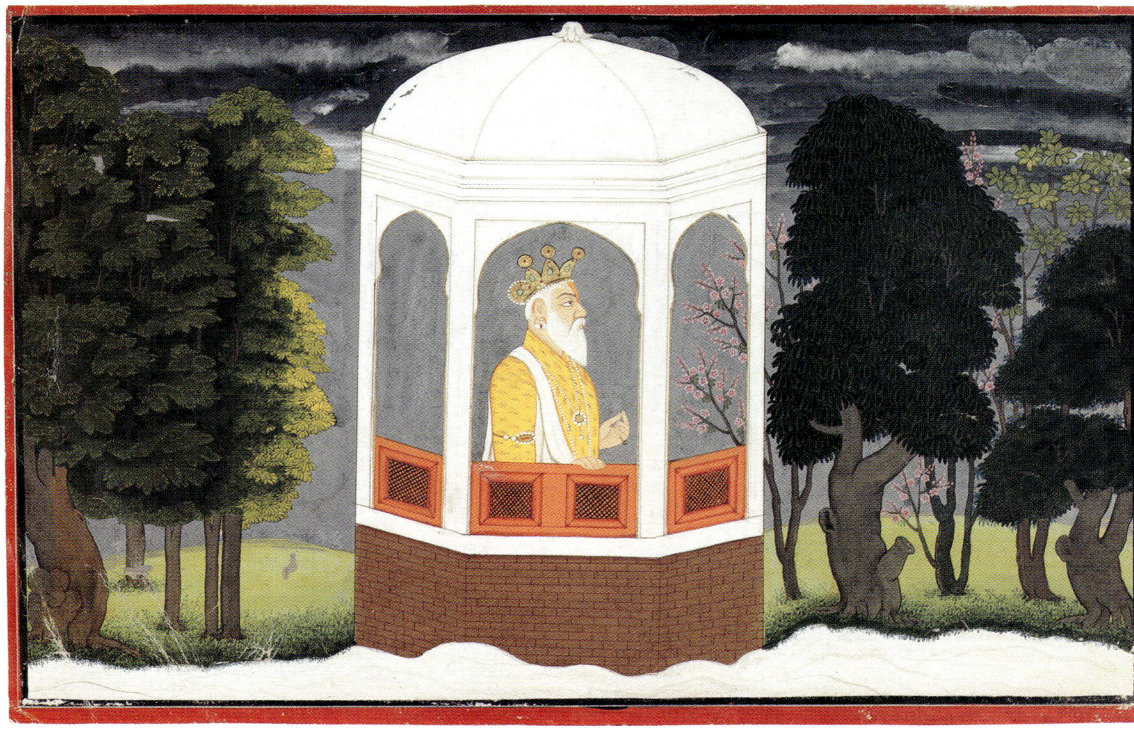

34

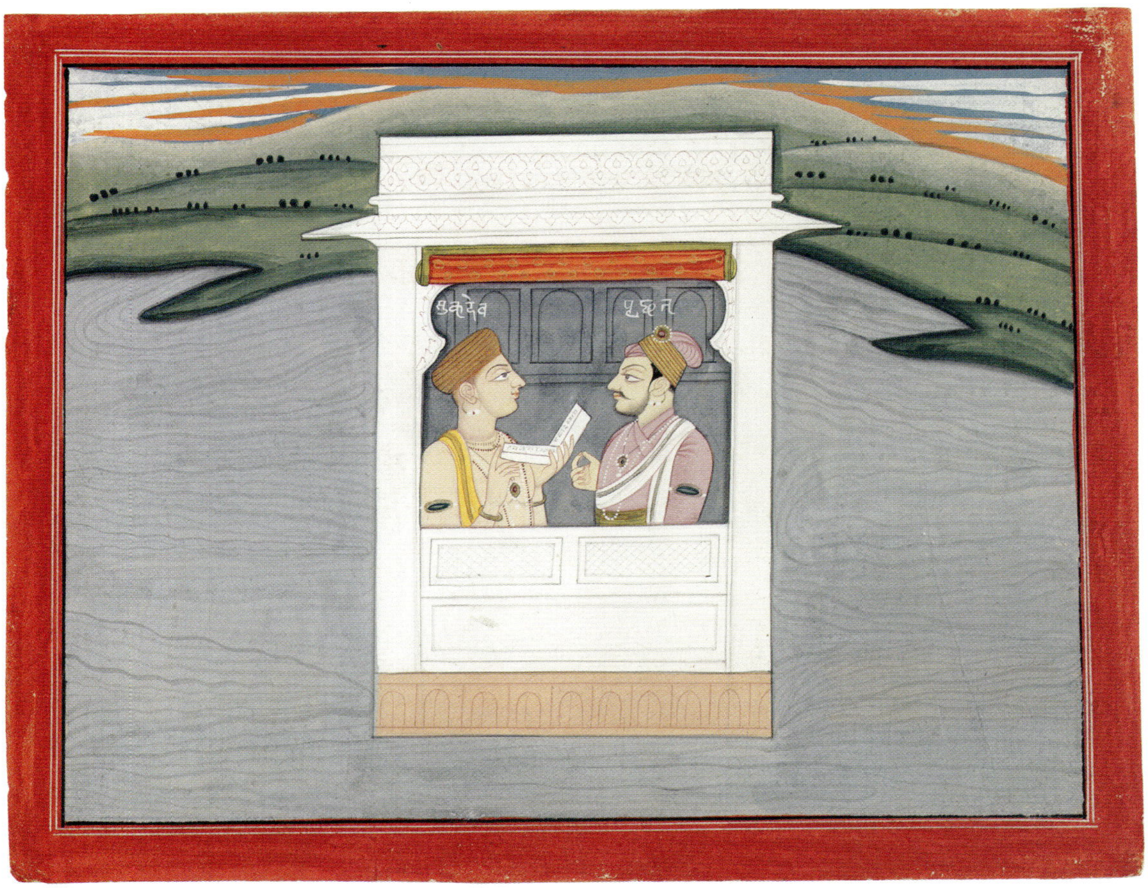

35

36 Folio from a *Bhagavatapurana* Series: King Yudhisthira Performs the Rajasuya Sacrifice

Himachal Pradesh, Kangra workshop, 1825–50
Opaque watercolor and gold on paper
Sheet: 12 ¼ x 17 in. (31.1 x 43.2 cm)
Image: 10 ½ x 15 ⅝ in. (26.7 x 39.7 cm)
Gift of Ramesh and Urmil Kapoor; p.2003.2.2

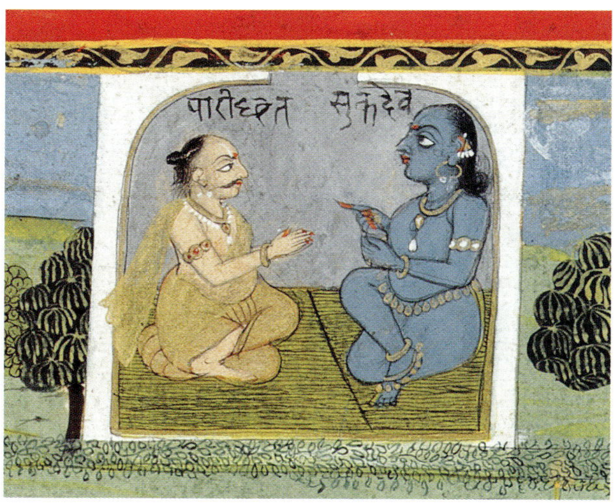

The subject represents the performance of the Rajasuya, or Royal Consecration sacrifice, by King Yudhisthira, as described not in the *Mahabharata* but in the *Bhagavatapurana*. The Sanskrit text from chapter 75 of the tenth book is given on the back. Short inscriptions written in Devanagari within the picture identify some of the scenes (see Appendix).

At the summit of the composition is an inset representation of the sage Sukdeva narrating the text to King Parikshit, the grandson of Yudhisthira [35]. Immediately below, under a makeshift awning, the sacrifice is being performed in front of the sacred fire. The entire left third represents the kitchen, whose superintendent is Bhimasena, as well as the place where guests are eating. The blue boyish figure of Krishna is shown twice: once in the foreground center, being greeted officially with water, and again, swimming in the water. To the right, King Yudhisthira is seen bathing and then donning his royal robes on the bank. Behind, musicians accompany him as he approaches the water. He is also shown seated in the gazebo-like structure with a thatched roof, bidding farewell to departing guests.

Curiously, among the five brothers, only Bhimasena and Sahadeva are identified by name. Yudhisthira is simply addressed as *raja*. Draupadi, the common wife of the five siblings, is also named, as are Duryodhana and Karna of the rival group. Curiously, Krishna is depicted as a boy rather than a grown-up, as he is in the saga. In this large composition, note the generous use of gold for the clothing, utensils, musical instruments and streaks of clouds.

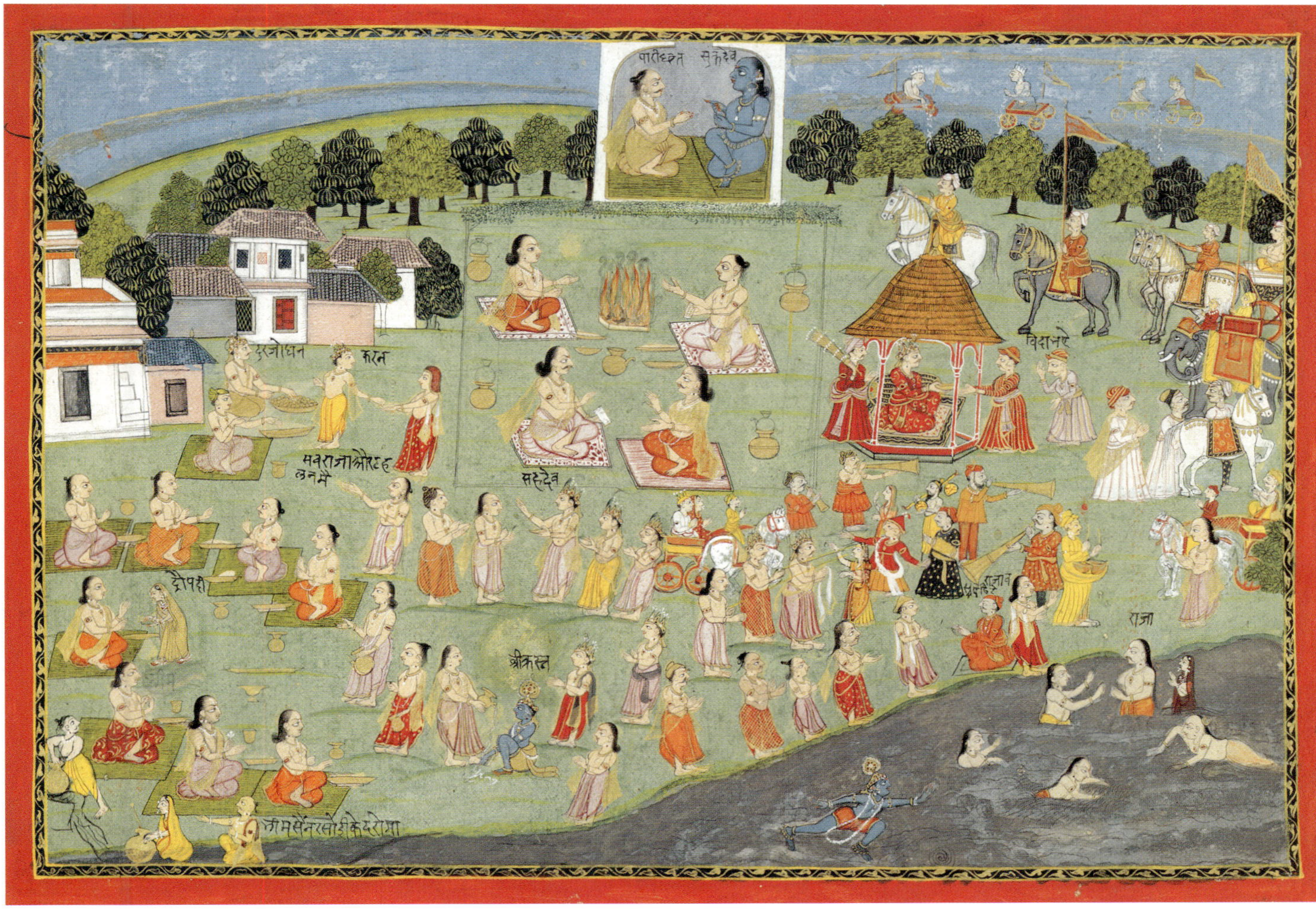
दुरजोधन
करन
सहदेव
द्रौपदी
श्रीकृस्न
राजा

37 Folio from a *Bhagavatapurana*: Priests Perform a Sacrifice

Orissa, Puri (?), nineteenth century
Opaque watercolor on paper
Sheet: 9 ¼ x 12 ¾ in. (23.5 x 32.4 cm)
Image: 8 ⅜ x 11 ⅝ in. (21.3 x 29.5 cm)
Gift of Ramesh and Urmil Kapoor; P.2003.2.3

Both the illustration and the text, written in the Oriya script (see Appendix), are accommodated within the red border. The five-line text is written in the slightly narrower bottom half in a beautiful calligraphic hand with bold lettering. The figures in the illustration above are arranged in two tiers, rather than around the fire. The four men in the upper register seem to be engaged in a heated debate, judging from their attitudes, expressions and gestures. Perhaps they express the disagreement narrated in the text below as to whether a brahman should eat rice cooked by milkmen, who are not of the same caste. In the lower register, one of the four brahmans offers oblation into the sacred fire. Looking on are two boys standing in reverential attitude and three women inside two separate buildings. The inscription next to the boys alludes to the sacrificial garden and the *gopavalaka*, or cowherds.

Paper was adopted rather late in Orissa, both for texts and illustrations. Instead, the preference was for palm leaves, especially for sacred books, and the stylus. Obviously such works as these were inspired by Rajput illustrated books, which seem to have become available in Orissa by the eighteenth century. Except for the horizontal format, little influence of Orissa's traditional manuscript illuminations is evident in these works in terms of figural forms, foliage or coloring. Closely related in broad elements of style is a contemporary *Gopa-lila* manuscript in the Bhuvaneshwar Museum (see Fabri 1974, pl. CLXXVII).

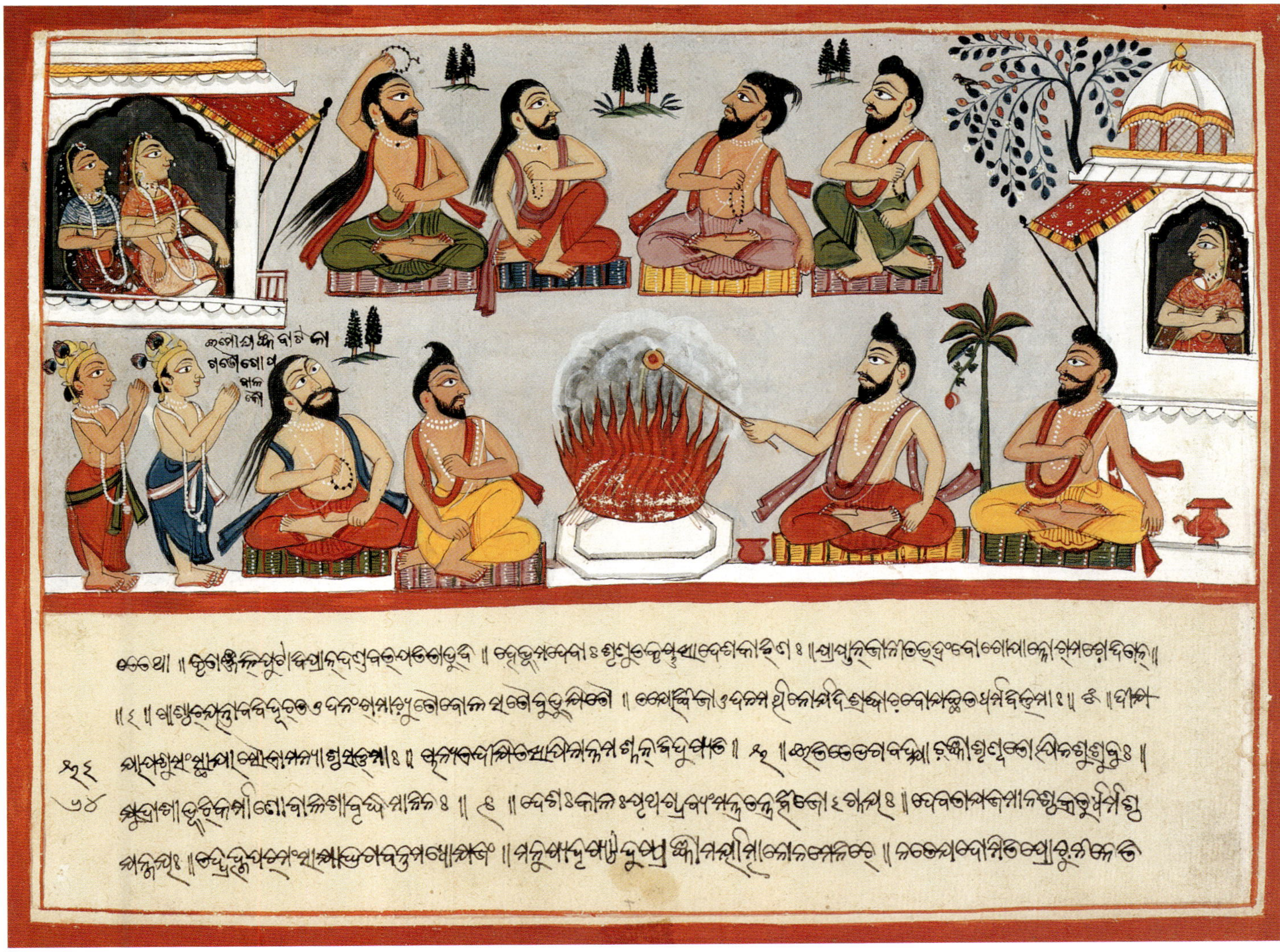

Illustrations from an "Abduction of Rukmini" Series

38 Rukmini and the Messenger

Himachal Pradesh, Guler workshop,
c. 1775–1800
Opaque watercolor on paper
Sheet: 7 7/8 x 11 1/2 in. (20 x 29.2 cm)
Image: 7 1/8 x 10 7/8 in. (18.1 x 27.6 cm)
Gift of Ramesh and Urmil Kapoor; P.2000.9.9

39 Rukmini and Entourage Leave for the Temple

Himachal Pradesh, Kangra workshop, c. 1800
Opaque watercolor on paper
Sheet: 14 x 19 1/2 in. (35.6 x 49.5 cm)
Image: 12 x 17 1/2 in. (30.5 x 44.5 cm)
Lent by Ramesh and Urmil Kapoor

40 The Marriage of Krishna and Rukmini

Himachal Pradesh, Kangra workshop, c. 1800
Opaque watercolor on paper
Sheet: 9 7/8 x 13 3/8 in. (25.1 x 34 cm)
Image: 7 3/4 x 11 7/8 in. (19.7 x 30.2 cm)
Gift of Vineet and Floretta Kapoor; P.2001.15

These three pictures, though stylistically related, are from three different series of a tale of romance and chivalry that was particularly popular with Pahari patrons around 1800. Known as *Rukmini-haran*, or the Abduction of Rukmini, the story forms part of the *Bhagavatapurana*, but was illustrated as an independent tale. The story is about a princess called Rukmini who was betrothed by her brother to Sishupal, the powerful Chedi king. Rukmini, however, had lost her heart to Krishna. After receiving a message from her through a brahman, Krishna told the brahman to instruct Rukmini to visit a temple on the morning of the wedding day. Doing so, she was abducted by Krishna while Balarama and their companions fended off the chase given by her brother and others. On reaching Krishna's palace in Dvaraka, the couple were married and lived happily ever after.

In the first of the three pictures [38] we see the brahman messenger returning to Rukmini with Krishna's message. The threatening gesture of his right hand may indicate that he is telling her not to forget the instructions he has conveyed to her. In the second painting [39], Rukmini leaves her palace for the Gourja temple with much pomp and ceremony, as befits a princess. Dressed in a golden sari with her head completely covered, she stands in the middle of the group of ladies. Two companions hold the fly-whisk and the peacock-feather *morchal* behind her. (For other examples from the same series, see Fogg 2003, no. 45 and Galloway 2000, no. 11.)

In the third picture [40] the bride and groom—Rukmini and Krishna—are being welcomed at the palace by the ladies, as is still done in traditional Hindu weddings when the groom returns home with the bride. Usually the groom's mother performs the ceremony, but the lady here is unlikely to be Krishna's mother. Nevertheless, the scene is remarkably true to life and reflects the artist's familiarity with the occasion. He has not forgotten the auspicious floral drawing with rice powder below the couple, or the custom of covering the shy bride's head. *(continued on page 90)*

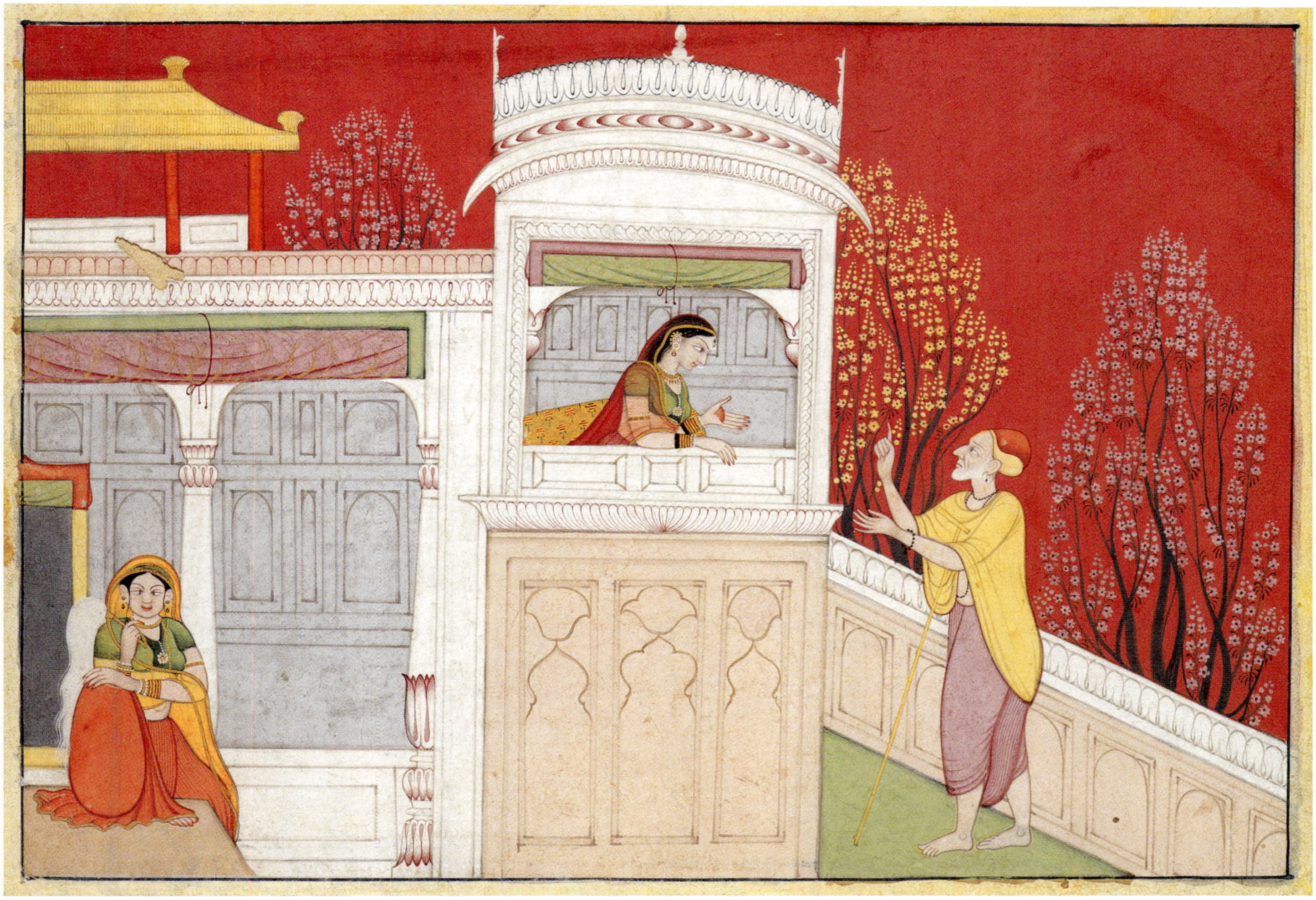

38

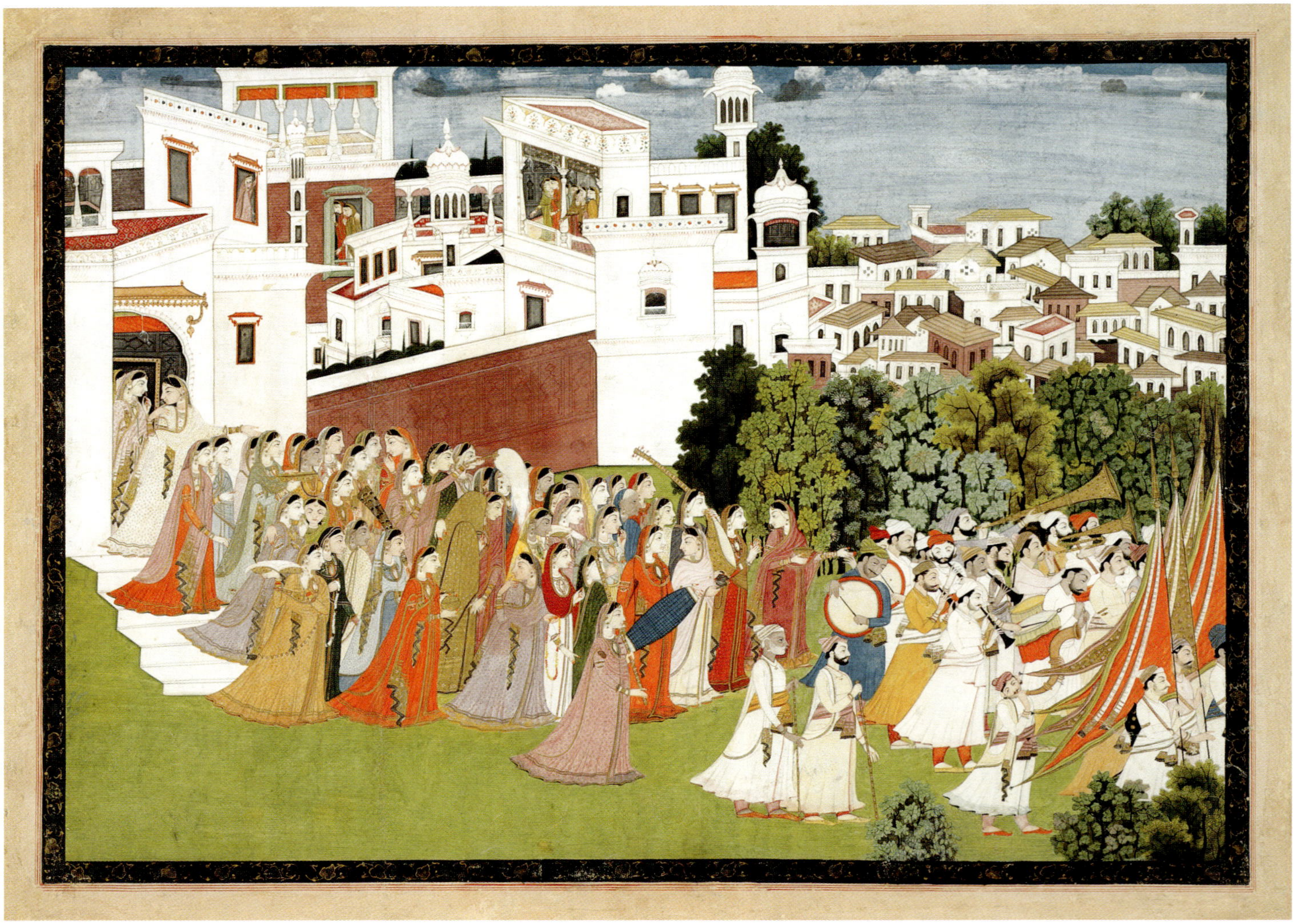

39

At least two other versions of the return of the messenger have been published: one in the Bhuri Singh Museum in Chamba (Goswamy and Fischer 1992, no. 147 and Ohri and Craven 1998, fig. 11) and a second in the Victoria and Albert Museum, London (Archer 1973, vol. 2, pl. 83, fig. 12). William Archer assigned the Victoria and Albert picture to Garhwal between 1775 and 1785. While the Chamba example is considered by the authors to be a work between 1790 and 1800, of a "master of the first generation after Nainsukh," V. C. Ohri has suggested that it was painted by the Guler artist Nikka at Chamba between 1775 and 1780. Nikka was in fact a son of Nainsukh (d. 1728), who was one of the great Pahari masters of the Guler *gharana*. It should be noted that the Garhwal ruler, Pratap Shah (r. 1872–87), was married to a Guler princess; hence, the presence of Guler pictures at the court is not surprising.

The differences between the three pictures are only in minor details. In [38], flowering plants replace the green trees of the other two paintings, and there is no indication of sky above the sweep of the red background. Another noteworthy difference is the close-up view of the scene in this and the Victoria and Albert Museum versions, as opposed to the wide-angle view in the Chamba rendition. The squint eyes of the maid and the stronger characterization of the messenger's physiognomy are other distinguishing features of the painting under discussion. Whether such differences have chronological implication or are simply idiosyncratic nuances of individual artists is not possible to assert. Nor can we be certain where it was painted. However, it is certain that all three reflect the same Guler manner.

In the panoramic procession and marriage pictures we encounter complex renderings of architecture, with multiple perspectives, as if each artist were observing the scene from an exalted vantage point on a rooftop or balcony. Such deft and idiosyncratic manipulation of architectural forms to enliven a composition was a peculiarity of Phurku, whose career and corpus have been extensively discussed by Goswamy and Fischer (1992, pp. 368–73). Active from 1782 to 1820, he was one of the artists who worked for Raja Sansar Chand of Kangra. Phurku, who had a keen eye for details, was also adept at handling compositions with multiple figures, situating them naturalistically in unconventional architectural settings. Noteworthy is the considerably larger size of the procession painting, which adds to the drama of the composition and the visual effect. According to Galloway (citation above) the series to which this belongs may have been commissioned by Lajna Singh Majithia (of unknown date but of the early nineteenth century), who was the Sikh governor of the Hills and retained in his service descendants of the great Nainsukh.

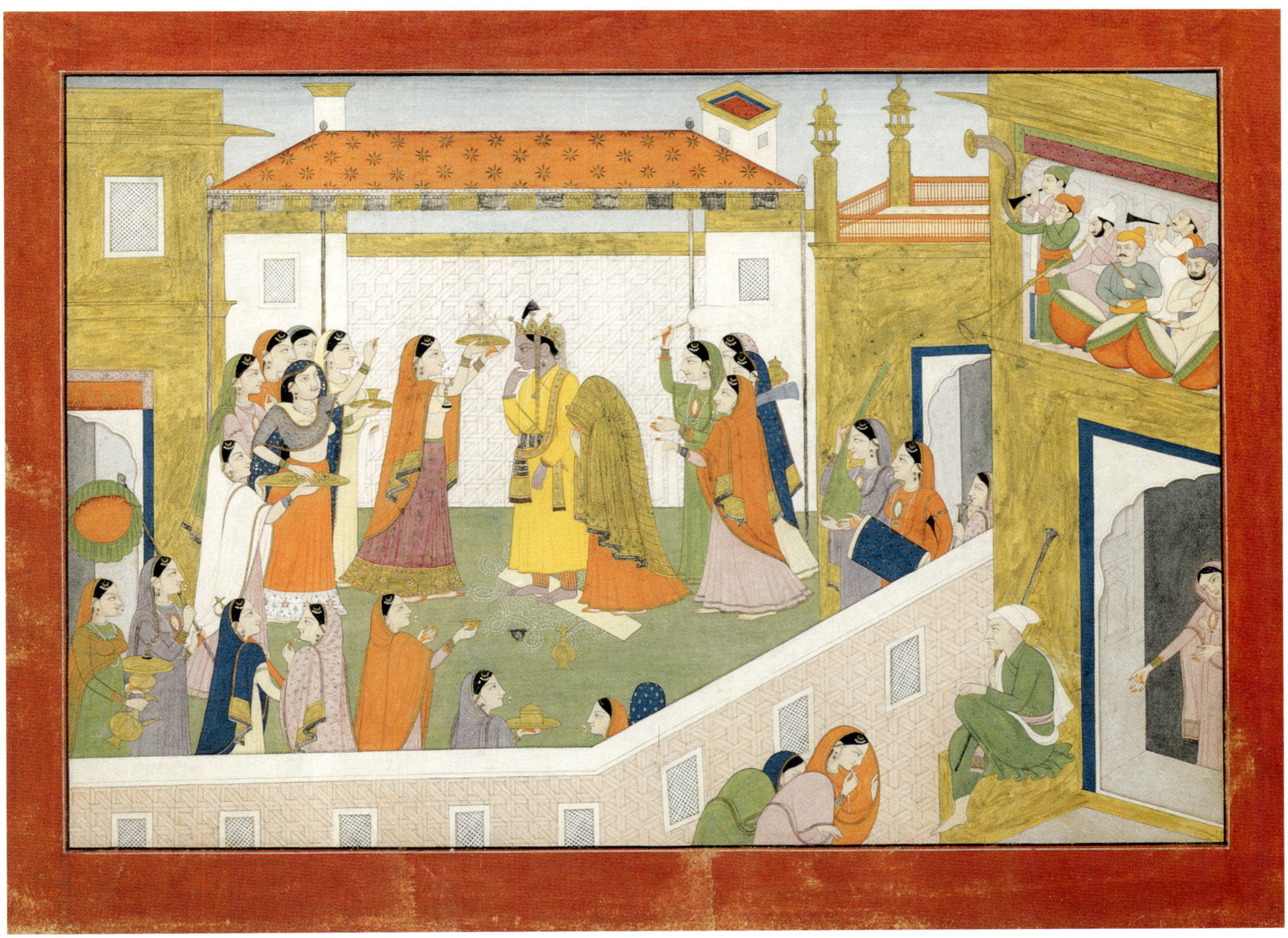

40

41 Krishna Offering Parijata Flowers to Rukmini

Himachal Pradesh, Tira Sujanpur (Kangra) workshop, c. 1760
Opaque watercolor on paper
Sheet: 11⅜ x 8⅜ in. (28.9 x 21.3 cm)
Image: 9⅜ x 6⅜ in. (23.8 x 16.2 cm)
Lent by Ramesh and Urmil Kapoor

42 Parvati Extolling Punyaka Rite to Wives of the Sages

Himachal Pradesh, Kangra workshop, 1800–1825
Opaque watercolor on paper
Sheet: 16⅛ x 22⅝ in. (41 x 57.5 cm)
Image: 15 x 21½ in. (38.1 x 54.6 cm)
Lent by Ramesh and Urmil Kapoor

Both paintings relate to the myth of Parijata-harana (theft of the Parijata [tree]), recounted in the *Harivamsa*, an important Vaishnava text. The myth is followed by three chapters extolling the efficacy of certain rites and fasts (*vrata*) that pious women should perform to ensure the well-being of their husbands. This is what Parvati is discussing in the later of the two paintings here [42], as indicated by the text quoted on the back (see Appendix).

In the earlier painting [41], the first part of the myth of the theft is represented. The divine sage Narada, the mischievous minstrel and messenger of the gods, has brought a flower from the Parijata tree; Krishna hands it over to Rukmini. Narada promptly proceeds to the pavilion of Krishna's other wife, Satyabhama, and tells her how Krishna has favored Rukmini. Jealous and angry, Satyabhama nags Krishna and refuses to be appeased until he brings the entire tree to her. Krishna departs for the god Indra's celestial garden, the only place where the tree grows. Indra is unable to prevent Krishna's aggression. A second picture depicting the battle between Krishna and Indra is in the collection of the Lambargaon court, also in Kangra (see Randhawa 1959, pl. 15).

In the later picture [42], Parvati, seated in a pavilion on a lake, discourses to the wives of the sages, some of whom are also present in the audience led by Narada holding his *vina*. Parvati has all the trappings of royalty, and the scene is set in the high mountains, perhaps representing Shiva's palace on Mt. Kailash, the lake being Manasarovar.

The two paintings differ considerably in style, the earlier one continuing what is generally characterized as the Basohli manner. The series, however, is said to have been painted in Tira Sujanpur, the new capital of Kangra, when the older fort was occupied by the Mughals, around 1760. The artist was probably from the family of Pandit Seu of Guler, for the style has clear affinity with pictures rendered by Pandit Seu's third-generation descendants in the mid–eighteenth century for various patrons, shortly before the style changed dramatically around 1775 to that seen in the later picture. The painting could have been done *(continued on page 95)*

41

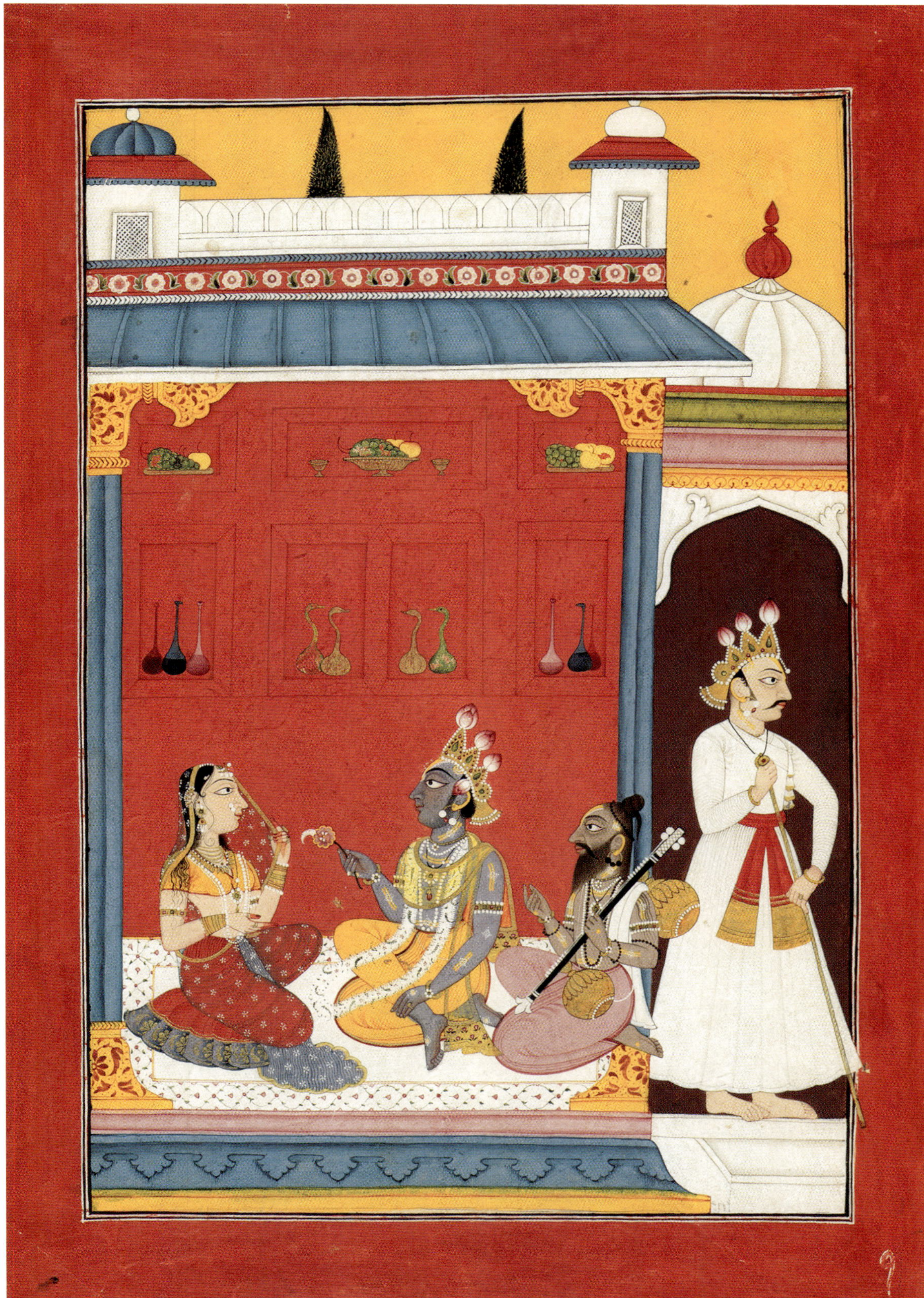

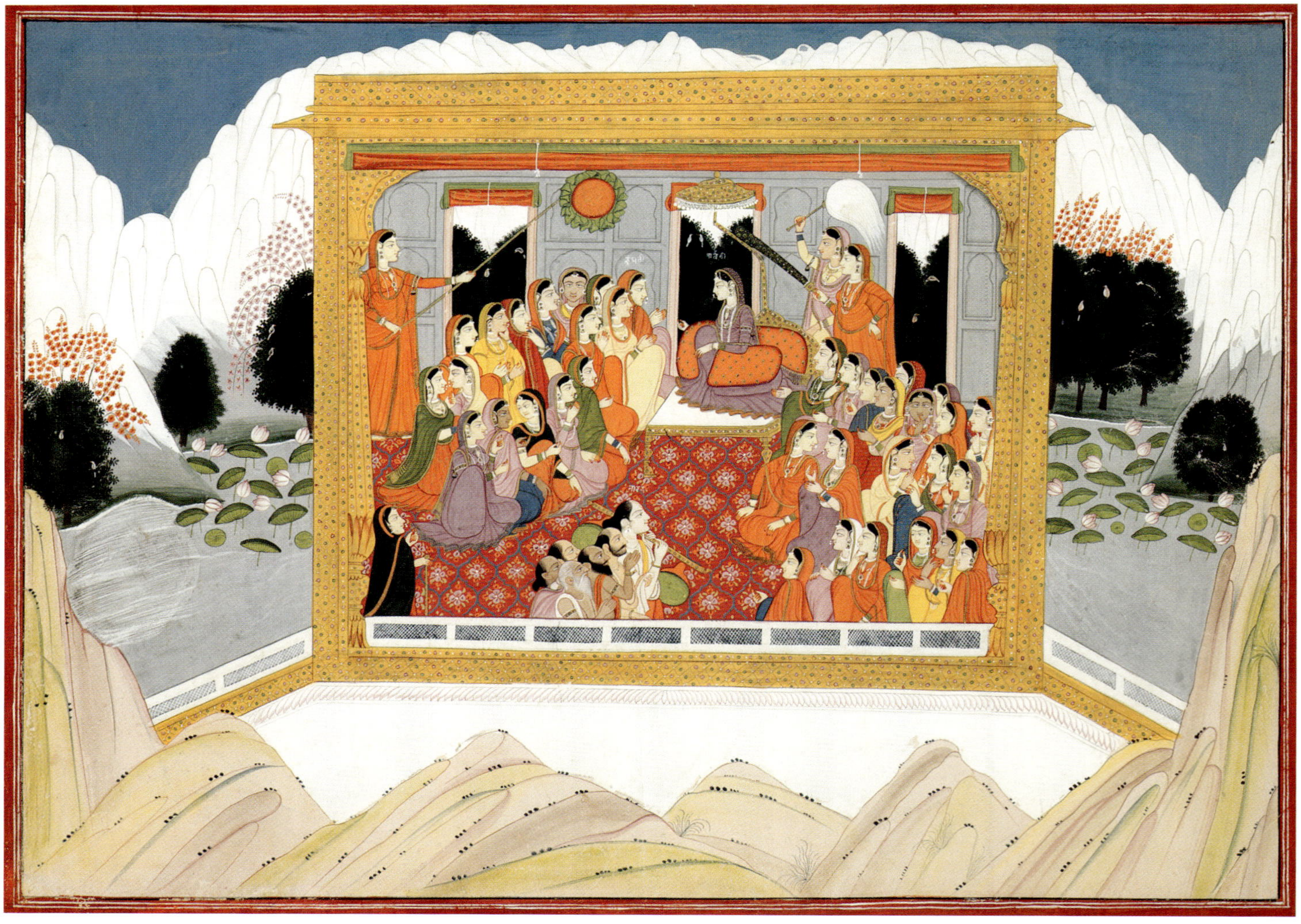

42

for Raja Ghamand Chand (r. c. 1751/1761–1774), a powerful ruler who restored Kangra to its former size and made it the most powerful southern state. It is interesting that his predecessor, who in 1748 built the fortress palace at Tira Sujanpur, gave his daughter in marriage to Amrit Pal of Basohli.

The later picture [42] is closely related to two paintings published by Goswamy and Fischer (1992, nos. 166–67), who have ascribed them to the painter Phurku of Kangra. Not much is known about him except that he flourished between 1780 and 1820, was attached to the court of the Kangra ruler and avid patron of the arts Sansar Chand (r. 1775–1823) and belonged to a family originally from Guler (Goswamy and Fischer 1992, pp. 368–73).

As is clear from his other pictures, Phurku was not bashful in manipulating forms, especially of architecture and landscape elements, in order to enhance the mythic elements of his narrative. Realistic spaces and optical veracity were not his concerns. Pushed back to the far edge of the white terrace without imparting any sense of volume, the golden pavilion looks like a giant framed picture. Inside, the figures are deftly arranged in diagonal rows to create perspective space and to emphasize Parvati's eminence.

43 Leaf from a Manuscript of Jayadeva's *Gitagovinda*: Dalliance of Krishna and Radha

Attributed to Govinda (fl. 1580–1611)
Gujarat, c. 1600
Opaque watercolor on paper
Sheet: 5 x 10 in. (12.7 x 25.4 cm)
Gift of Ramesh and Urmil Kapoor; P.2002.2.6

The verses on top of each page are from Canto 11 of the *Gitagovinda* of Jayadeva (fl. twelfth century). The following translations are by Barbara Miller (1977, pp. 120 and 163):

[A]
She (Radha) saw her passion reach the soul of Hari's mood—
The weight of joy strained his face; Love's ghost haunted him.
He toyed with ropes of clear pearls lying on his chest,
Like the dark Jumna current churning shining swells of foam.

[B]
The soft black curve of his body was wrapped in fine silk cloth,
Like a dark lotus root wrapped in veils of yellow pollen.
Her passion rose when glances played on his seductive face,
Like an autumn pond when wagtails mate on lotus blossom hollows.

The first couplet is a refrain that is used for each of the verses from number twenty-four to thirty-one. It should further be noted that only very minor variations occur between the text here and the published edited text, although the numbering is different.

As has been discussed elsewhere (see Pal 1993, pp. 147–49), almost certainly the artist responsible for this series of the *Gitagovinda* was Govinda, who painted a Jain text in the same style at Matar in Gujarat in 1583. His name is also found in two *Bhagavatapurana* manuscripts, one of 1598 (City Palace Museum, Jaipur) and one of 1610–11 (formerly in the Jodhpur Royal Library). Eighteen painted folios from this manuscript are in the Maharaja Sawai Man Singh II Museum (Vatsyayan 1980). Typically, the figures are represented in a single plane against a red background, whose undulating upper edge forms the horizon. Natural forms are stylized and minimal—a tree or two with bees, and water rendered in a basket-weave pattern. Also characteristic of the series is the rather vague nexus between the verses and the illustrations. The composition seems to be divided into two by a vertical line. On side [A] on the left, Radha is shown twice approaching Krishna, while Love in the form of Kamadeva wearing stitched clothes "haunts" him by shooting an arrow.

Changing his costume, Kamadeva does the same as Radha turns and looks at Krishna across the vertical stream of the river Yamuna. He is not toying with his ropes of pearls. The relationship between the verbal and visual narratives is even less clear in the second composition [B], except for the darker shades of Krishna and the inclusion of the autumn pond with a pair of birds.

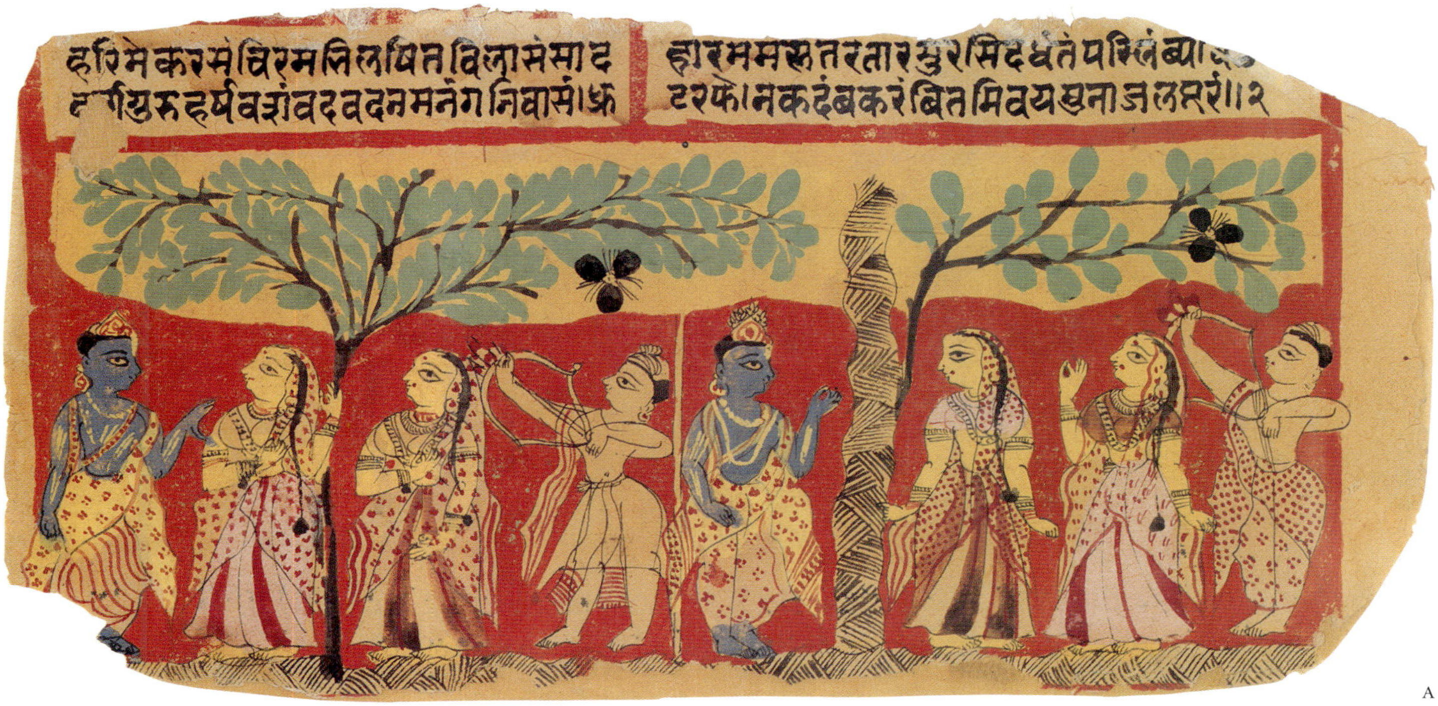

A

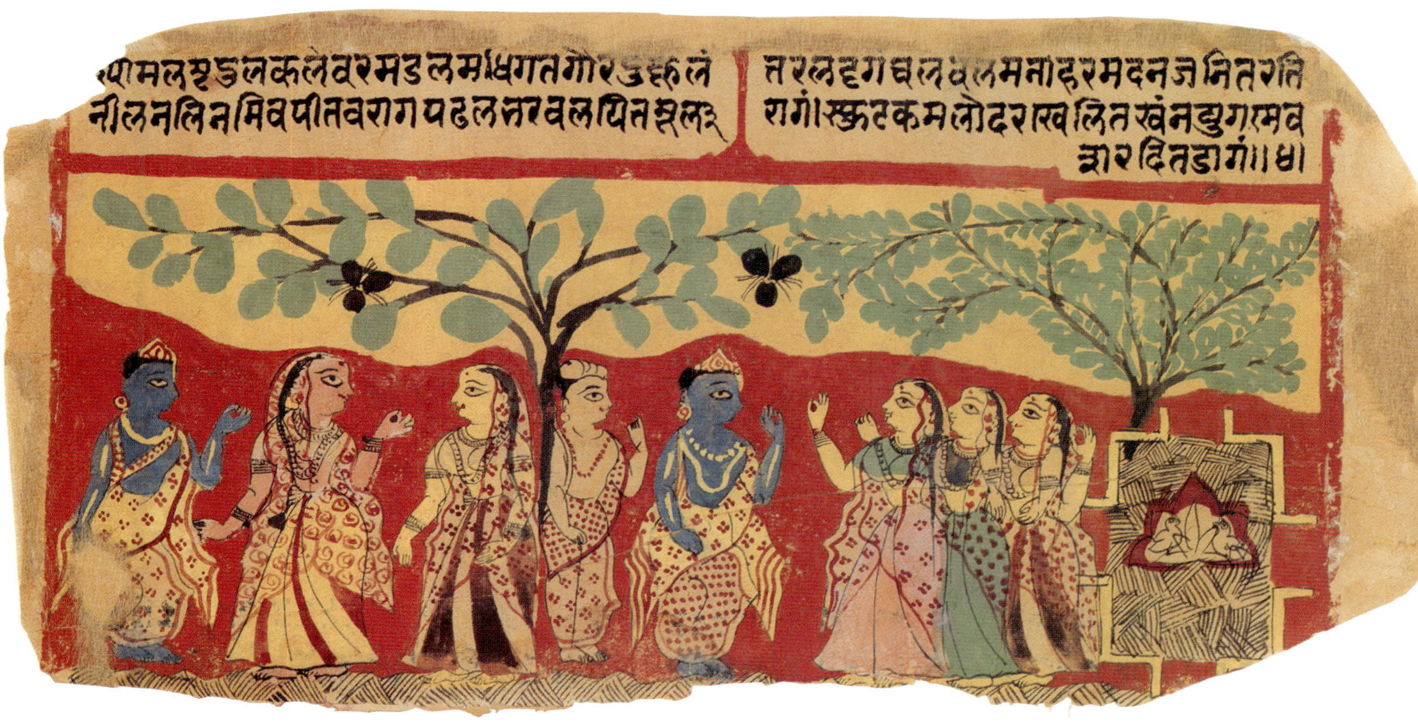

B

44 Illustration to a Verse from Jayadeva's *Gitagovinda*: The Charming Flautist

Himachal Pradesh, Guler or Kangra workshop, c. 1775
Opaque watercolor and gold on paper
Sheet: 7 x 10 ¾ in. (17.8 x 27.3 cm)
Image: 6 x 10 in. (15.2 x 25.4 cm)
Lent by Ramesh and Urmil Kapoor

The verse on the back (see Appendix) is the inspiration behind this lyrically beautiful picture. According to the inscription following the verse, it is from the ninth canto of Jayadeva's *Gitagovinda*, but elsewhere (Randhawa 1963, p. 74 and George Kyt as quoted in the Appendix) it is included in the eighth canto. However, the verse is not included at all in the most recently published edition of the text (Miller 1977), which needs to be examined further.

The painting is from what has come to be regarded as one of the finest series illustrating the long lyrical poem. With the river Yamuna and the rolling hills of the Aravalli range in the background, Krishna, clothed in yellow garb, stands in his popular iconic form playing the flute. A group of *gopis*, or milkmaids, surround him with rapturous attention, though the artist chose not to depict flowers falling from their hair (as is mentioned in the verse). Each of the ladies is a paragon of beauty with delicate, graceful features, a depiction characteristic of Guler/Kangra artists. While their faces show little variation, the subtle gestures of their hands and body language express their emotions.

William Archer was the first scholar to suggest that this series was probably painted by two cousins: Kushala (1730–1790) and Gaudhu (c. 1740–1820). The former was the son of the master Manaku, whose sibling Nainsukh was the father of Gaudhu (Archer 1973, vol. 1, p. 292). Goswamy and Fischer (1992, p. 312), however, regard the series as the work of a solitary "master of the first generation after Nainsukh." In no way does the uncertainty of the identity of the painting's creator detract us from admiring this lyrical and joyous visualization of Jayadeva's sublime poetical composition.

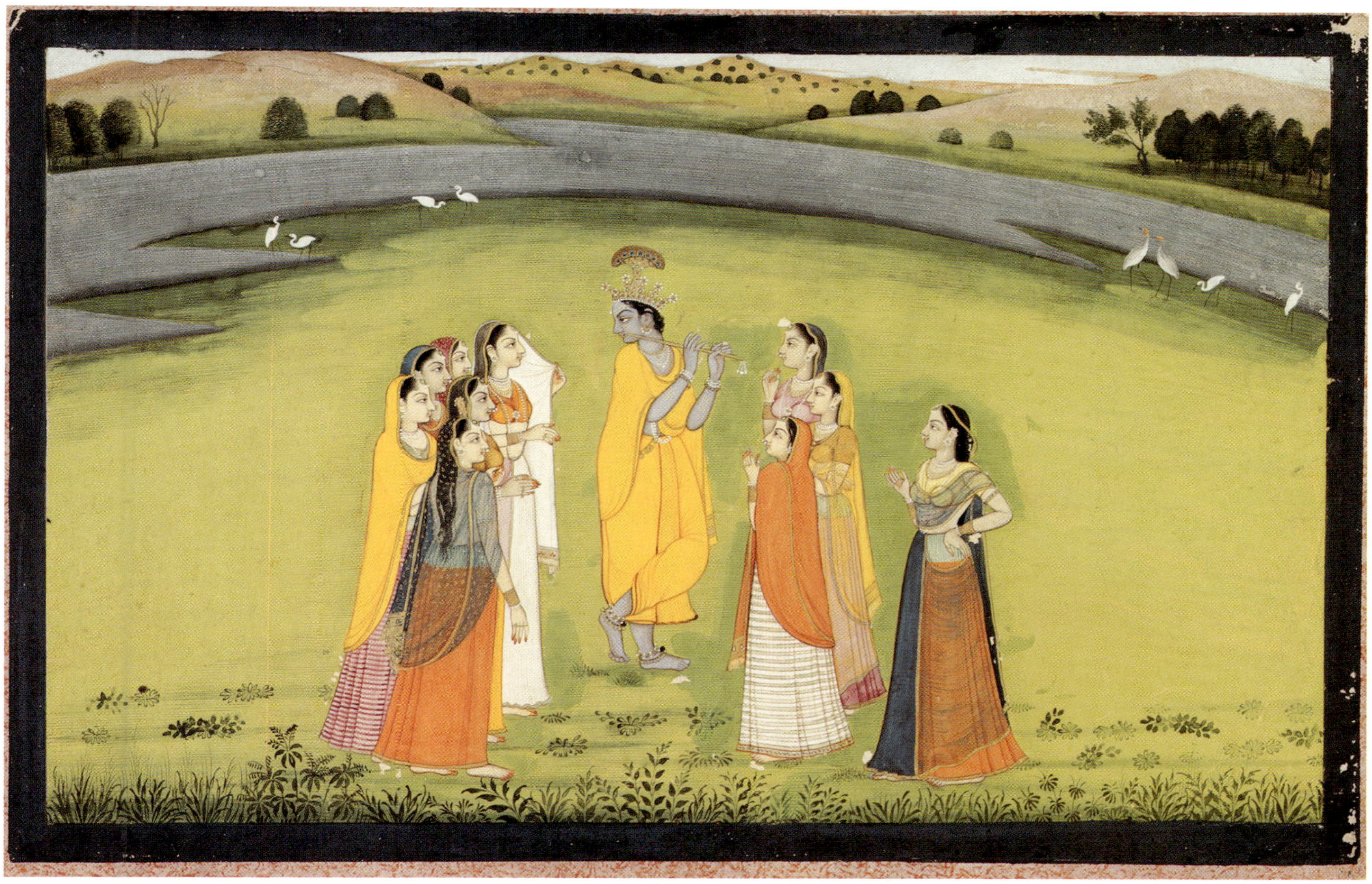

45 Krishna Demands a Toll

Himachal Pradesh, Kangra or Uttaranchal, Garhwal, c. 1825
Opaque watercolor on paper
Sheet: 11 ¾ x 9 ¾ in. (29.8 x 24.8 cm)
Image: 9 ⅛ x 7 ⅛ in. (23.2 x 18.1 cm)
Gift of Ramesh and Urmil Kapoor; P.2000.9.2

The story depicted here appears to have been particularly popular with Pahari artists and patrons, as several versions have been published. It is a charming tale of "eve teasing," in today's parlance. Once when Radha and her milkmaids of Brindavan were taking their dairy products to the market, Krishna and his cohorts waylaid them and demanded their share of the goods as a toll tax. (Alternatively, he was fresh and demanded a kiss.) The theme is known as *danalila*, which literally means "gift play." The name likely derives from the mountain pass of Dana-ghati (Toll pass), where the milkmaids were accosted.

In this rather elaborate composition, a palace—perhaps representing Mathura—forms an architectural background beyond the rolling verdant meadow. In the foreground two cows, a frisky calf and the cowherd companions watch; it is Radha who has grasped the arm of Krishna rather than the reverse. A female companion turns her head back to speak with a third woman, who is carrying a large tray with pots of curds. Two of the ladies wear turbans that are somewhat reminiscent of those seen on the heads of men in nineteenth-century Sikh paintings.

Indeed, the picture could have been painted somewhere in the Punjab plains by an artist trained in the Kangra tradition. Another possibility is Garhwal. Be that as it may, it is an interesting version of a popular story, with a lively arrangement of figures. Although Krishna and Radha stand in rather stiff postures, the others, including the bovines, interact with unaffected animation.

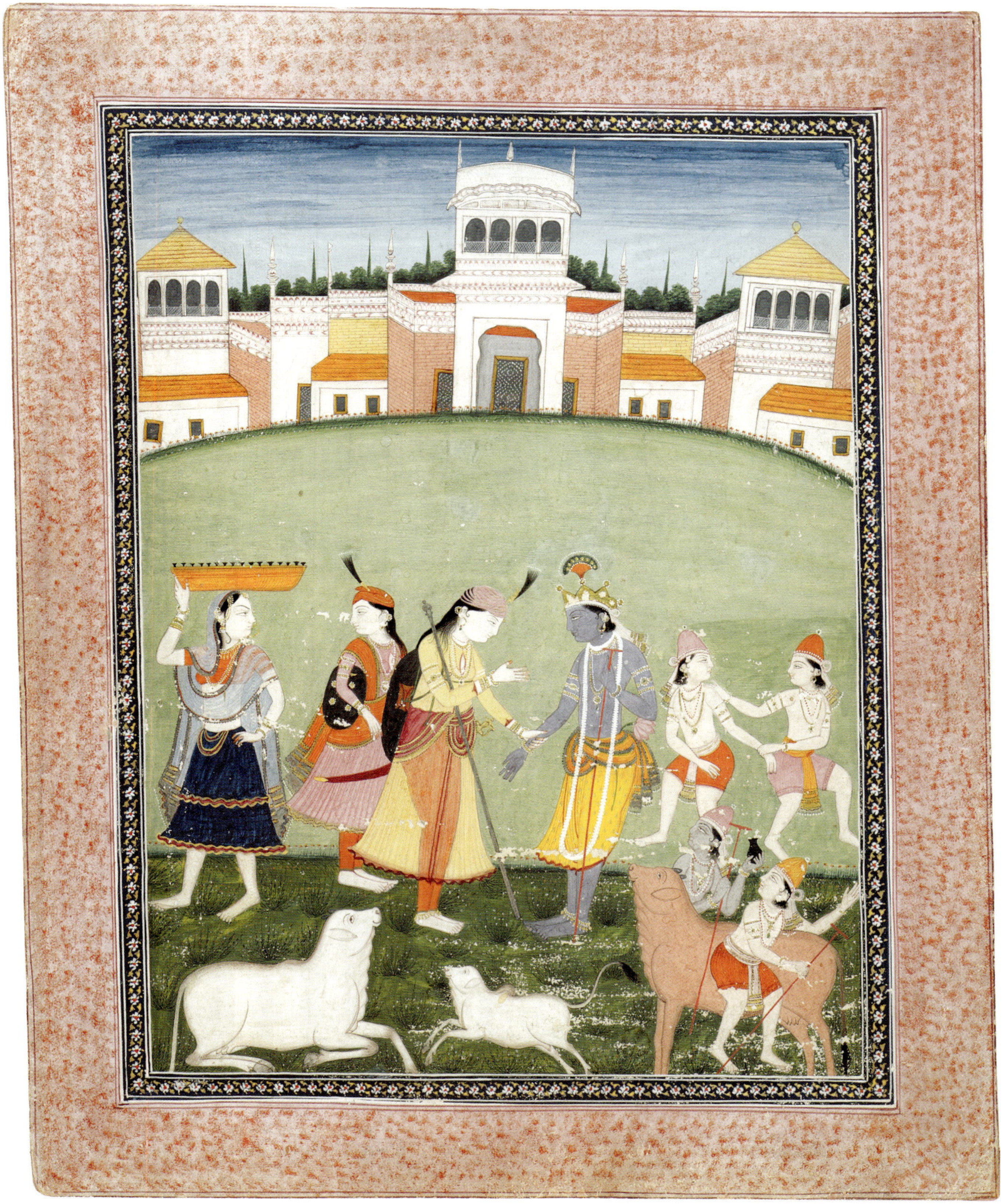

46 Sheltering from the Rain

Uttaranchal, Garhwal or Himachal Pradesh, Nurpur, 1775–1800
Opaque watercolor on paper
Sheet: 10 x 6 ¼ in. (25.4 x 15.9 cm)
Image: 9 ½ x 5 ½ in. (24.1 x 14 cm)
Lent by Ramesh and Urmil Kapoor

A sudden cloudburst provides an opportunity for Krishna and Radha to snatch a few moments of physical intimacy. They take shelter under a stately mango tree and are given additional protection from the rain by a leafy parasol held by an obliging cowherd companion. A second cowherd stands discreetly behind Radha with his eyes lowered. He offers a lotus, perhaps meant for Krishna. He has already plucked one from the tank nearby and given it to Radha. Krishna, however, has eyes only for Radha, whose face he raises in anticipation of stealing a kiss.

This subject was certainly popular in the Garhwal region, though in a different version (see Pal 2001, no. 66 and citations therein for others). This is a simpler composition with fewer figures and a sparser landscape, as if the artist wanted to emphasize the intensity of the lovers' desire to unite.

There is no unanimity among scholars in regard to where the other versions were rendered. Arguments have been made for both Kangra and Garhwal. With this delightful rendering, too, one cannot be certain. It could have been painted in a Kangra workshop or that of Golu of Nurpur (see Goswamy and Bhatia 1999, no. 204). However, Garhwal remains a distinct possibility. The tall, elegant figures are remarkably similar to those in a series depicting the story of Rukmini, which was rendered in Garhwal in the last quarter of the eighteenth century (see Lal 1968, pl. xx-xxiv and Archer 1973, vol. 2, pl. 85). No matter where it was painted, it remains a charming picture of delicate but assured drawing, subtle coloring and tender feeling.

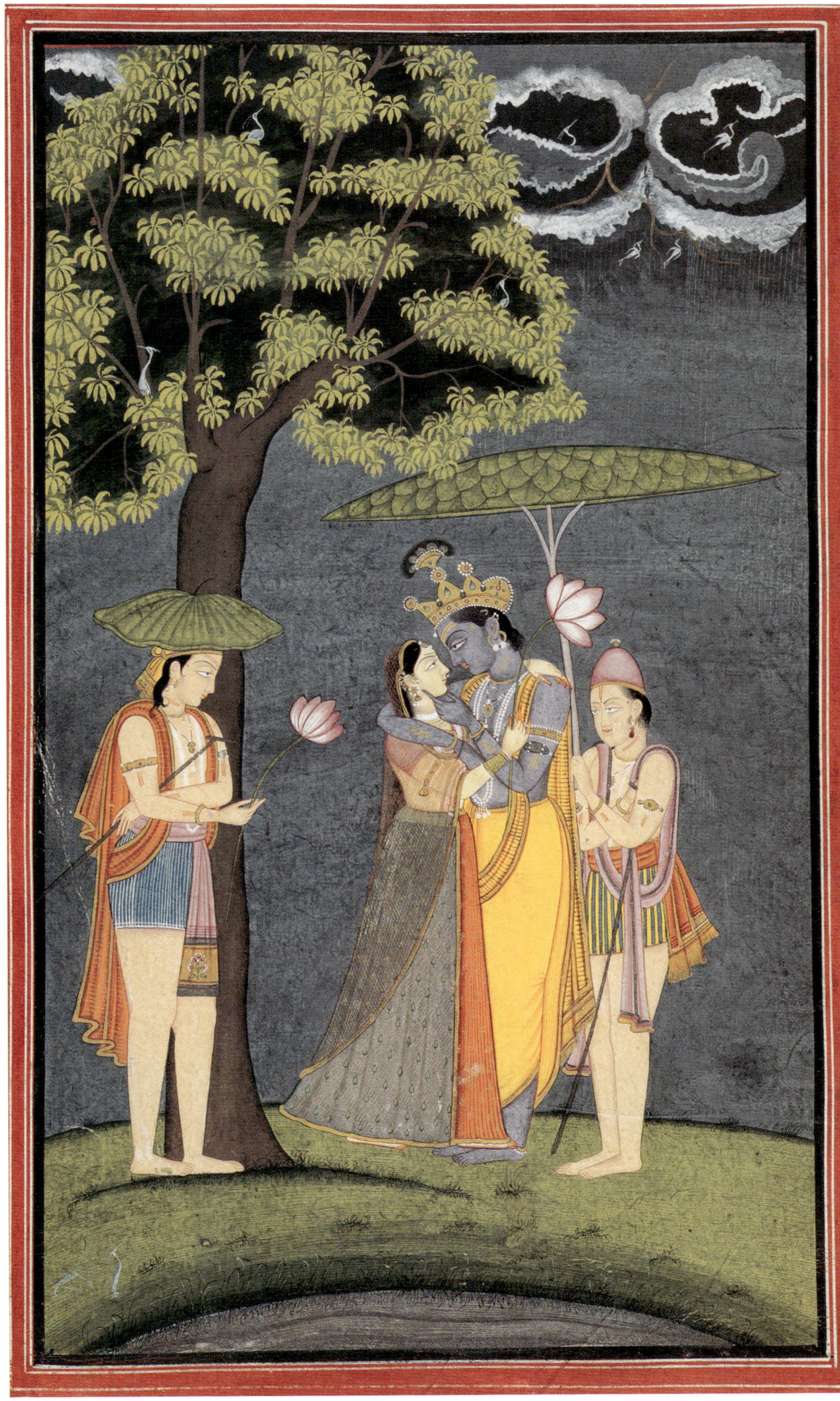

47 The Captive Krishna

Painted by Prag Chand (fl. c. 1780–1820)
Himachal Pradesh, Kangra workshop,
1775–1800
Opaque watercolor on paper
Sheet and image: 7 ⅝ x 10 ⅞ in. (19.4 x 27.6 cm)
Lent by Ramesh and Urmil Kapoor

The painting is based on a Hindi poem by Bhagwan, which is written on the back (see Appendix). The name of the artist is given as Prag Chand, who, according to artist/scholar Vijay Sharma of Chamba (personal communication, 2002) was from the village of Chari in the Kangra valley and visited the pilgrimage site of Hardwar in 1820. The fact that neither the poet nor the artist is known from other sources enhances both the literary and pictorial interest of the work.

Prag Chand has not followed the poem literally but still has accurately conveyed the essential sentiments. Standing below a tree, wearing his yellow dhoti and holding the branch of a tree, Krishna is clearly captivated by the charm of the fair Radha, who stretches her left arm to grasp a flowering spray and turns back to look at him. Her dusky companion seems to be startled by Krishna's gaze. The encounter occurs in sylvan surroundings on a riverbank during the day, rather than at night as indicated in the poem. Nevertheless, the accomplished Prag Chand has expressed the flavor (*rasa*) of the poem with delicacy and cool elegance. Clearly his manner is related to the lyrical and lush compositions of the great *Bhagavatapurana* and *Gitagovinda* pictures generally ascribed to the family workshop of the master artist Nainsukh.

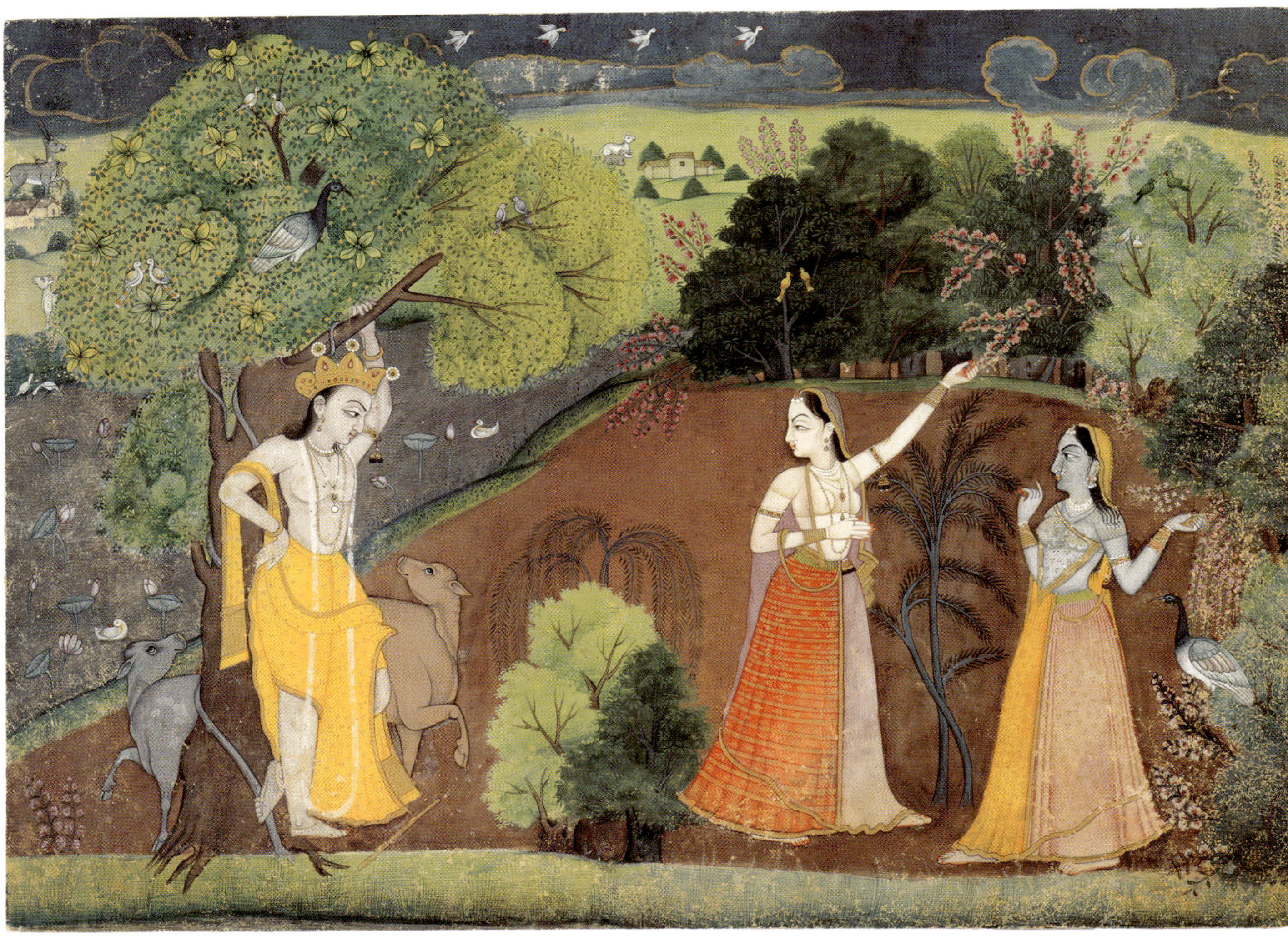

48 Krishna Converses with a Messenger

Himachal Pradesh, Kangra workshop, c. 1800
Opaque watercolor on paper
Sheet: 9 ½ x 6 ⅞ in. (24.1 x 17.5 cm)
Image: 7 ¼ x 4 ⅝ in. (18.4 x 11.7 cm)
Gift of Ramesh and Urmil Kapoor; P.2002.2.1

We do not know the exact message being delivered by the young lady, but we can be certain that she has come to plead for her mistress Radha. The gesture of her hand would indicate that Radha awaits Krishna's arrival, perhaps not far from the pavilion beside the pool where Krishna pines away for his beloved. The unknown artist has emphasized Krishna's divine nature by providing him with a lotus seat, while the flower in his hand symbolizes his playful mood (*lilakamala*). All the lotus flowers are in full bloom, for it is a moonlit night made clear by the pale moon in the upper left.

The picture could well be from the same series as another in a private collection (Spink 1971, fig. 98). Almost of the same size, and with similar blue borders with floral decorations, the two pictures are stylistically so close that they must be from the same workshop, if not the same series. In both pictures the architectural forms are rendered with exquisite detail, though here the artist has added glass vases to the wall niches. There is a strong possibility that the picture is from the family workshop of Phurku (active 1780–1820) of Kangra (see Goswamy and Bhatia 1999, nos. 211–12). Those two paintings of Krishnavite themes reflect a similar lively and lush treatment of the foliage, lotus pond and figural forms.

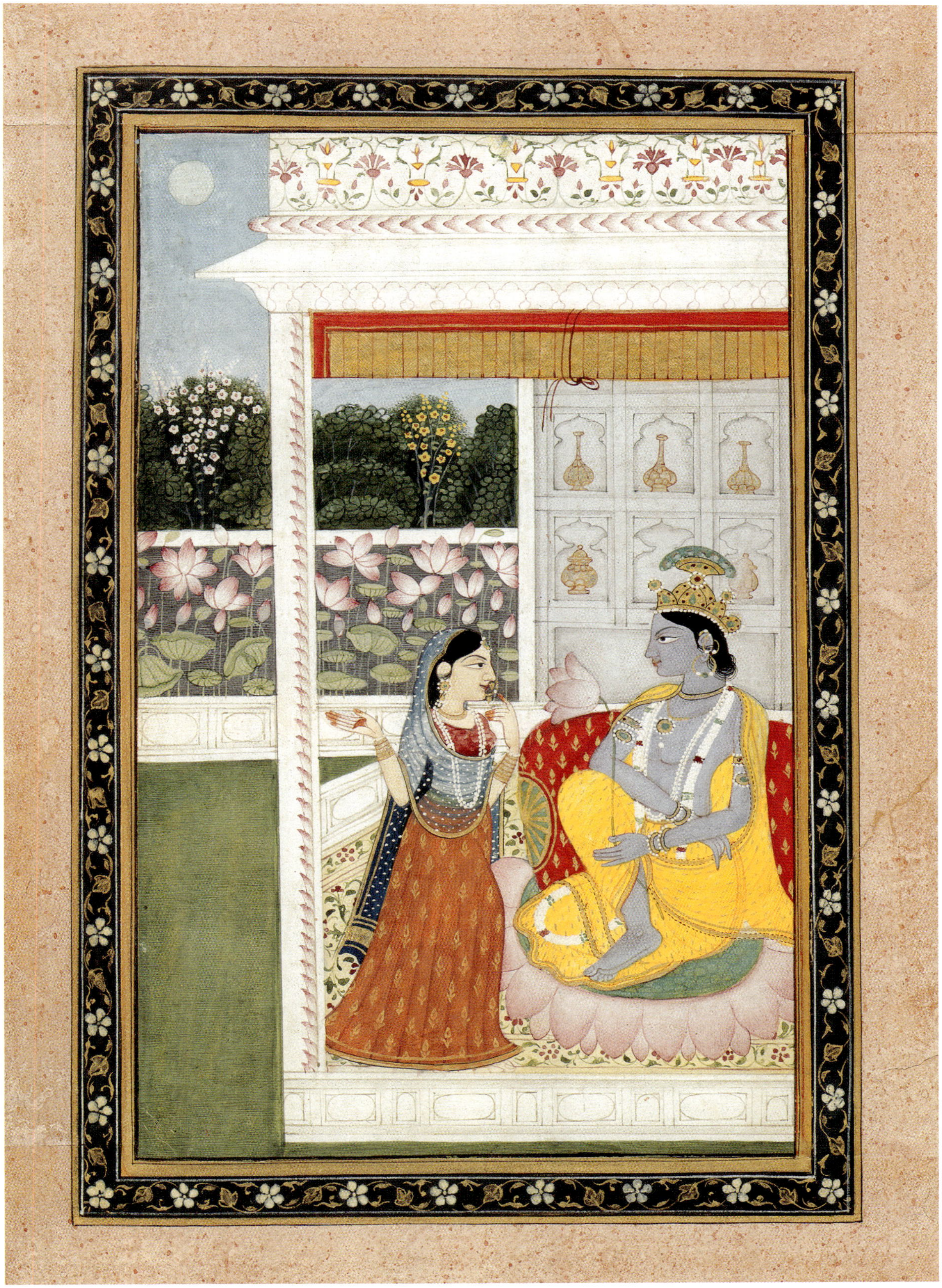

49 The Hour of Cowdust

Himachal Pradesh, Kangra, 1800–1825
Opaque watercolor and gold on paper
Sheet: 9 x 11 3/8 in. (22.9 x 28.9 cm)
Image: 6 7/8 x 9 3/4 in. (17.5 x 24.8 cm)
Lent by Ramesh and Urmil Kapoor

In the sales catalogue (Sotheby's 2002, no. 63) this painting is described as illustrating a theme from the *Bhagavatapurana*. However, the two verses found on the back are from a *Rasikapriya* (see Appendix). This theme was popular with Pahari artists, but no known Rajasthani version is known to exist. Ever since Ananda K. Coomaraswamy (1927, fig. 270) published the Boston version and used the title "Hour of Cowdust," the English translation of the Sanskrit expression *godhuli*, it has become emblematic of the romance and lyricism that one associates with Kangra pictures.

The poem on this painting does not use the expression *godhuli* at all, though it does describe the beauty of the dusky Krishna, punning as well on the dark storm clouds gathering above the trees. The divine cowherd is returning after a long, hot day of grazing with his companions and cows, whose hooves throw up the dust from the parched land—hence, the poetic expression used to describe dusk as the "hour of cowdust." It is also an auspicious time for Hindus to perform the evening (*sandhya*) rituals and a romantic time for lovers to meet. This hour is also considered an ideal time for viewing potential brides in the soft light of dusk. That romance is indeed involved here is clearly expressed by the eager solitary woman framed in the doorway. She must be Radha, which also rules out the *Bhagavatapurana* as a literary source for the theme.

More acceptable is the Sotheby catalogue's suggestion that the picture may have been painted by an artist in the circle of Sajnu and is stylistically close to an 1808 picture of a fire in Vraja that was given to the artist as a tribute (*nazar*), perhaps by a gifted progeny and pupil (Goswamy and Fischer 1992, no. 154). The detailed rendering of the architecture and the bovines and the fondness for whites are some of the common features of these two paintings.

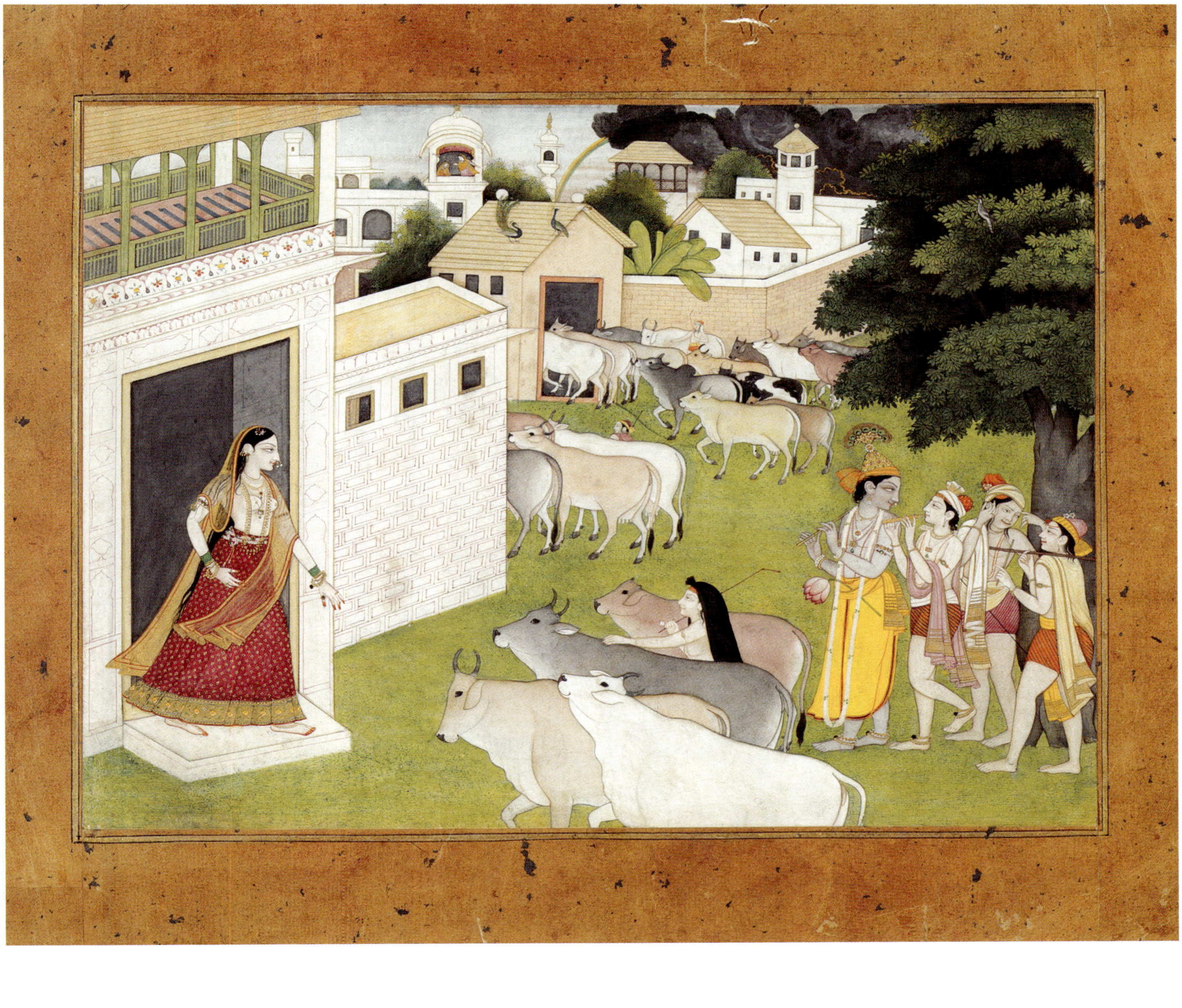

50 A Folio from the *Satsai* (?): Ravishing Revelation

Uttaranchal, Garhwal workshop or Himachal Pradesh, Kangra workshop, c. 1825
Opaque watercolor on paper
Sheet: 9 ¾ x 7 ⅛ in. (24.8 x 18.1 cm)
Image: 7 ⅝ x 5 ¼ in. (19.4 x 13.3 cm)
Gift of Ramesh and Urmil Kapoor; P.1999.3.2

The *Satsai* of 700 verses was composed by the Hindi poet Bihari (1595–1663), who was the court poet of Mirza Raja Jai Singh (1625–1667) of Amber, Rajasthan. The verses are considered to be among the finest examples of short lyrical poetry in the Hindi language, extolling the various moods and situations of love. The protagonists are of course Radha and Krishna.

The verses illustrated in this Pahari picture (see Appendix) were quoted by M. S. Randhawa (1966, p. 68) along with another version of the subject in an Indian private collection. They describe Krishna's enchantment with Radha's physical charms as she walks away from his house with a bowl of curds. These verses, however, are not the ones written on the back of the picture, as is the case with others from the series published by Randhawa. Nor do the verses match the version of the text translated by Holland (1969).

The sensual beauty and erotic charm of a partially revealed female body has remained a perennial theme with Indian poets and artists and also in contemporary films. Bihari uses this concept frequently in his *Satsai*. Apart from the verses that inspired this beautiful picture in another typical example, the poet says: "Though concealed under a simple white bodice, her young and coming breasts reveal themselves as clearly as the meaning concealed in the words of a great poet" (Mathur 1973, p. 67). Thus, in the painting Krishna remains transfixed in the doorway, unable to move, even as Radha turns her back and walks away. In a second vignette above, the seated Radha is engaged in a conversation with a companion.

The artist responsible for this painting undoubtedly used the same source as that published by Randhawa. He made some alterations, however, in the forms of Radha and Krishna, their attire, the architectural details and the coloring. The proportions of the figures here are different. Krishna has a more robust torso and the outline of Radha's lower body is not revealed as articulately and sensuously as in the other version. Her breasts, however, are more prominently delineated. Her hands and feet too are rather long and not as naturalistically drawn as in the other picture. The designs used in the corners beyond the oval frame are also different in the two renderings.

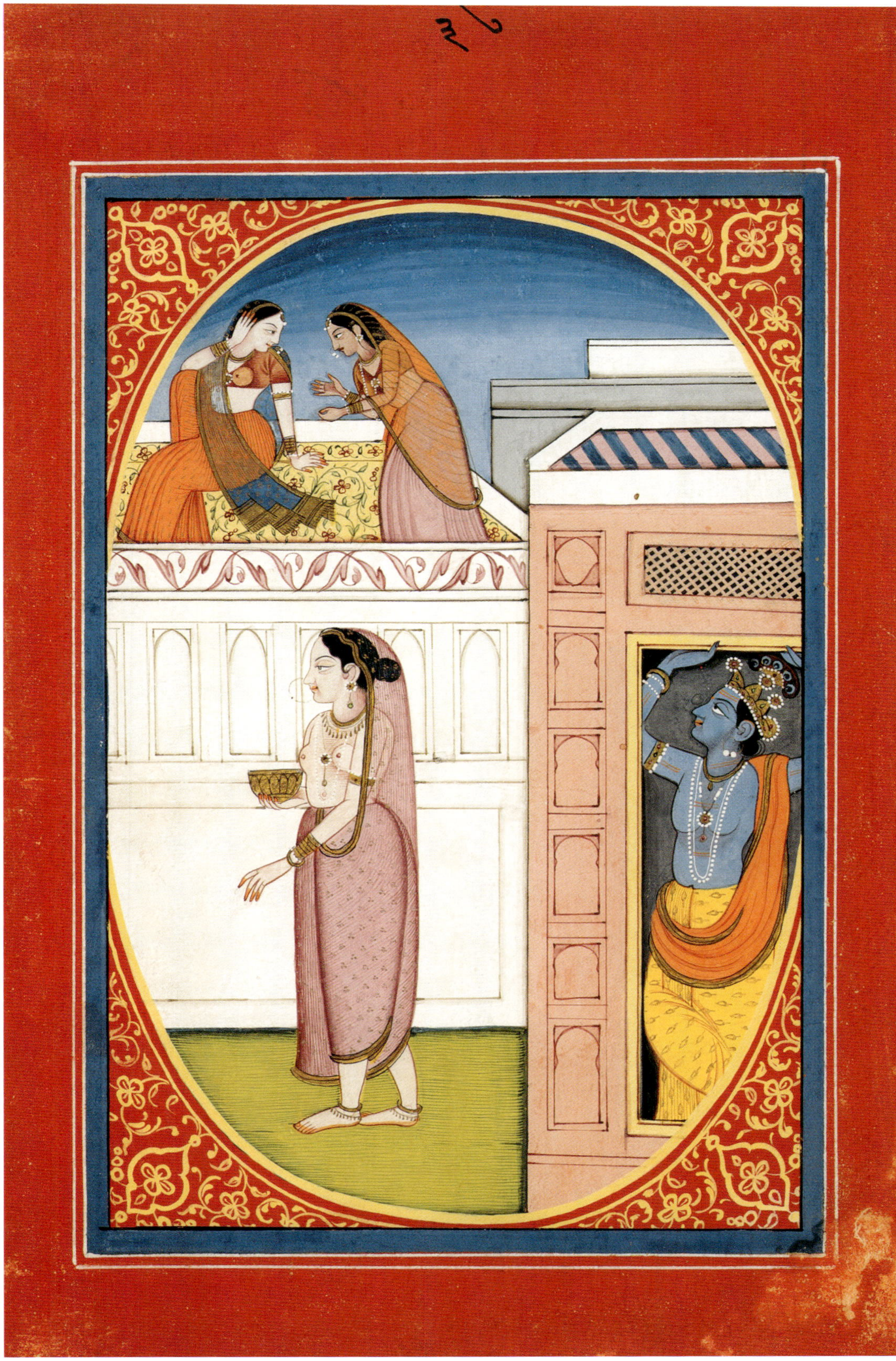

51 A Sketch for a *Satsai* Illustration (?): Peeping Tom

Himachal Pradesh, Guler or Kangra workshop, 1800–1850
Ink and graphite on paper
Sheet and image: 5¾ x 4⅜ in. (14.6 x 11.1 cm)
Gift of Ramesh and Urmil Kapoor; P.2003.2.12

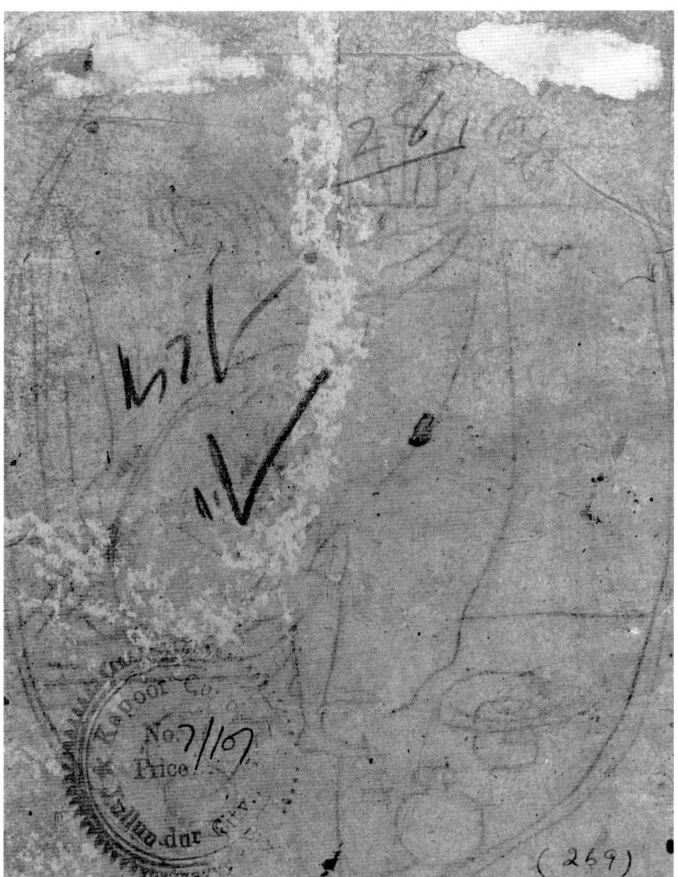

The same subject is sketched on both sides, the depiction on the back being a mirror composition, more faintly and summarily executed. It appears that two separate pieces of paper were glued together, the mirror composition being perhaps the result of an attempted transfer. There is also a rubber stamp on the back that reads "Kapoor Curio [House], Jullundur City, No. 7/107." The price—7 rupees—is handwritten.

Both scenes depict Krishna as the Peeping Tom standing beyond a wall and watching a semi-naked Radha bathe. Seated on a low stool, she seems to be aware of Krishna's gaze as she demurely pulls one end of the cloth that her companion holds up to shield her modesty. Her other hand is coyly raised to her chin. A spittoon, two water pots and a spouted jug appear in the foreground within the oval frame. That the picture was meant to be colored—probably by a junior artist of the family or workshop—is clear from the color notations (see Appendix). The boldly drawn outlines reveal the hands of a deft and mature artist.

The popular subject could have been meant as an independent picture or an illustration to a *Satsai* series [50]. A finished picture with a more elaborate composition is published by Randhawa (1966, pp. 66–67, pl. XI) with the following verse:

The lotus-eyed Nayika [Heroine] sits arranging her hair after her bath;
She peers at Krishna with gaze fixed between her fingers and tresses.

In style, the sketch is comparable to another picture of Radha's toilette (*sringara*) attributed to Guler by William Archer (1973, vol. 2, pl. 118, fig. 68).

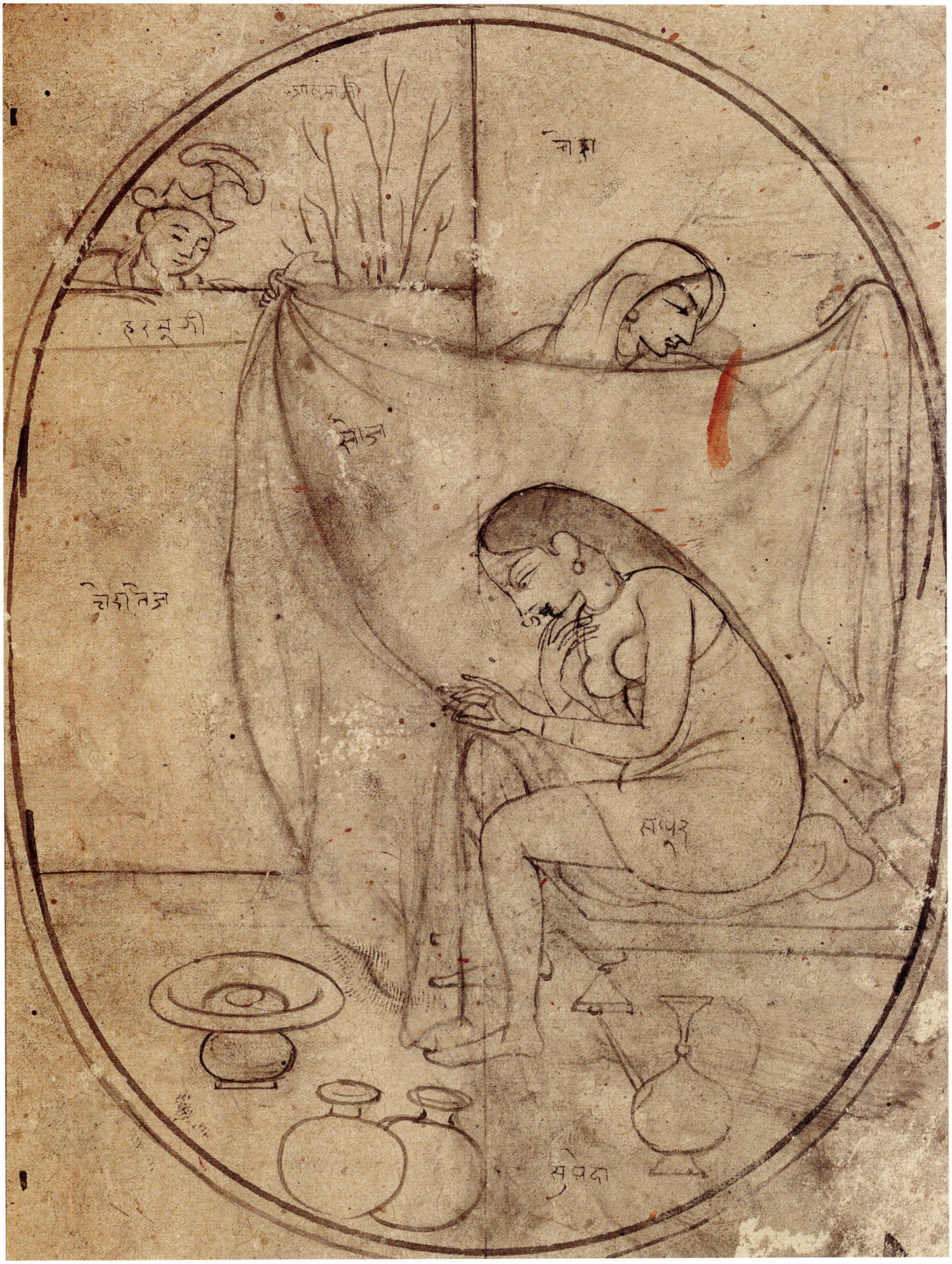

52 Toilette on a Terrace

Rajasthan, Kishangarh, 1800–1825
Opaque watercolor on paper
Sheet: 16 7/8 x 11 1/8 in. (42.9 x 28.3 cm)
Image: 13 1/4 x 8 1/8 in. (33.7 x 20.6 cm)
Promised gift of Ramesh and Urmil Kapoor

The Hindi inscription on the top of the yellow border of the painting may be loosely translated as follows: "The shimmering beauty of the heroine's body behind the transparent garment glitters like the graceful water drops on the leaves of the wish-fulfilling tree drenched in the ocean" (see Appendix). Characteristically, an unknown Kishangarh artist has given us an equally lyrical composition of this charming poetic conceit. The fair heroine is contrasted with her darker-skinned companion, who is no less attractive. She holds the mirror with her left hand and balances a plate and garland with her right. The mistress stands on a stool, proud of her assets, as she wrings her wet hair and looks into the mirror. There is no doubt of the provocativeness of her posture.

Typical of Kishangarh pictures, the space within the composition is given enormous depth by the solid expanse of water in shades of gray. Beyond is an imposing but empty palace, mostly in white, against a backdrop of dark-green dense foliage with a wide expanse of blue sky. The flowering foliage along the front balustrade of the white terrace is rendered with greater definition and in a brighter and more soothing shade of green. A pair of blue and pink birds, a lamp and a table with small bottles of perfume animate the terrace.

The picture was likely painted shortly after 1800, since the verse is quoted, as pointed out by Naval Krishna (see Appendix), from the *Lalachandrika*, a commentary composed in 1799/1800 by the Gujrati poet Lallulala, based on Bihari's *Satsai* [50–51]. One cannot be certain whether the picture illustrates the poem or the poem was added as a literary embellishment for the painting. There is no hint that the lady is Radha, nor is she likely to be an actual princess, who would not bathe in so public a place. Nonetheless, the landscape is the royal setting of the lake and palace complex of Kishangarh, and the lady a fictive princess of the poet's romantic imagination.

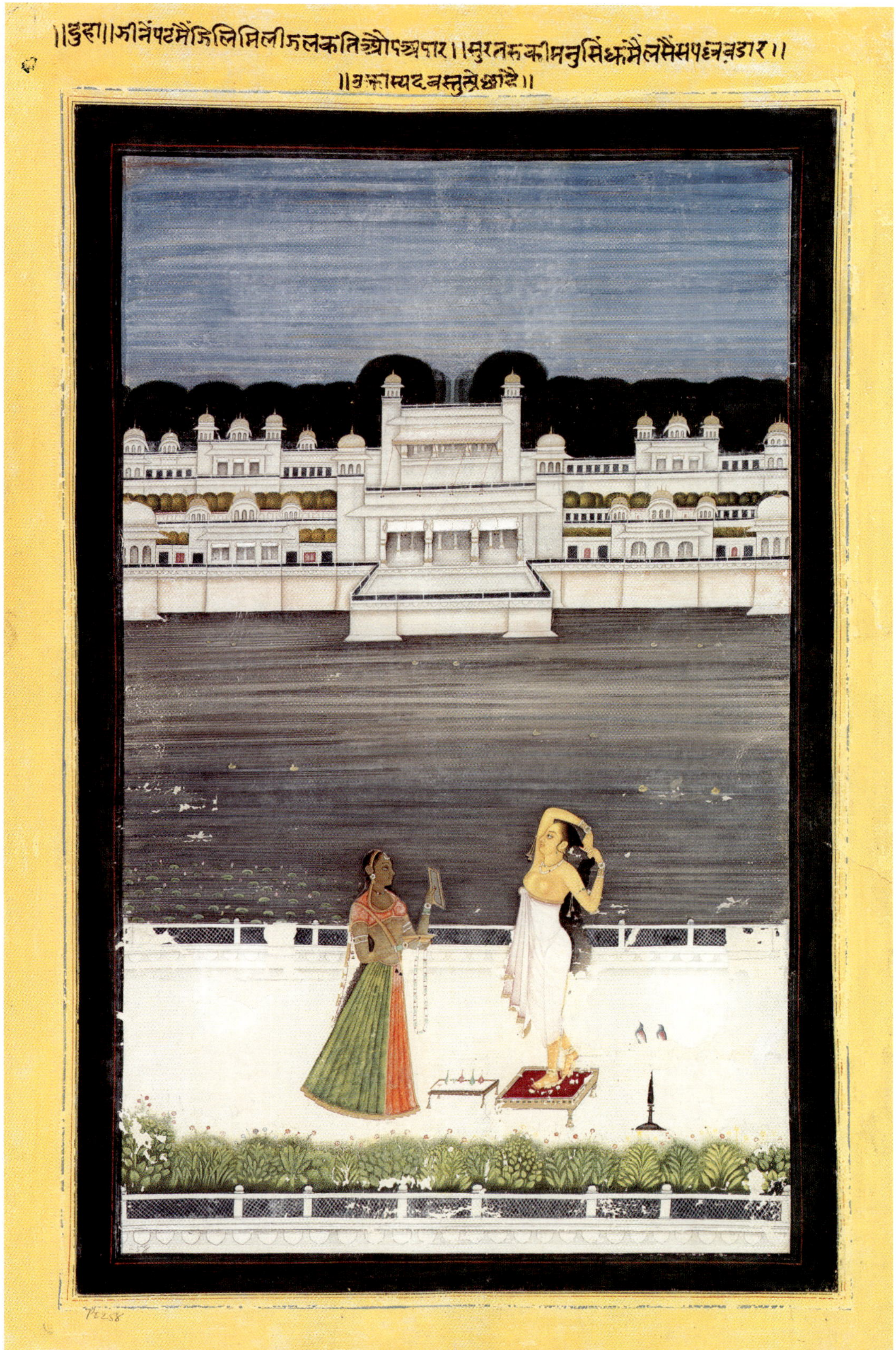

53 The Month of Bhadon (August–September)

Rajasthan, Bundi or Uniara workshop, c. 1750
Opaque watercolor and gold on paper
Sheet: 9 ½ x 6 ⅝ in. (24.1 x 16.8 cm)
Image: 9 ⅜ x 6 ⅜ in. (23.8 x 16.2 cm)
Gift of Ramesh and Urmil Kapoor in honor of Pratapaditya Pal; P.2003.2.9

The purple clouds are gathering, the thunder rolls and rain pours in torrents. The winds blow fiercely, the cicadas chirp, the lions roar, and elephants fell the trees. The day is dark like night, and one's home is the best. Pray leave me not in the month of Bhadon, for separation pains like a poison.
(Randhawa 1962, p. 192)

The above is a translation of the Hindi verse quoted on the cover sheet of the painting (see Appendix). It is from the Hindi writer Keshavadas' *Kavipriya*, in which the poet has composed twelve odes to the twelve months of the year (Baramasa). Each ode provides reasons why the lovers should not part, as is the case here for the month of Bhadon at the height of the monsoon season.

The artist has followed the poet's literary conceits rather carefully, though not literally. The lovers—here Krishna and Radha—are shown in the upper pavilion, while a second female is engaged below in feeding a couple of pet peacocks. The full river flows by swiftly as the rain comes down in sheets across the entire surface. A solitary lion runs for cover on the opposite bank and three elephants seem to be in disarray. Against the dark sky is a heraldic, winged griffin-like animal crowning an outcrop of purple rocks and watching the gold streak of lightning.

The picture may well have been painted at Uniara, a feudatory of the state of Jaipur, in which the Bundi court manner was current in the mid–eighteenth century. The most noted artist was Mira Bagas, who may have been recruited from Bundi (see Beach 1974, pp. 23–27). Apart from Mira Bagas' *Bhagavatapurana* pictures (Beach 1974, figs. 48–49), closely comparable is a Nayika painting (fig. 54) attributed by Beach to the same artist. Noteworthy for its deft composition, the picture is admirable for its nuanced coloring and evocative mood. (For a contemporary Kota version see Welch 1997, no. 41).

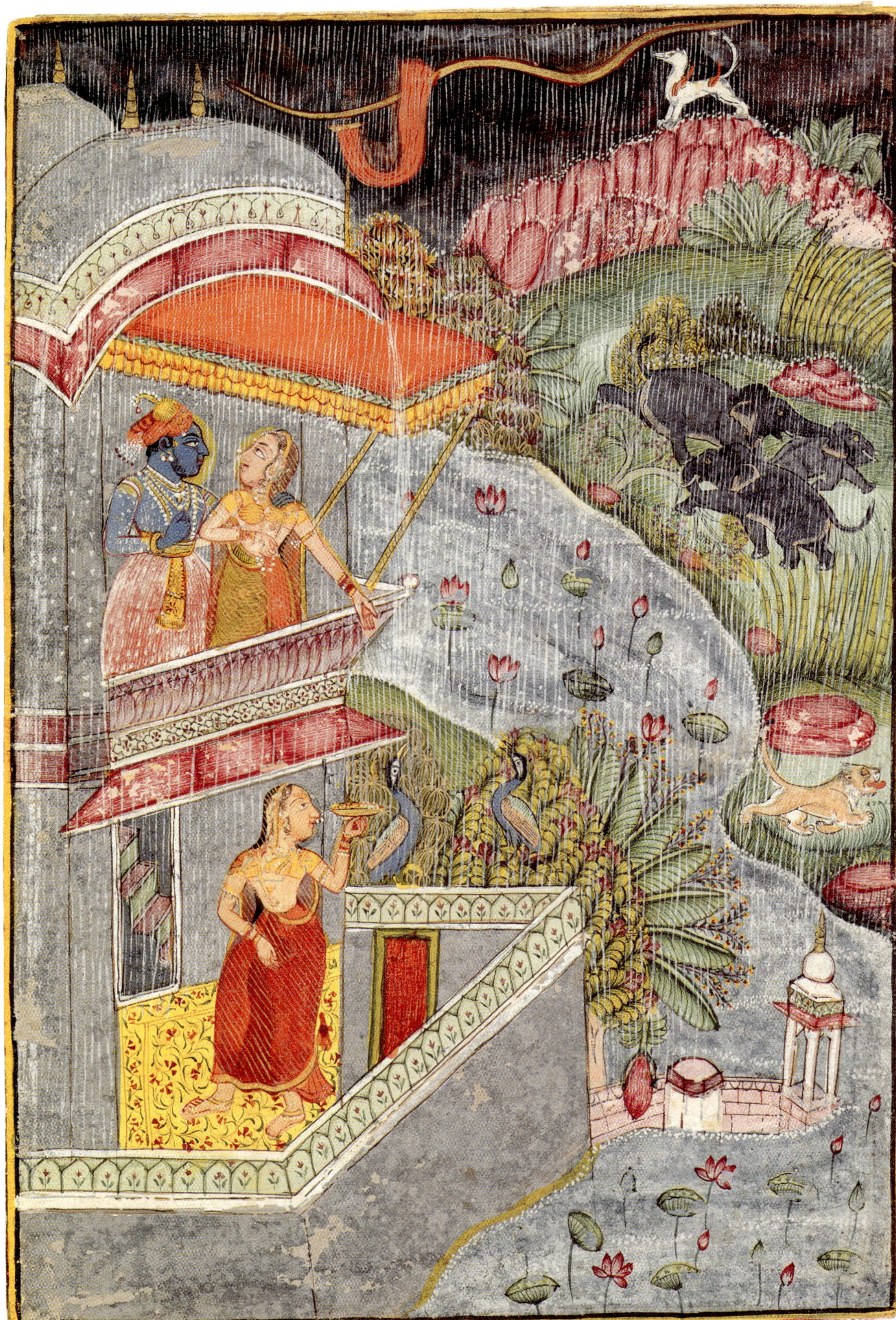

54 Ladies Worship Krishna and Radha

Painted by Harinarayan
Rajasthan, Jaipur, c. 1900
Opaque watercolor and gold on paper
Sheet: 16 ¼ x 12 ¼ in. (41.3 x 31.1 cm)
Image: 13 ¾ x 9 ¾ in. (34.9 x 24.7 cm)
Gift of Ramesh and Urmil Kapoor; P.2002.2.2

At the bottom of the painting a short inscription informs us that it is the brushwork of the artist Harinarayan (Naval Krishna, personal communication, 2002). Stylistically the large picture is related to works of the Jaipur school of around 1900. Although the name of the artist does not occur in any other Jaipur painting, it is clear from this dazzling picture that he had a dramatic sense of composition and was a consummate colorist.

Although the two deities are presented iconically, perched on large lotuses on a lotus-filled pool, they seem to be involved in a pas de deux. Their lively postures, swirling skirts with golden borders, self-absorption and dynamic interaction are all enhanced by the sparkler-like, bold golden rays radiating from their haloes. The backdrop of this vivacious performance is formed by densely foliated trees sprinkled with clusters of tiny white flowers and flanked by mango trees with luscious ripe fruits. In the foreground are six ladies who have come with offerings and two pairs of cranes. The abundant use of gold indicates that this was probably a picture for the court to which the artist was attached.

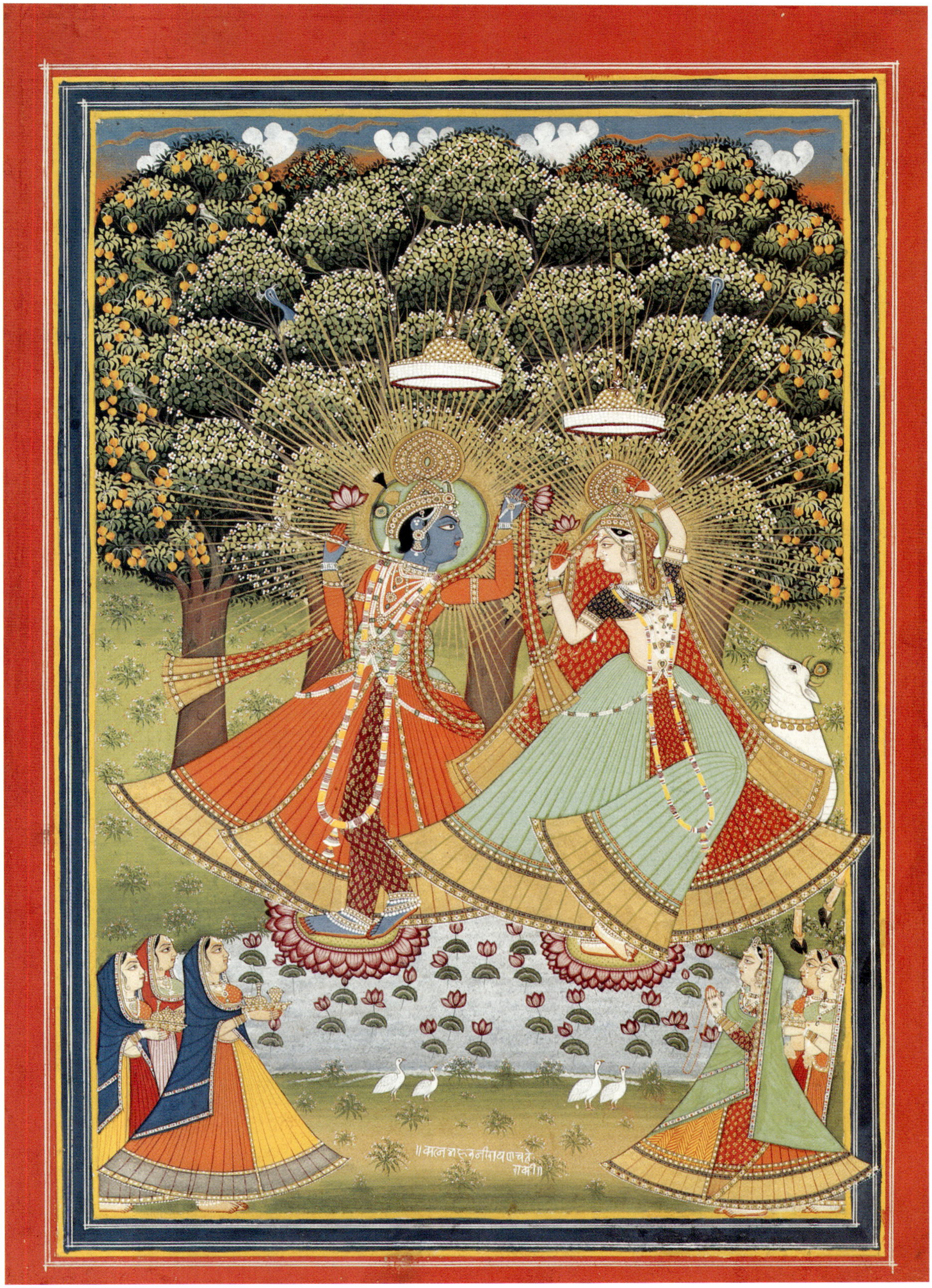

Musical Modes (Ragamala)

55 ILLUSTRATION FROM A *RAGAMALA* ALBUM: BHAIRAVA RAGA

Andhra Pradesh (Deccan), Hyderabad, 1700–1750
Opaque watercolor and gold on paper
Sheet: 14 1/8 x 9 5/8 in. (35.9 x 24.4 cm)
Image: 11 1/4 x 7 in. (28.6 x 17.8 cm)
Gift of Ramesh and Urmil Kapoor; P.2002.2.5

ARABIC INSCRIPTIONS ABOVE THE PICTURE identify the subject as the representation of Raga Bhairava. One of the principal musical modes in the *Ragamala* classification, Bhairava is a name of Shiva, especially in his angry form. The iconography of the *raga*, however, varies considerably, sometimes with minimum religious nuance, as is the case here. Except for the ascetic male within the pavilion, the scene essentially represents "amorous pleasure," as is described in some texts (see Ebeling 1973, p. 120; Waldschmidt 1975, pp. 330–31).

In this vibrant and richly colored visualization, an unknown Hyderabadi artist appears to have added elaborations. It would seem he was well aware of the iconographic tradition of the older Uma-Maheshvara themes in which Shiva is shown in dalliance with Parvati while being entertained, though not in such luxurious surroundings. Two maids stand chatting behind, one holding a beautifully detailed peacock-feather fan. Even though Bhairava is an ascetic, the urbane couple is enjoying music provided by a couple of ladies seated on the white terrace. A young moon in the sky indicates that it is nighttime, even though there is no other indication of a nocturnal soiree and bright light suffuses the scene. Bhairava is generally regarded as an early morning *raga* symbolizing the separation of lovers, while this particular iconography is more appropriate for a nighttime *raga* such as Malkos.

Nevertheless, the picture is a highly accomplished example of the Mughal-influenced style that prevailed in eighteenth-century Hyderabad. As is typical, it combines perspectival rendering with a strongly decorative flair and flights of imagination, seen in the delineation of the large tree behind the empty gazebo and the passage with the crescent moon, the rich blue ground enclosed by irregular clouds against a steel gray flat sky. The graceful figures, manicured setting, variegated palette and generous use of gold not only evoke the splendor of a handsome mansion but also the affluence of the patron who commissioned the piece.

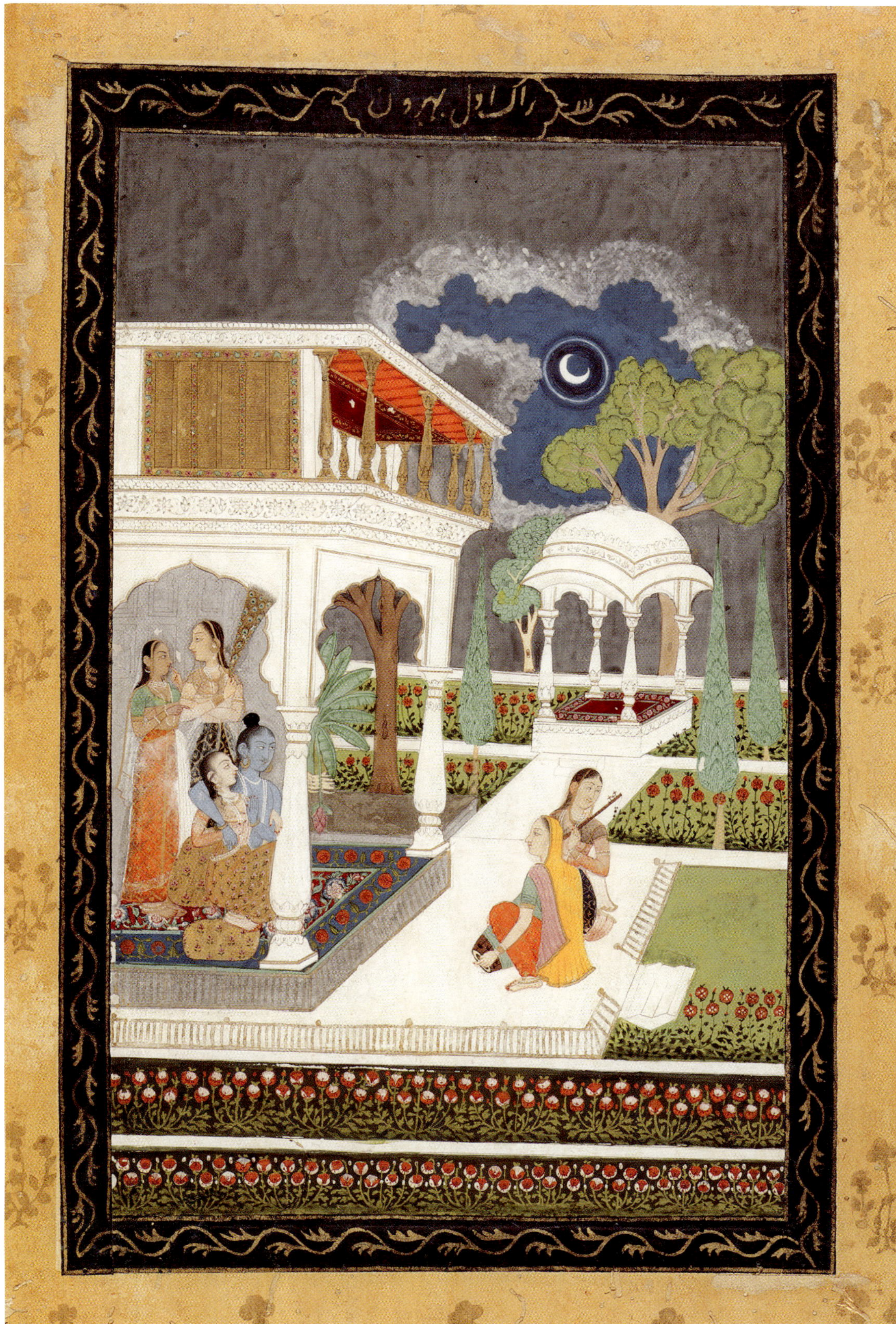

56 Illustration from a *Ragamala* Album: Bhairava Raga

Rajasthan, Amber, early eighteenth century
Opaque watercolor on paper
Sheet: 13 x 9 ¼ in. (33 x 23.5 cm)
Image: 11 ⅛ x 7 ⅜ in. (28.3 x 18.7 cm)
Promised gift of Ramesh and Urmil Kapoor

A short inscription above the central couple states "*raga bhairu*," which is a colloquial but common name of Bhairava. Unlike the elaborate and secularized representation from Hyderabad [55], the unknown Amber artist has given us a more religious version. Bhairava here is fair, has a third eye, a snake and the crescent and the river Ganga on his head. He does not have additional arms, but his bull is seated below and looks up adoringly at his master. That the lady offering him a drink in a small golden cup is Parvati is clearly indicated by her iconographic signifier, the lion, also within a smaller pavilion. A maid approaches the divine couple with a covered golden tray, perhaps containing betel quids (*pan*). A further indication of their divinity is the lotus mat placed on the carpet. Thus, although the architecture has no religious character, the scene is more iconic than the Hyderabad picture. It is not a garden scene and there is no music, but the pair is engrossed in entertaining each other.

Amber is the name of a fort and a town of the state known by the same name. After a new capital was established at Jaipur by Maharaja Jai Singh in 1727, the state became more familiarly known as Jaipur. Stylistically, the Kapoor picture compares with others given an early-eighteenth-century date (see Ebeling 1973, pp. 29, 186, 188). The artist may well have adopted ideas from two poetic descriptions of the *raga* commonly encountered in Rajasthani paintings (Ebeling 1973, p. 120) or based his representation on an unknown text. What he has graphically expressed is the amorous and playful mood of the divine couple.

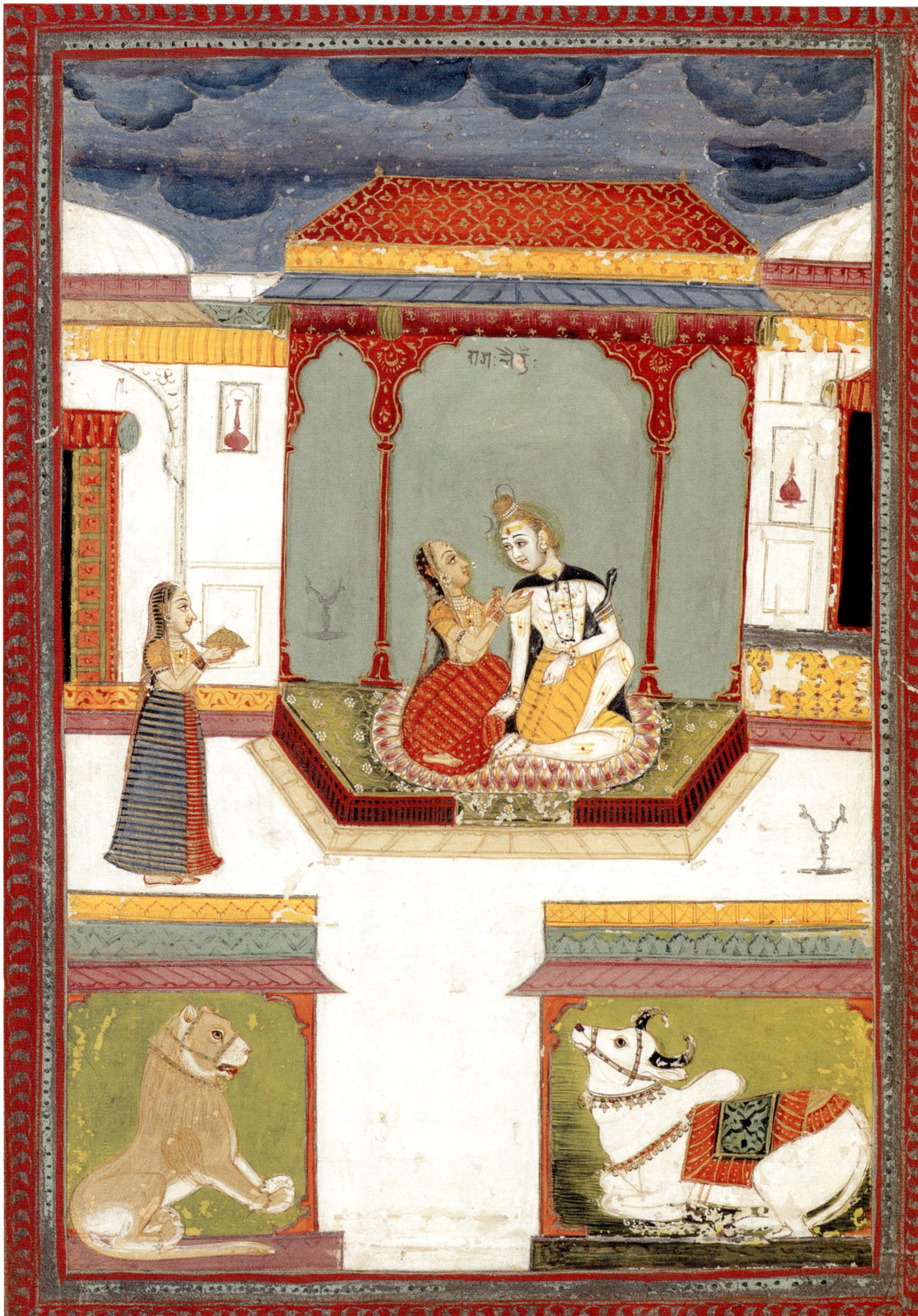
राग:

57 Folio from a *Ragamala* Series: Bhairavi Ragini

Madhya Pradesh, Malwa, c. 1625–50
Opaque watercolor on paper
Sheet: 8 ¾ x 6 ¼ in. (22.2 x 14.9 cm)
Image: 7 ¼ x 5 ⅞ in. (18.4 x 14.9 cm)
Gift of Ramesh and Urmil Kapoor; P.2002.2.4

An inscription on the back of the painting identifies the subject as Bhairavi Ragini, number six in the family of Raga Hindol. This is unusual, as she is generally classified as the first wife of Raga Bhairava [55–56]. Whether this is a scribal error—not uncommon among such paintings—or indicates a hitherto-unknown classification remains unknown.

Most familiar verses describe the *ragini* as a fair damsel engaged in worshiping the emblem of Shiva, known as a *shivalingam*, at a shrine on the lakeshore of Manasarovar, below Mt. Kailash in the Tibetan Himalayas. Here, however, the artist has not provided any indication of water but rather given us a colorful representation of a temple raised on a platform. Four women provide music while the personified mode offers flowers on the god's emblem of black stone. Below is the impressive figure of Vrisha (generally known as Nandi), the god's bull mount.

The picture likely belongs to the Boston *Ragamala* series, which originally belonged to Ananda K. Coomaraswamy and is now dispersed in several American museums (see Ebeling 1973, pp. 171–72). All have similar short identification labels on the reverse, and some have even more cryptic labels on top. In its more variegated hues and especially in its figural forms, the picture shares similar stylistic traits with the Boston series. The ladies in this series are distinguished by their tall proportions and long faces with prominent noses (Ebeling 1973, pl. [C7]). Characteristically, the *ragini* is depicted against a red panel, while the bull is against a deep brown favored by Malwa artists. Generally dated to around 1640, the series is perhaps the earliest one known from this school of painting.

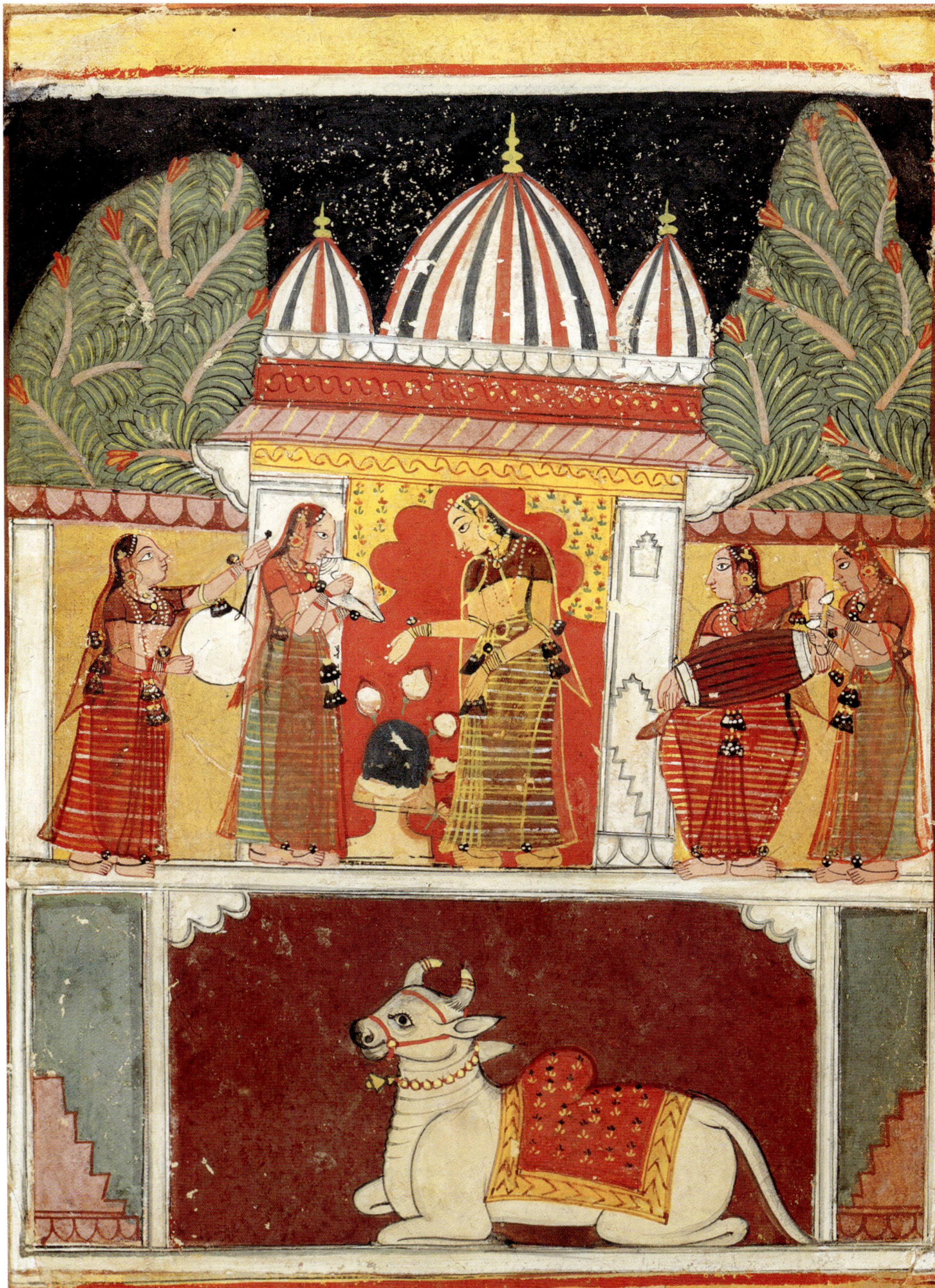

58 Folio from a *Ragamala* Series: Agada Ragaputra

Jammu and Kashmir, Mankot workshop, 1750–75
Opaque watercolor on paper
Sheet: 10 ¼ x 8 ⅛ in. (26 x 20.6 cm)
Image: 8 ⅛ x 6 ⅛ in. (20.6 x 15.6 cm)
Gift of Ramesh and Urmil Kapoor; P.2000.9.1

This picture is from a *Ragamala* series, from which two others are in a private collection in India (see Goswamy and Bhatia 1999, nos. 175 and 177). The Takri inscription on the red border at the top of the painting reads "Raga Agada the son of Sri Raga, folio 3" (V. C. Ohri, personal communication, 2002).

The painting shows a young nobleman taking leave of a lady who stands on a terrace outside a pavilion. The horse that will carry the lover away stands behind him. It should be noted, however, that this visualization of the mode differs from other published examples. In a Berlin picture (Waldschmidt 1967, fig. 18), no horse is included, though the couple does stand together on a terrace. In a sketch published by Ebeling (1973, p. 287, box 383) the mode is called Achada, the female is seated and there is no horse. In the Berlin album, however, the exact same composition—including the horse—is used as a mirror image for another *ragaputra* called Vardhana (Waldschmidt 1967, fig. 17). As quoted in Waldschmidt (1967, p. 187), M. S. Randhawa opined that the cavalier taking leave of his beloved is traditionally the iconography of the Vardhana in the Kangra tradition. Thus, there appears to have been some confusion between the representations of these two modes, which cannot be resolved here.

B. N. Goswamy (citation above) has attributed the other two pictures from this series to a Mankot workshop of the third quarter of the eighteenth century, which is endorsed by Ohri (personal communication). In an extensive discussion of the style of the Berlin series, Waldschmidt (1967, pp. 85–99) agrees with other scholars that the pictures are derivative of Basohli style but were executed in Bilaspur. There can be little doubt, however, that the same workshop produced the two *Ragamala* series, no matter where they were done.

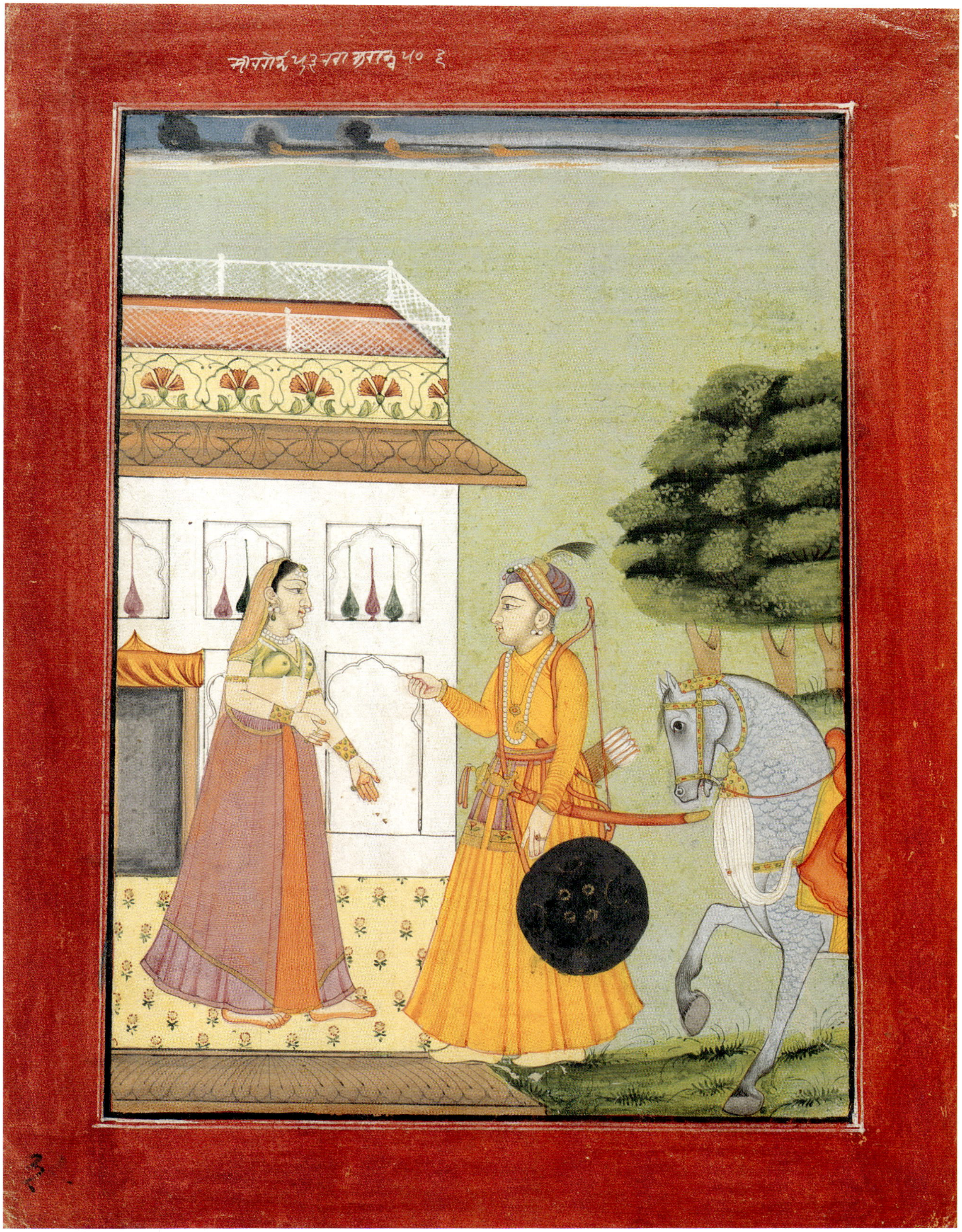

59 Illustration from a *Ragamala* Album: Saranga Raga

Northern Deccan or Central India, eighteenth century
Opaque watercolor and gold on paper
Sheet: 16 ½ x 11 ⅞ in. (41.9 x 30.2 cm)
Image: 15 x 10 ⅜ in. (38.1 x 26.4 cm)
Promised gift of Ramesh and Urmil Kapoor

"Fond of learning and culture, knowledgeable in the mortal and celestial music, Saranga is a youth of dark complexion, as has been declared by the sages." This is how Saranga is described in the Sanskrit verse at the top of the painting, which also contains the number 32. On the back of the picture (see Appendix), a local poet's verse in a Hindi dialect is added, with an additional line dedicating the painting to the Diwan Prithivi Singh (Naval Krishna, personal communication, 2002). The word *diwan* generally means the chief secretary of a state. Since this could not have been an isolated work, Prithivi Singh must have commissioned the entire series. It is probable that the Hindi poem was composed by the poet to flatter the patron for his taste in music and culture, like Saranga, which is derived from Sarngadeva, the thirteenth-century musicologist and author of the treatise *Sangita Ratnakara*.

That a double entendre is intended here is also clear from the opulent setting in which the prince is given a fair rather than dark complexion, as required by the verse, and holds a large lotus of dalliance (*lilakamala*), a sign of a cultured man. A beautiful lute stretches across his lap as he discourses with two sages seated on the carpet. Across from the ascetic pair are four female attendants with a cloth fan, a peacock-feather *morchal* and offerings. A fifth woman is busy preparing the narcotic bhang (?), while four other musicians, male as well as female, are seated on the terrace. Beyond the lotus pond is a pastoral scene with a woman feeding a deer below a tree. Two others return to the mansion, having filled their pots in the watering hole. The time of day (noon?) is indicated by a golden sun dominating the bright sky streaked in gold.

The exact place of origin for this sumptuous picture is not known, but it was likely painted in northern Deccan for a patron whose mother tongue was Hindi. The artist may have been from Hyderabad, which would explain the Mughal elements encountered in Deccani pictures in the eighteenth century after the region was conquered by the Mughal emperor Aurangzeb (r. 1658–1707). ❦

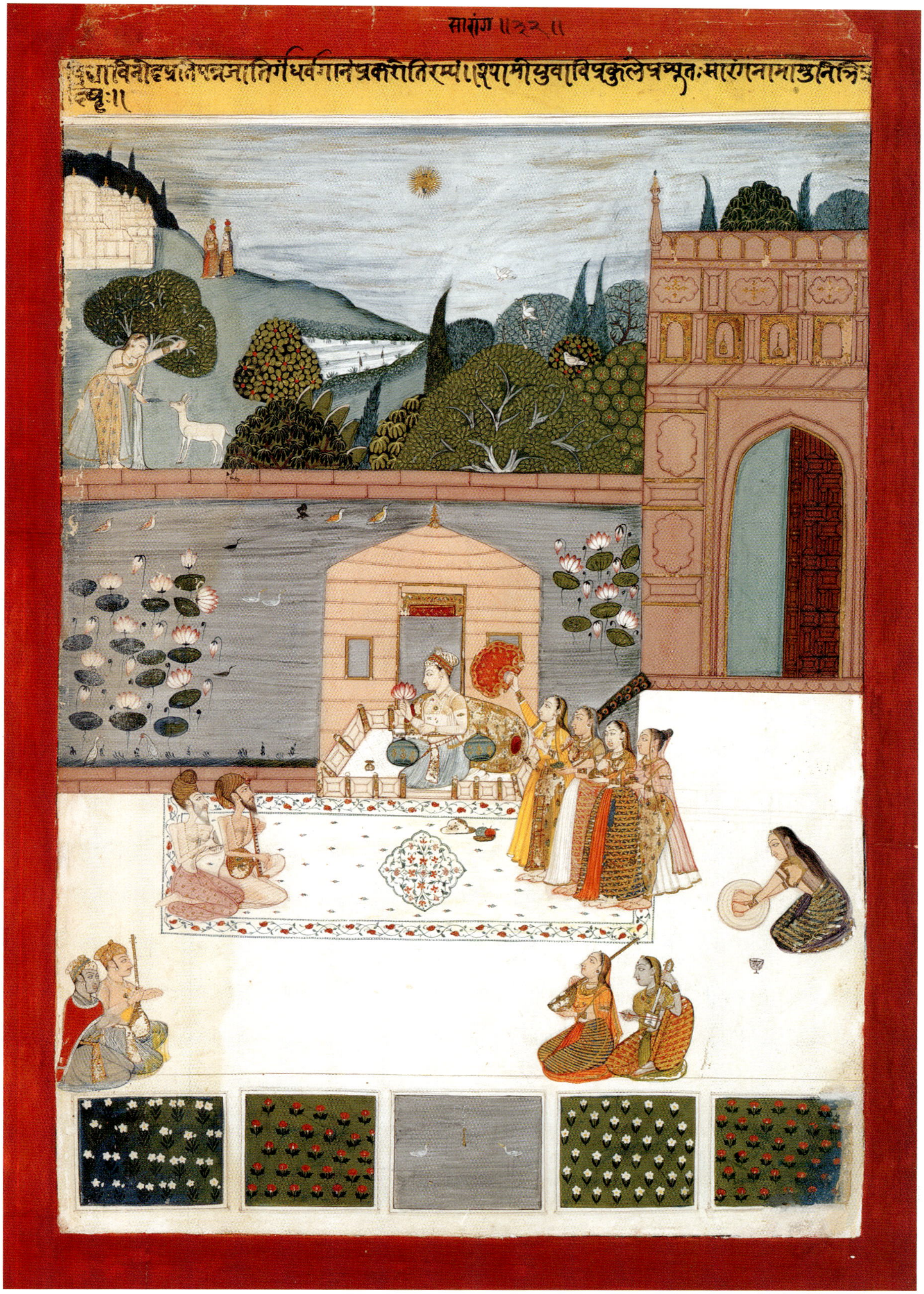
सारंग ॥२२॥

Kings and Courtly Pursuits

60 Leaf from an Album: Sultan Abu Sa'id

Mughal style, 1650–75
Opaque watercolor on paper
Sheet: 13 ¾ x 8 ⅞ in. (35 x 22.5 cm)
Image: 5 ⅞ x 3 ¼ in. (14.9 x 8.3 cm)
Gift of Ramesh and Urmil Kapoor; P.2001.13.6

A typical leaf from a Mughal album, it includes a formal portrait on one side and a calligraphic panel on the other side. Likely, it was assembled for a Muslim patron, but neither its exact provenance nor its date can be easily ascertained. The calligraphy in the *nashtaliq* script may be older than the painting, but neither a date nor the name of the calligrapher is provided. The verse written in the central panel was probably written by Sa'adi, a popular Persian poet who lived in the thirteenth century (see Appendix). Two additional strips on the side contain prose texts accommodated in decorative cartouches; these provide historical information about Sultan Mahmood and have no relation to the verses. Such whimsical juxtaposition of unrelated calligraphic panels with adornments and decorative borders was popular among Muslim connoisseurs.

The portrait is characteristically formal with a plain, buff background. The inscription not only identifies the enthroned monarch but also provides some chronological information (see Appendix). A Timurid sultan of Central Asia, Abu Sa'id ruled from 1451/52 until his death in 1469. He was the grandfather of Babur, the ruler of Fergana who invaded India and began the Mughal dynasty. Thus, it is likely that other portraits in the album included his other ancestors, beginning with Timur (1336–1405), the founder of the Timurid dynasty of Central Asia and Persia, as well as of Mughal successors. Although the representation is idealized, the Sultan has an individualized face, which may have been based on an accurately drawn earlier portrait. For two other portraits, inscribed similarly in Arabic or Devanagari script, one of which depicts Sultan Timur and probably belonged to the same album, see Pal 1976, no. M32–M33.

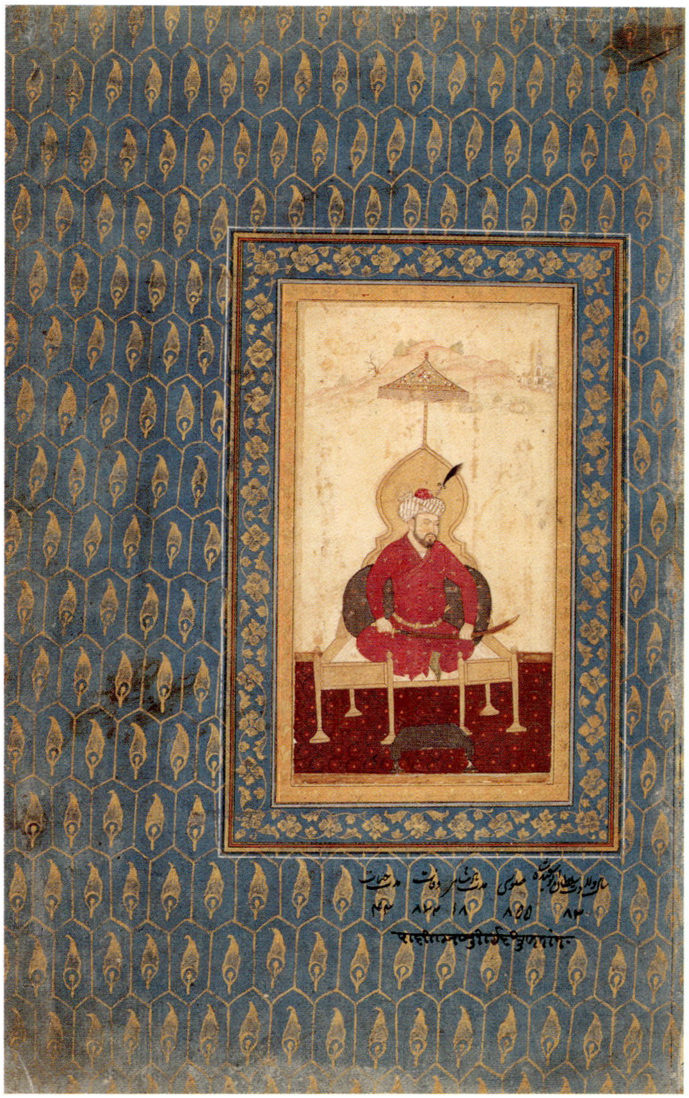

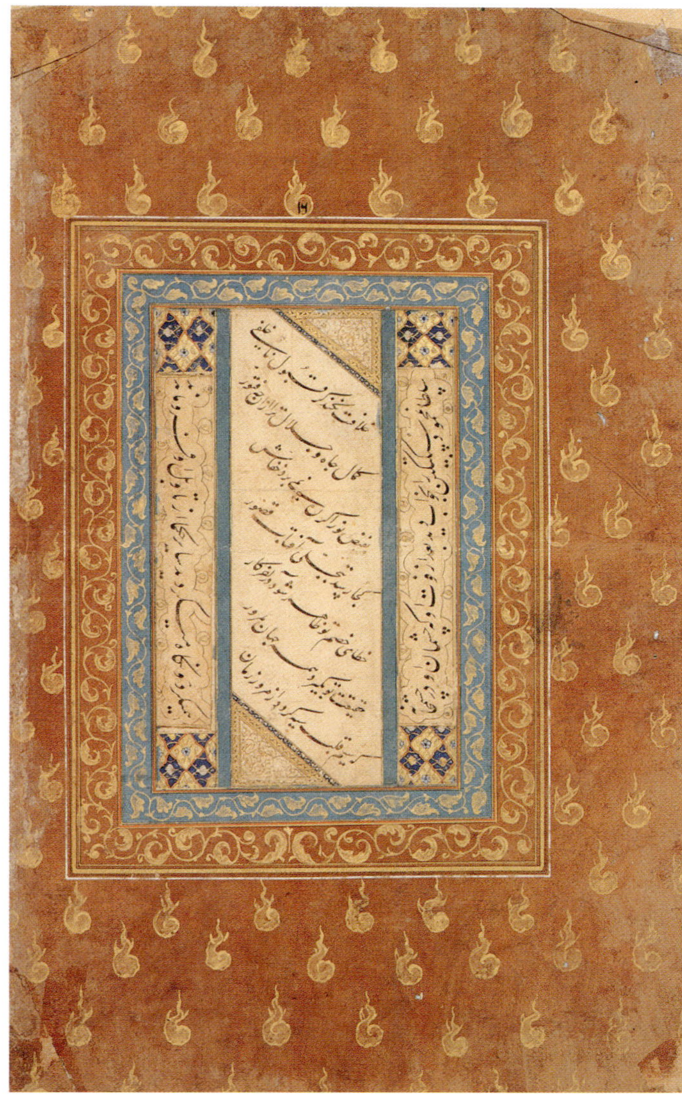

61 Maharana Sangram Singh II Watching Elephant Combat

Rajasthan, Mewar, Udaipur, c. 1725
Opaque watercolor on paper
Sheet: 17 ½ x 28 ⅛ in. (44.5 x 71.4 cm)
Image: 15 ⅜ x 26 in. (39.1 x 66 cm)
Gift of Ramesh and Urmil Kapoor; P.2001.13.7

Although the back has no inscription, the scene is easily identified. The haloed figure on the terrace center foreground is Maharana Sangram Singh II, who ruled from 1710 to 1734. The monarch was a punctilious recorder of all court events, festivals and pastimes, which were painted in large, sprawling and crowded compositions by his artists (see Topsfield 2002, pp. 141–78 for a detailed assessment of painting during his reign).

The scene shown here is a combat between two elephants—although at first glance, one may think scores of pachyderms are involved. In fact, the composition shows various stages of the encounter between the two elephants as a continuous narrative, disregarding temporal dimensions. Typical of Udaipur, this narrative strategy appears to have been employed by the artist, perhaps to add dramatic energy to his compositions and to make them grandiose, which is what the patron preferred. Two other relevant pictures of the genre may be cited here. One captures in a similar mode the death of a mahout by an elephant (Topsfield 2000, fig. 146), and the other, an elephant fight that takes place in the Chaugan arena of the palace (Topsfield 1980, no. 74). In that painting, the entire arena is depicted, but the combat is portrayed minimally. Here, only a part of the arena is visible, but the long sequence of combat is made clear by the multiple frames.

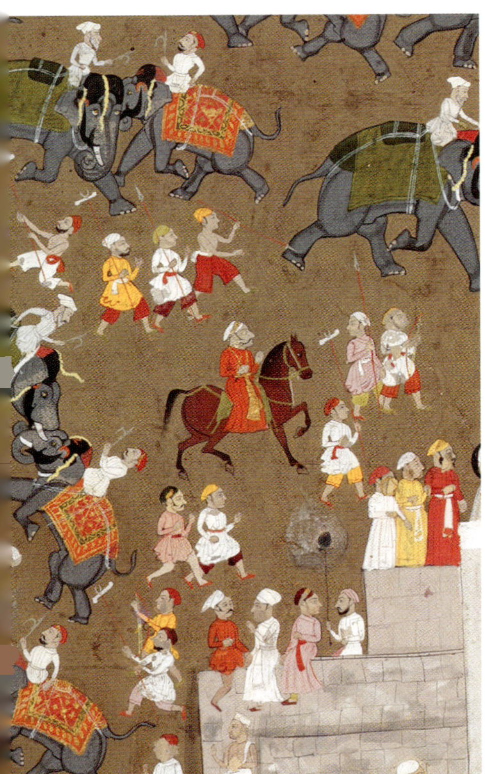

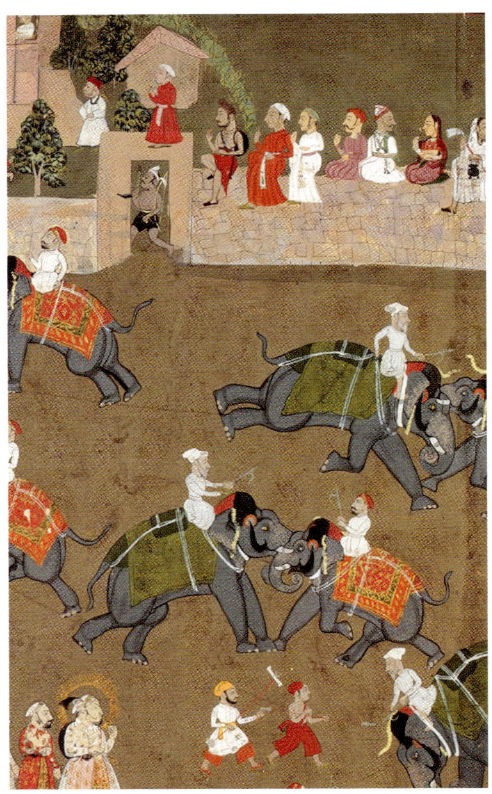

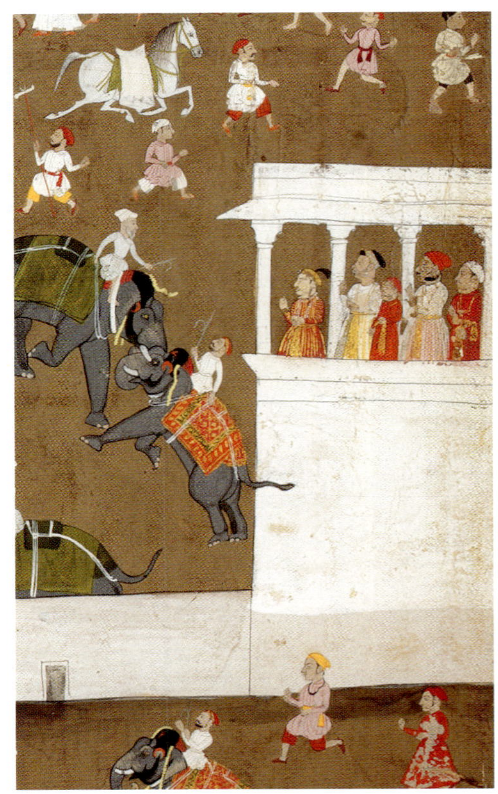

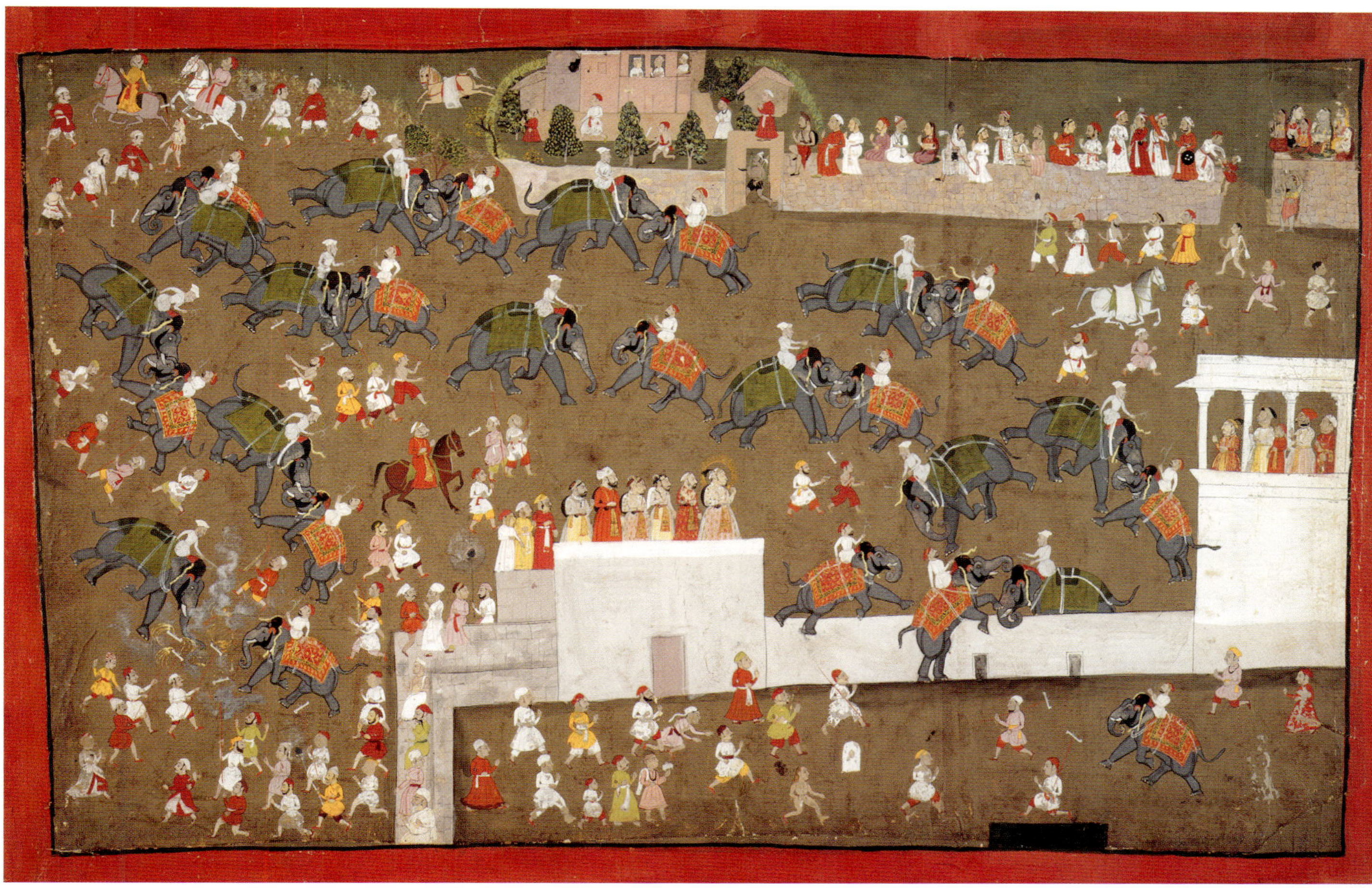

62 Ladies Watching a Cockfight

Rajasthan, Bundi school, c. 1725
Opaque watercolor on paper
Sheet: 11 7/8 x 9 in. (30.2 x 22.9 cm)
Image: 10 1/4 x 7 1/4 in. (26 x 18.4 cm)
Gift of Ramesh and Urmil Kapoor; P.2001.13.5

In this lively picture we are given a glimpse into life in the *zenana* (ladies' quarters) of a Rajput palace. Two elegant ladies, perhaps both princesses, are whiling away the afternoon watching a private cockfight. That it is still quite warm on the terrace is clear, as a maid holds a fan behind one of the ladies, who is perhaps the hostess. Behind the other lady stands a second maid, with a third cock waiting to be tested. In the foreground, a third woman, perhaps a nurse, restrains a boy from joining the contest of the birds. Cockfighting was a favorite pastime in India from antiquity, and was mostly indulged in by men. This Bundi picture is therefore a rare piece of evidence showing that upper-class females patronized the sport as well. The excitement and intensity of the occasion is clearly evident, as the princesses have abandoned the carpeted seat beneath the baldachin and are seated on the ground.

Not much has been written about the life of court ladies as reflected in Rajput pictures. It is also not known whether such genre paintings were commissioned by individual female patrons or were imaginary exercises by artists. In any event, this Bundi artist appears to have preferred drawing freely rather than meticulously. The ladies' dresses and the various implements strewn all over the terrace are deftly but swiftly rendered, with bold, rather than careful, brushstrokes. The floral designs of the parapet adorning the terrace, however, reflect a delicate touch.

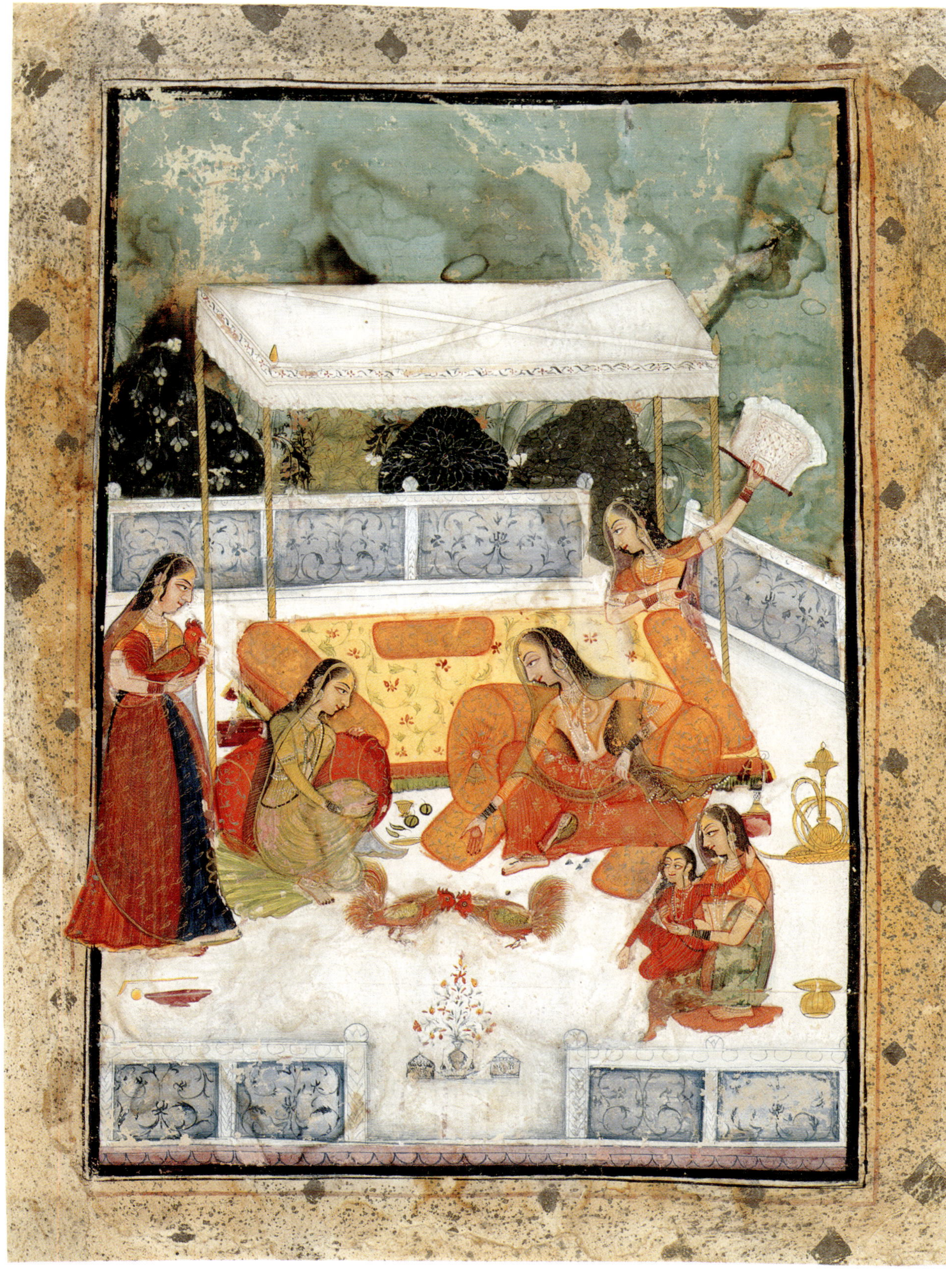

63 A Forlorn Lady and a Musician

Uttar Pradesh, Lucknow (?), c. 1750
Opaque watercolor and gold on paper
Sheet: 18 x 12 in. (45.7 x 30.5 cm)
Image: 9 x 7 in. (22.9 x 17.8 cm)
Promised gift of Ramesh and Urmil Kapoor

The setting is idyllic—an open terrace overlooking a formal garden. Beyond, clouds tinged with pink, mauve and orange float across the blue sky. The time is dusk, perhaps after a storm. In the clear air, the spruced-up elegant lady sits on a carpet strewn with glass flasks of wine, plates heaped with delicacies and a betel box filled with *pan* quids. A musician sitting at the edge of the rug sings and strums an instrument. However, our lady seems interested in neither the music nor in smoking, for she grasps the snake of the hookah idly with her left hand. She is clearly ruminating about her absent lover, and perhaps, her past trysts.

Clearly, the theme is one of love in separation according to the Indian rhetorical tradition. This could easily be the painted version of the following passage describing the heroine's secret reveries of her absent hero: "Her anguish has increased so much that she does not like talk, nor play, nor laugh, nor likes the sight of anything...she looks as if searching within herself for some lost thing...who should devise a diversion for her, or play on the *vina*, for her mind is lost in her own thoughts" (Randhawa 1962, p. 103).

The picture is rendered in what is known as the later Mughal style, perhaps at Lucknow, and mounted on a large sheet speckled with gold, as one sees in an album. At the bottom of the mount are two letters written in Devanagari script that, according to Naval Krishna, may be an abbreviation of the word for "chapter" (personal communication, 2002). The manner of mounting indicates that it once belonged to an album. One or more ladies on a terrace was a popular theme of eighteenth-century genre paintings for both Muslim and Hindu patrons. The lyrical, realistically detailed and romantic style preferred by the later Mughal patrons considerably influenced some Rajput court paintings.

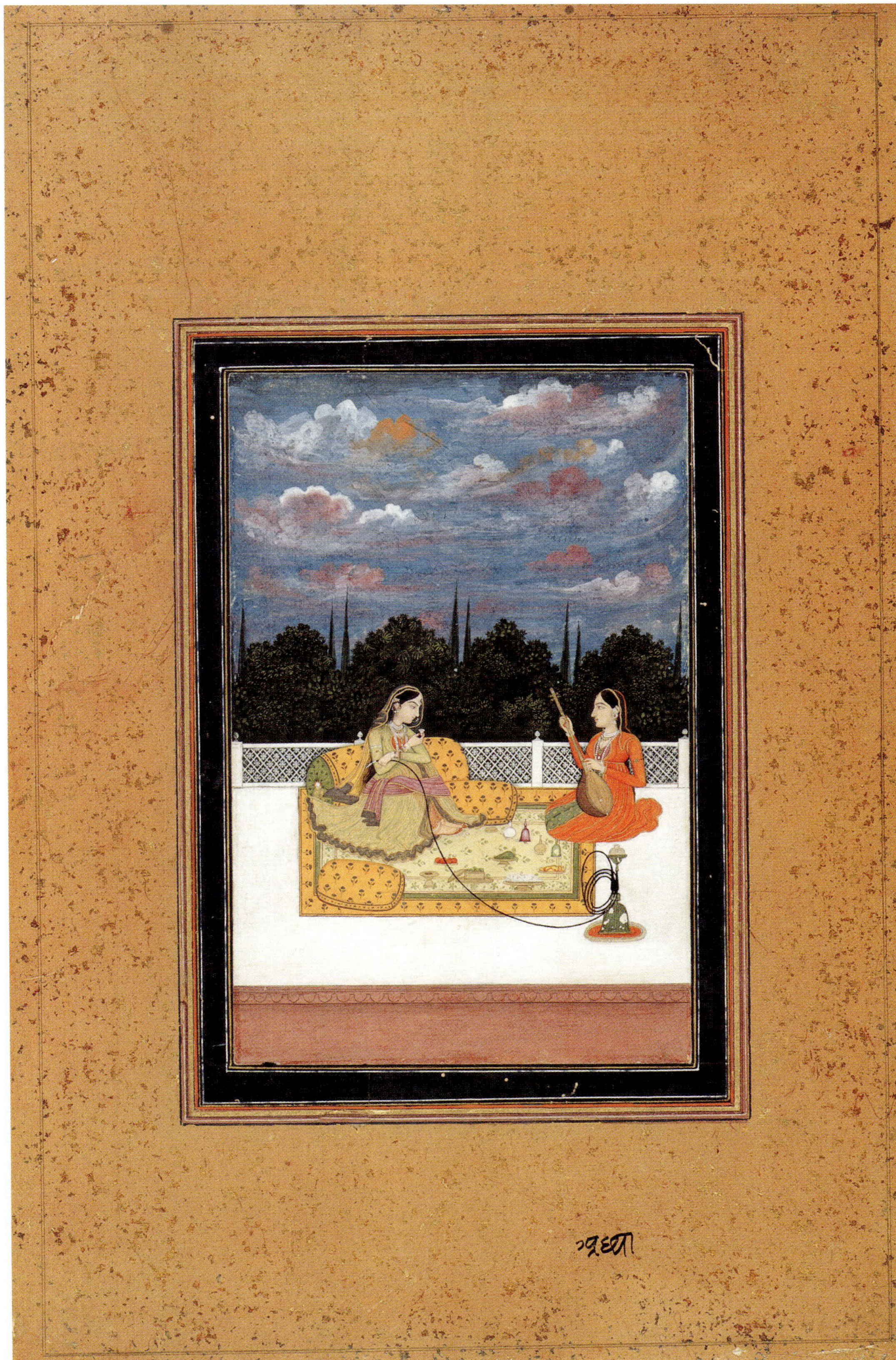

64 Raja Kailash Pal of Nurpur

Himachal Pradesh, Nurpur workshop, 1700–1725
Opaque watercolor on paper
Sheet: 10 ½ x 7 ½ in. (26.7 x 19.1 cm)
Image: 8 ⅝ x 5 ¾ in. (21.9 x 14.6 cm)
Lent by Ramesh and Urmil Kapoor

The inscriptions on the back and front identify the figure as Kailash Pal (1353–1397) (see Appendix). Although he died a little more than three centuries before this portrait was painted, he was a popular historical personality in the state. He was remembered particularly for defeating a Muslim general named Tatar Khan, so much so that a ditty commemorating the victory is still familiar in the region:

> *When he sees his face in the heart-rending mirror*
> *Tatar Khan sees on his forehead*
> *A Kailash-inflicted sear.*
> (Hutchinson and Vogel 1933, p. 221)

Tatar Khan was likely a governor of the Punjab under Muhammad Tughlaq (r. 1325–51).

It is not possible to determine whether this picture was based on an earlier portrait or was simply a figment of the artist's imagination. Cosmeticized though the face is, it still can be recognized for its individualized features, such as a strong nose and prominent and stylish facial hair. The face does convey a heroic and powerful personality, further augmented by the falcon the subject holds with his right hand. A second portrait—not as polished and with a hooked nose—was published by William Archer and wrongly identified with a seventeenth-century Nurpur ruler (see Archer 1973, vol. 2, pl. 76). Both are likely contemporaneous renderings, perhaps even by the same workshop, which produced several other sensitive and strong characterizations for the Nurpur court around the turn of the eighteenth century (see Archer 1973, vol. 2, pl. 302–3, figs. 1–2, 5–6).

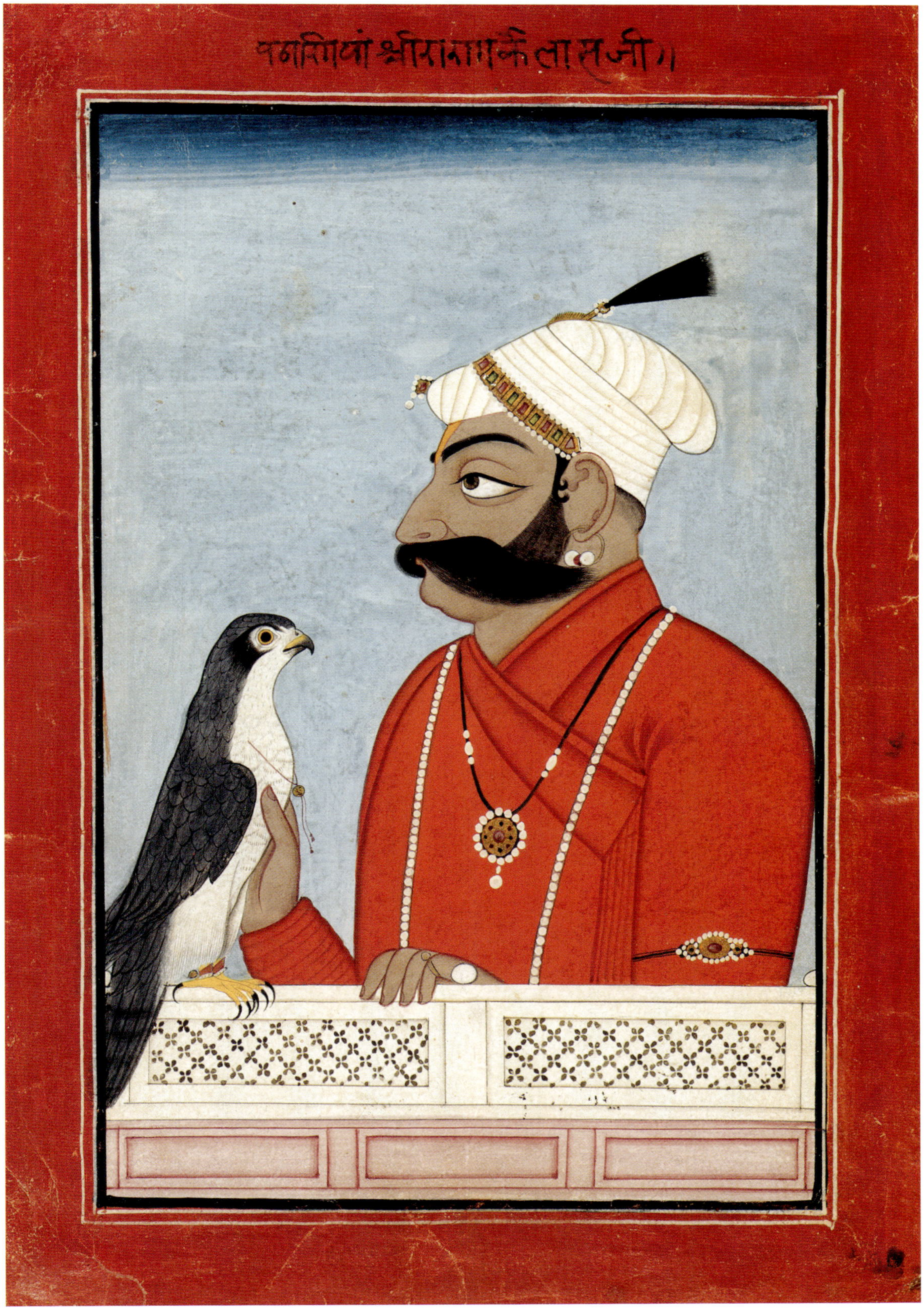

65 Raja Devichand of Bilaspur

Himachal Pradesh, Kangra workshop, c. 1775
Opaque watercolor on paper
Sheet: 9 ¾ x 6 ½ in. (24.8 x 16.5 cm)
Image: 7 ⅞ x 4 ⅞ in. (20 x 12.4 cm)
Gift of Ramesh and Urmil Kapoor; P.2000.9.8

This is an accomplished formal portrait of a hill *raja* rendered by an artist of the Kangra school. The sitter is likely Raja Devichand, who ruled the state of Bilaspur (or Kahlur) between 1741 and 1778. This identification is based on the subject's resemblance to another Kangra portrait of Devichand seated with a contemporary Kangra ruler (see Archer 1973, vol. 2, pl. 194, fig. 1).

This portrait, however, is probably by a different hand, as the characterization is much stronger, revealing the artist's familiarity with the ruler. The details of the facial features as well as of the garments are sensitively rendered with incredible accuracy and finesse. The composition, however, is typical of such formal Pahari portraits, in which the sitter is shown in profile, smoking a hookah, while an attendant stands behind with a tall fan (*morchal*), a symbol of sovereignty. The floor of the terrace is usually carpeted, and a large bolster and two cushions with soft purple covers are used as supports. The *raja* wears matching dress, shawl and turban, all in pale green and delicately embroidered.

Devichand enjoyed a long reign and was an able ruler and general. His only wife was a Kangra princess and an aunt of the famous Kangra ruler and patron of the arts, Sansar Chand (r. 1775–1823). This portrait by a Kangra artist may have been rendered either on a visit to that state or while working at his court in Bilaspur. The painting is certainly from the circle of the famous Nainsukh of Guler, to whom another portrait of the *raja* is ascribed (Goswamy and Fischer 1992, no. 121). It could have been rendered by one of his sons, either Kama or Ranjha (Aijazuddin 1977, pl. 68).

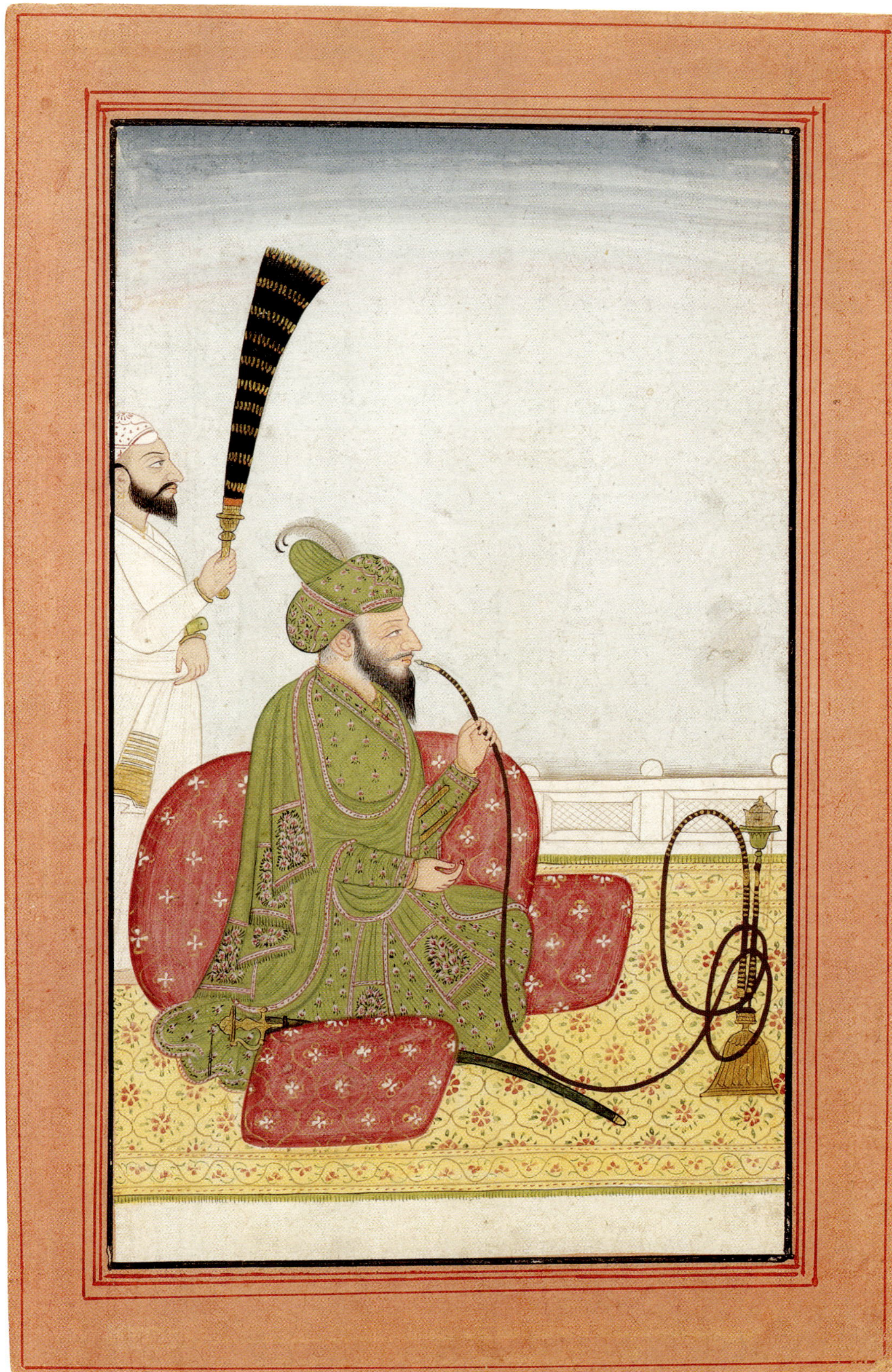

66 Raja Ranjit Sen of Suket and Family

Himachal Pradesh, Kangra workshop, c. 1775
Opaque watercolor on paper
Sheet: 10 ¼ x 8 ½ in. (26 x 21.6 cm)
Image: 8 ⅛ x 6 ½ in. (20.6 x 16.5 cm)
Gift of Ramesh and Urmil Kapoor; P.2003.2.4

The inscriptions in Persian script on the front and in Devanagari on the back (see Appendix) identify the figures as Raja Ranjit Singh Sen (r. 1762–91), holding the pipe of an unseen hookah and being fanned by an attendant, with his son and heir, Bikram, conversing with Kishan Singh and his son Bishan Singh. Kishan Singh was Ranjit Sen's younger brother, who, during a campaign against neighboring Mandi, was betrayed by Ranjit Sen on suspicion of disloyalty. Sometime after 1775, Kishan Singh returned with the help of his son-in-law Sansar Chand of Kangra to sack Suket and then retire to Jagannath. This meeting between the siblings probably took place before the relationship soured.

Another portrait, but without the two sons and the attendant, is published by Archer (1973, vol. 1, p. 283 and vol. 2, pl. 197, 8 [xv]); it, too, has Arabic lettering on the front. Indeed, it is likely that the writing is by the same hand and that both portraits are from the same workshop. Archer ascribes that portrait to Kangra around 1780. Comparable are two other formal durbars or audiences of hill rajas (Archer 1973, vol. 2, pl. 195), which may also be works by the same hands. Speaking of hands, it should be noted that the unknown artist of the portrait under discussion has attached a right hand to Kishan Singh's left arm. The same incongruity is repeated as well for his son, whose attire is identical to that worn by a prince in two Chamba pictures ascribed to the artist Ranjhha (Ohri and Craven 1998, figs. 17–18). The faces of both brothers are dominated by strong noses, large eyes and dense but well-groomed beards.

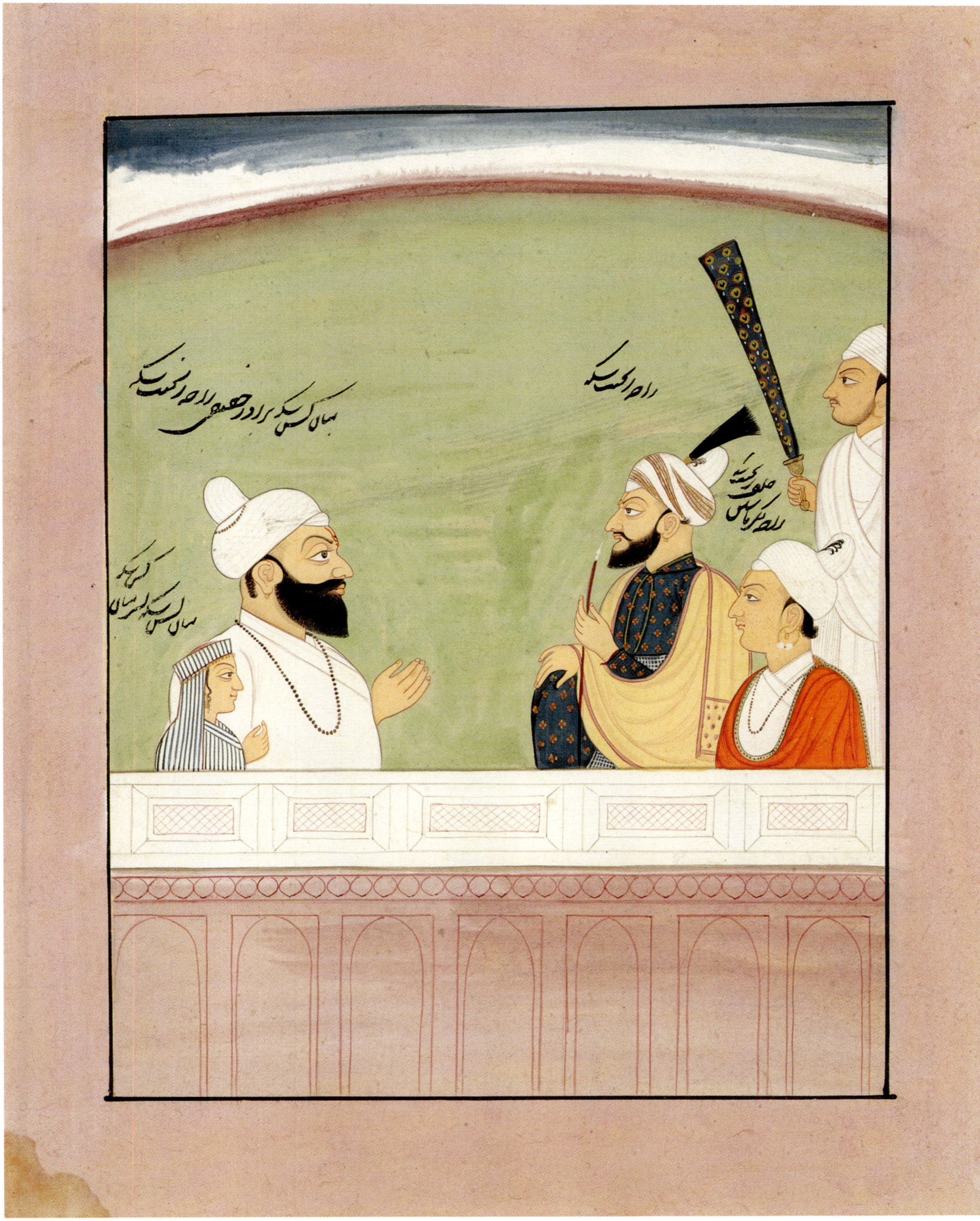

67 Maharao Basant Singh and Maharaja Sahab Prithivi Singh

Rajasthan, Kota (?), c. 1775
Opaque watercolor on paper
Sheet: 8 ¼ x 10 ½ in. (21 x 26.7 cm)
Image: 7 ¼ x 10 ½ in. (18.4 x 26.7 cm)
Gift of Ramesh and Urmil Kapoor; P.2002.2.8

Despite the white inscriptions in the upper margin that provide two names and titles, the two princes cannot be identified. The more important figure, with all the trappings of a ruler—a preeminent position, a halo, lavish ornaments and the *morchal* and flywhisk bearers—has been identified as Maharao Basant Singh, the other as Maharaja Sahab Prithivi Singh by Naval Krishna (see Appendix). Because of the style of the picture and the figures, a Kota association is most likely. However, although Kota rulers did assume the title *maharao*, there was no ruler by the name of Basant. There was a prince named Bakht Singh who ruled at Itawa, a fiefdom (*jagir*) of Kota, who was the brother of Maharao Ajit Singh (r. 1756–58). Prithivi Singh was the name of the father and also of a descendant three generations below. The visitor, however, could be a feudatory from another *jagir*.

In any case, the picture is a typical Rajput composition in which the figures are represented hierarchically and the ruler's exalted position is left in no doubt. The informality of the meeting is clear from the setting of a terrace, but this did not mean that there would have been any breach in etiquette in the behavior of the four figures. ❧

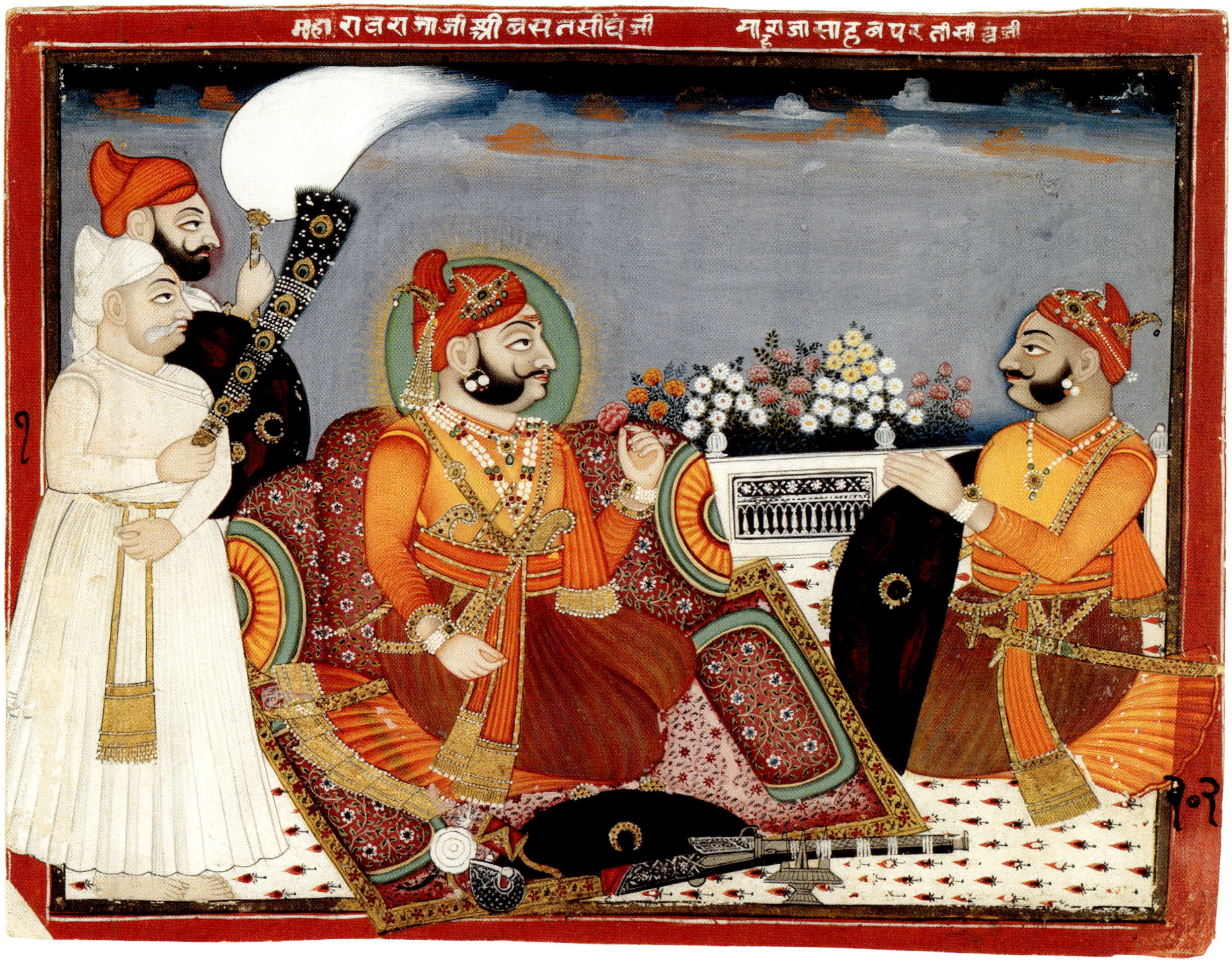
महारावराजाजी श्री बसतसींघजी
माहाराजा साहब परतीसींघजी

68 Dancing at Court

Rajasthan, Kota workshop, c. 1775
Opaque watercolor and gold on paper
Sheet: 13 5/8 x 8 3/4 in. (34.6 x 22.2 cm)
Image: 11 x 6 in. (27.9 x 15.2 cm)
Gift of Vineet and Floretta Kapoor; P.2002.3

This scene could be typical of any Rajput court. A prince waits on a terrace with attendants and watches a performance by a female dancer, who is accompanied by musicians. Watching from the roof of the pavilion is the first lady of the palace, whose status is clearly indicated by her peacock fan–bearing companion. She also has a female musician waiting to entertain her. Significantly, the foreground of the lower terrace is splattered with red powder, indicating that the occasion may be the spring saturnalia known as *holi* or *fagua*. What is distinctive about the picture is the dark-blue complexion of the prince, which identifies him as Brijnathji, a form of Krishna and the family deity of the Kota rulers. Such identification of the ruler with the divinity is a characteristic feature of Kota pictures.

The prince in this instance could be Maharao Umed Singh I (r. 1771–1819) of Kota. It is stylistically close to a genre picture of a prince's visit to a shrine attributed to the workshop of Sheikh Taju (Welch 1997, no. 43). In both pictures, the figures are embodiments of grace and elegance and the palette is bright and brilliantly varied. Especially noteworthy in the present picture is the abundant use of gold, which almost certainly indicates a court patronage. The border of the picture is adorned with formal floral sprays in mauve.

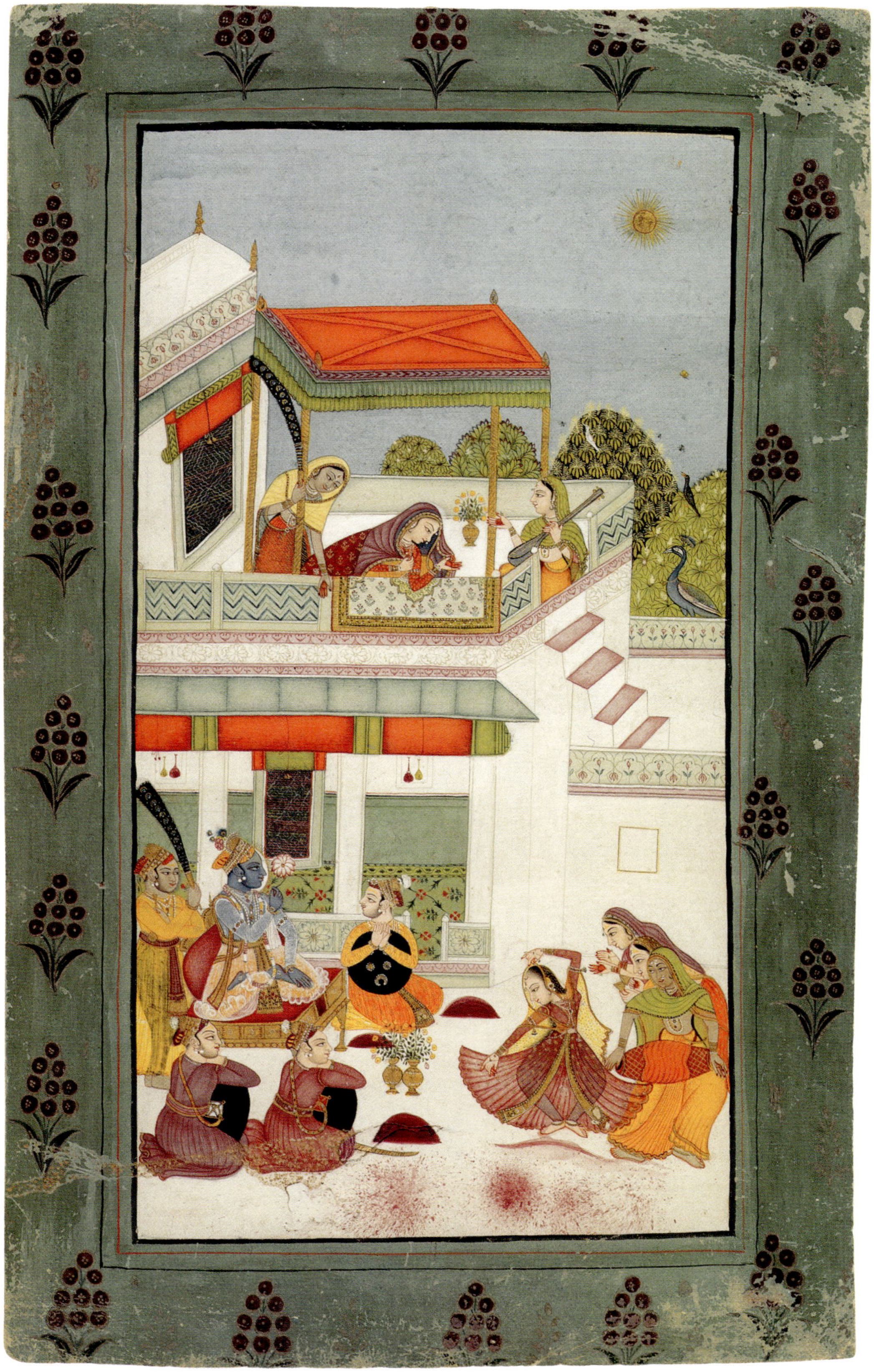

69 A Beastly Combat

Rajasthan, Kota, c. 1775
Opaque watercolor on paper
Sheet: 7 5/8 x 11 7/8 in. (19.4 x 30.2 cm)
Image: 6 5/8 x 10 7/8 in. (16.8 x 27.6 cm)
Promised gift of Ramesh and Urmil Kapoor

Elephants were a popular subject with Kota patrons and artists, who have given us a large corpus of both drawings and paintings (see Welch 1997 for a number of examples from the Kota royal collection). Most of these paintings show elephants sporting or in rut (*must*) and are remarkable for the power of their compositions and for the empathy with which the animals are rendered. This picture is thematically unusual, however, in that the unknown master artist has captured the violent occasion with controlled energy and expressive power.

The action takes place in an almost arcadian setting, with ornamental trees and leaves rendered with precision but almost as cutouts. The darker green scalloped hilly foreground is abruptly separated from a lighter green background filled with finely rendered grass; a deeper green edge marks the transition to the blue sky. The stillness of the landscape is effectively contrasted with the dramatic contest. The poor camel has no chance, as the elephant has not only crushed him but also driven both his tusks deep into the camel's shoulder. The two riders of the elephant clearly react in horror, and the mahout drives his dagger into the elephant's head. The fact that part of a chain is still attached to the pachyderm's leg indicates that he is likely a court elephant gone berserk.

A less dynamic version of this subject, but of an earlier date, is in the Art Institute of Chicago (Pal and Seid 2002, no. 26). The smooth and polished rendering of this Kota representation, the use of greens with mauve tree trunks, the fan-like spread of the roots of the larger tree and the assurance with which the two animals are drawn relates it to Kota hunting pictures of the second half of the eighteenth century—without, however, their ornamental bravura.

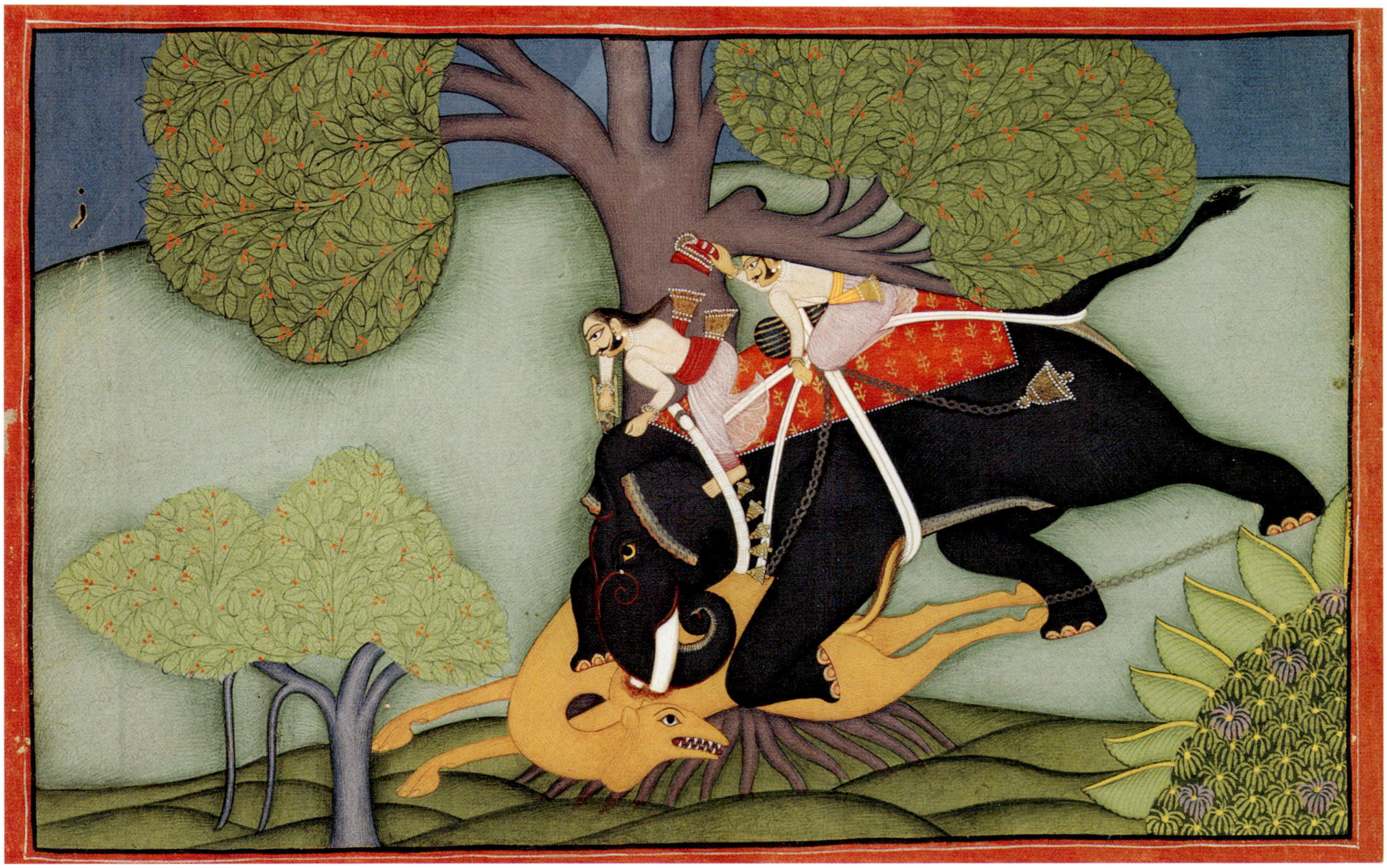

70 Ruler with Princes Giving an Audience

Rajasthan, Bundi, c. 1775
Opaque watercolor on paper
Sheet: 12¾ x 9⅝ in. (32.4 x 24.4 cm)
Image: 11⅛ x 9½ in. (28.3 x 24.1 cm)
Gift of Ramesh and Urmil Kapoor; P.2002.2.3

The rubber stamp on the back makes it clear that the painting once belonged to the collection of the Bundi court. That, however, does not necessarily make the subject represented here a ruler of that state, though it is likely. Without an identifying inscription, the ruler cannot be recognized with certainty. A possibility is Ajit Singh (r. 1770–73) or his son and successor, Bishen Singh (r. 1773–1821). The face is similar to an inscribed portrait of Ajit Singh (see Beach 1974, figs. 35 and 37), but the features differ somewhat, as do the shape of the sideburns. As Beach has commented (1974, p. 20), in such portraits, figure types conform to a similar formula and character depiction, though facial modeling is rare, as is clear from a comparison of all the adults in this picture. Along with the ruler are his two sons and two attendants with the regal symbols. The attitude of the five visitors is clearly reverential. The two white pigeons on the yellow carpet in front add a touch of informality to the occasion.

Whatever the identity of the ruler, the work is stylistically related to several paintings attributed generally to the second half of the eighteenth century and rendered both at Bundi and Uniara (Beach 1974, figs. 38–39 and 46). The palette is richly dominated by strident yellows and oranges. Notably, all the figures have been given an orangish-pink complexion.

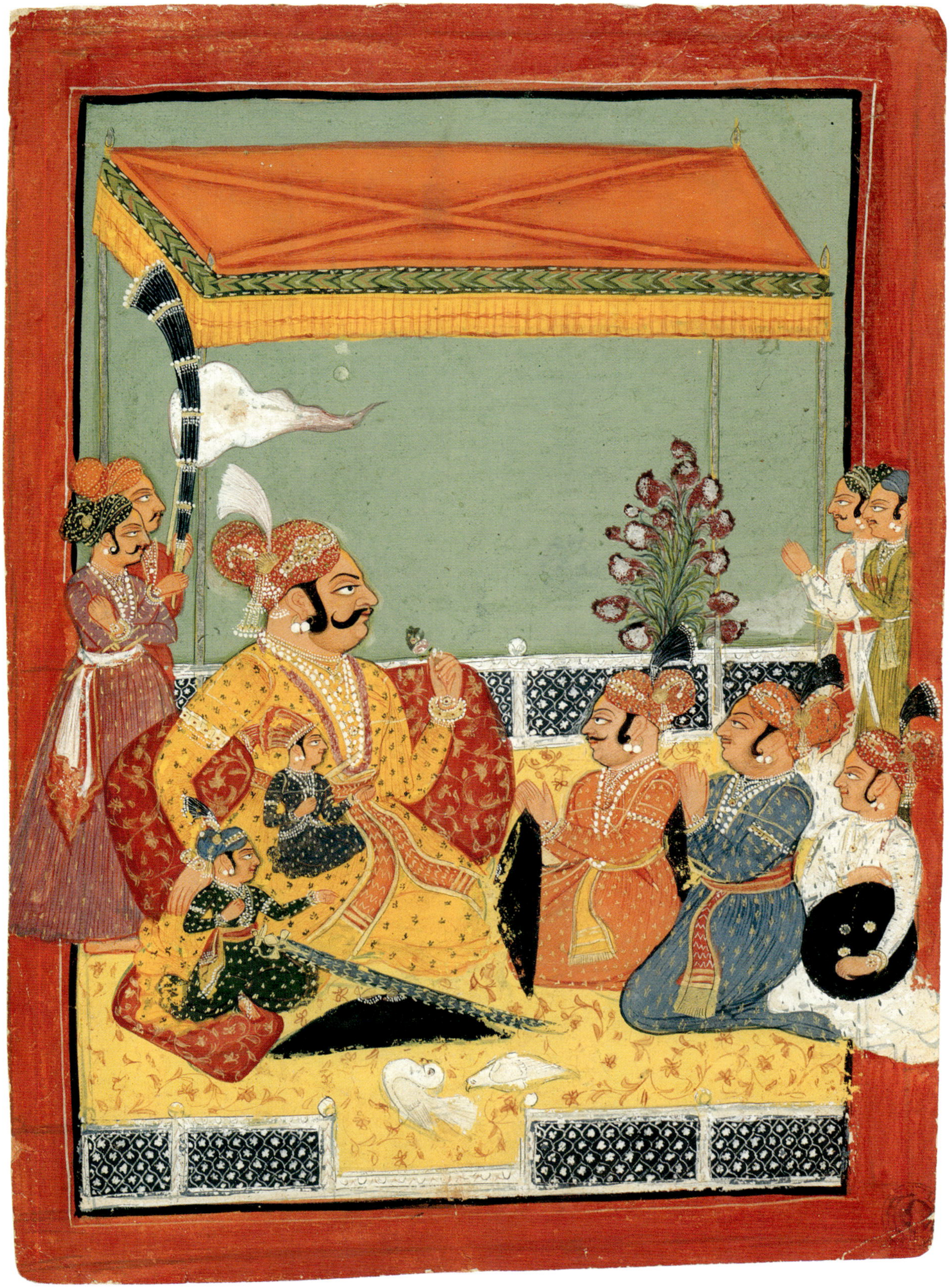

71 Prince Entering a Mansion

Himachal Pradesh, Guler workshop, 1775–1800
Opaque watercolor on paper
Sheet: 11 5/8 x 8 in. (29.5 x 20.3 cm)
Image: 9 5/8 x 6 1/8 in. (24.4 x 15.6 cm)
Gift of Ramesh and Urmil Kapoor; P.2003.2.5

Accompanied by an attendant, a prince in a white dress walks up the steps to the entrance of a mansion. It is likely that he is walking to an assignation, as he holds a flower in his left hand like a bon vivant. Beyond the cusped arch of the entrance, a man in a green dress stands at the landing of a narrow flight of stairs, chatting with another man seated in a loft with a musical instrument(?). Still higher up is a partially seen woman who seems to be attempting to restrain a child, who looks down at the man in the green dress.

Stylistically the picture is close to another more formal portrait of Raja Amrit Pal of Basohli, attributed to the "workshop of the first generation after Nainsukh of Guler" (Goswamy and Bhatia 1999, no. 198). Interestingly, that painting, too, has an identical design on the border but is differently colored. Thus, very likely the same unknown artist was responsible for both representations. The two princes are so similar in appearance that it is tempting to regard this as a portrait of Amrit Pal as well. On the other hand, there is a close physical resemblance between this prince and the portraits of Raja Prakash Chand of Guler (Aijazuddin 1977, pl. 38, fig. 17 and Archer 1973, vol. 2, pl. 114, fig. 52).

No matter which prince is represented in this sparingly colored and delicately drawn picture, it remains an unusual princely portrait in its spontaneity and informality of occasion, as compared to more standard renditions. Apart from the painting's interesting subject matter, the figures are drawn with acuity, whether in their apparel or in their facial features.

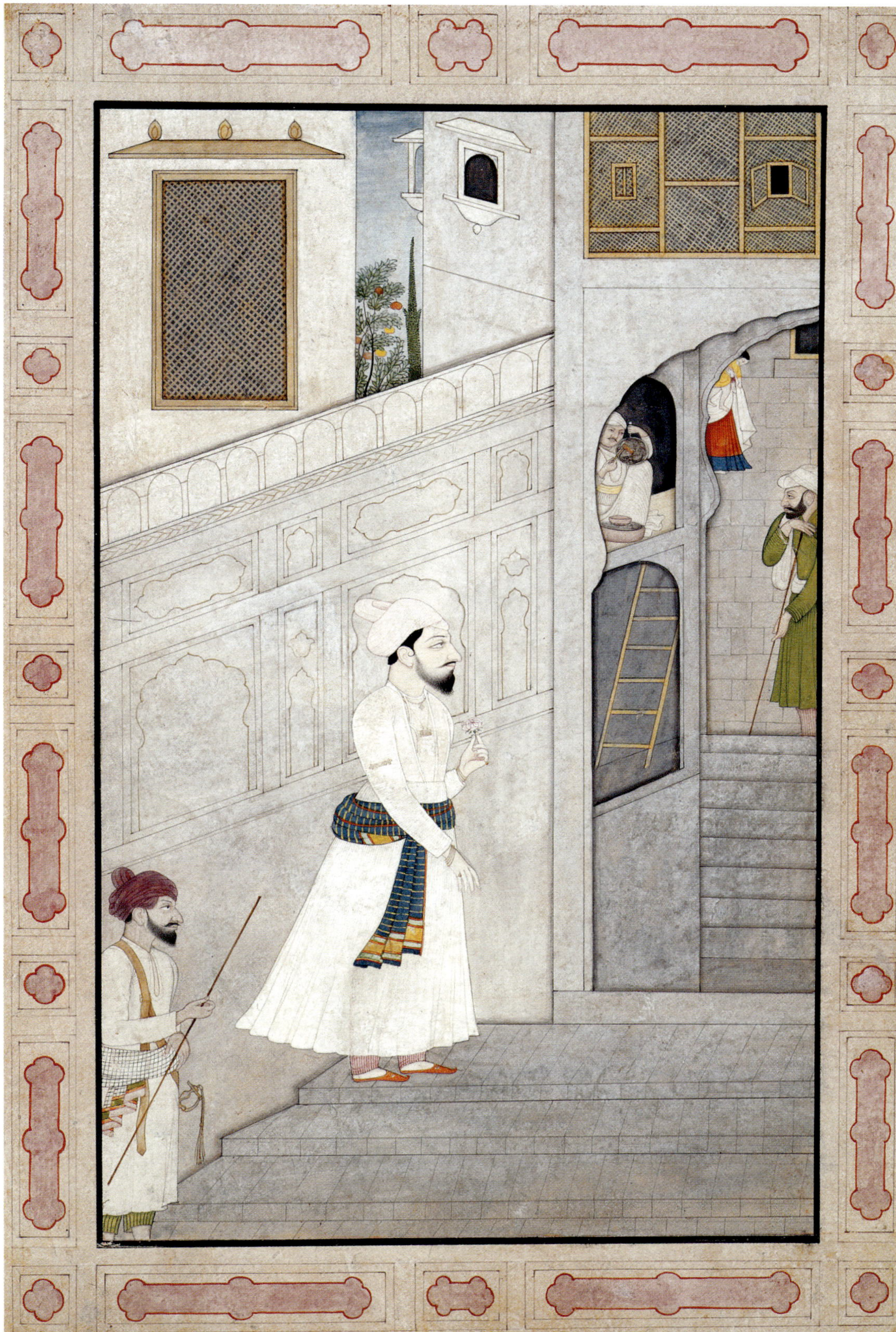

72 Ajit Singh of Ghanerao

Painted by Dana (active 1800–1825)
Rajasthan, Jodhpur, Nivajwala Palace, dated 1812
Opaque watercolor on paper
Sheet: 11 ½ x 9 ¼ in. (29.2 x 23.5 cm)
Image: 11 ¼ x 9 in. (28.6 x 22.9 cm)
Gift of Ramesh and Urmil Kapoor; P.2002.2.9

There are two inscriptions and a rubber stamp on the back, which provide a great deal of information about this formal equestrian portrait. The long, bold inscription, written when the painting was completed in 1812, informs us that the rider is Maharaja Ajit Singh (r. 1800–1856) and the mare's name is Gulab Kunvar. She was acquired from Khejarla for 1,800 rupees. The picture was painted by Dana at the mansion called Nivajwala (see Appendix). This is clearly a portrait of Ajit Singh of Ghanerao, a fiefdom under the state of Jodhpur, as is also confirmed by a faint later inscription. The Ghanerao chiefs were generally addressed as *thakur*, a lesser title than the exalted "maharaja" given in the inscription. Other paintings of Ajit Singh, who was a connoisseur, are said to be in the collection of the late Sangram Singh of Nawalgarh (see Crill n.d. [2000], pp. 130–31, figs. 101–2), whose seal also appears on the back of this painting.

The artist Dana was one of the court artists of Maharaja Man Singh (r. 1803–1843) of Jodhpur, the overlord of Ajit Singh. As Crill has mentioned (pp. 145–46), Dana painted other pictures for Ajit Singh as well. The Museum's painting is quite typical of the Jodhpur style, though perhaps less flamboyant than similar equestrian portraits rendered for Man Singh. There is no use of gold and the swagger of the textiles is more restrained. Nevertheless, the prancing animal adds a dynamic tension to the otherwise upright prince and marching retainers with drawn swords and royal trappings. Elegantly turbaned, Ajit Singh is portrayed as a dandy with a nosegay, rather than as a heroic figure.

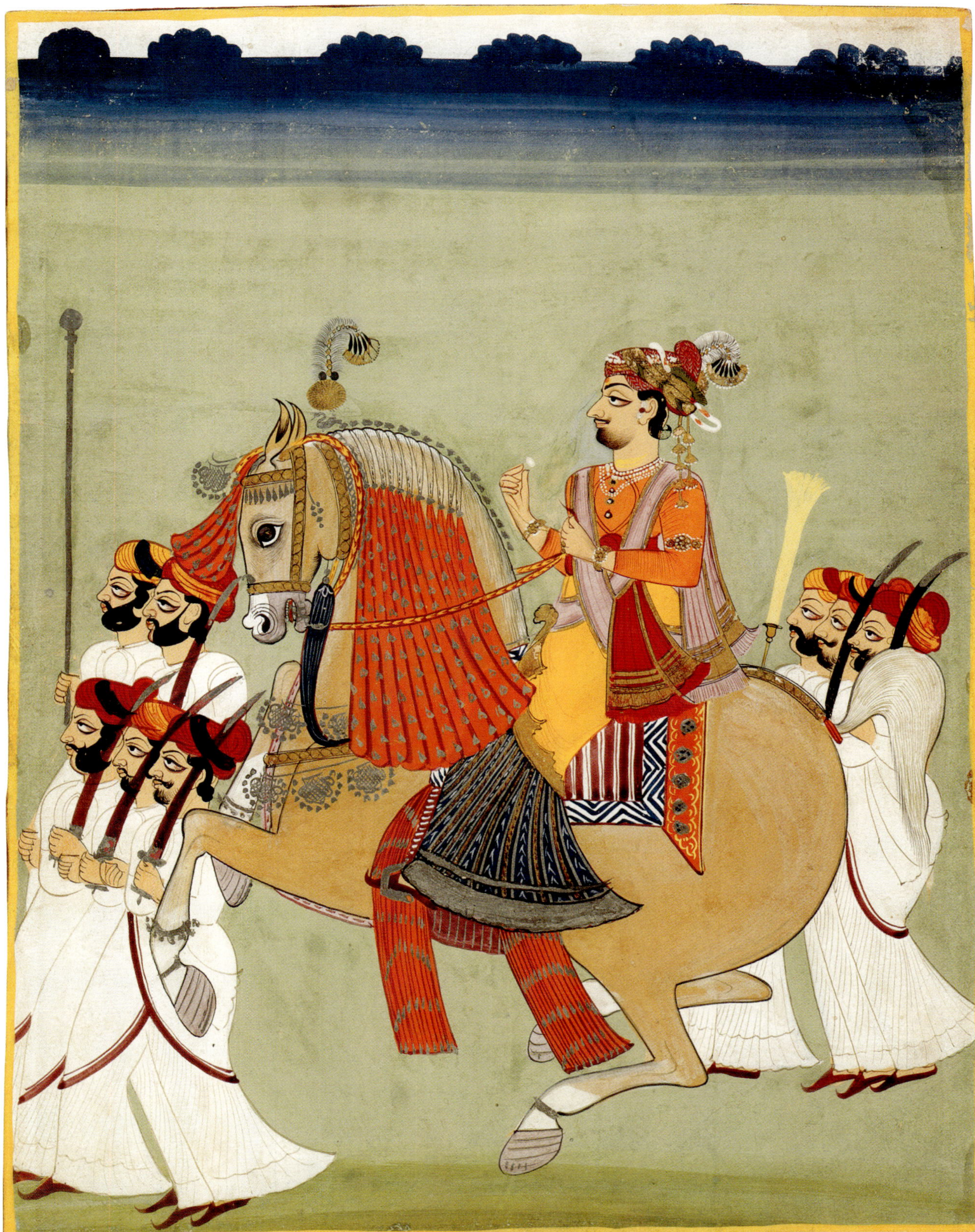

73 An Equestrian Portrait of a Sikh Prince

Himachal Pradesh, Kangra workshop, 1825–50
Opaque watercolor on paper
Sheet: 9 ¾ x 7 ½ in. (24.8 x 19.1 cm)
Image: 8 ¼ x 6 ⅞ in. (21 x 17.5 cm)
Gift of Ramesh and Urmil Kapoor; P.1999.3.3

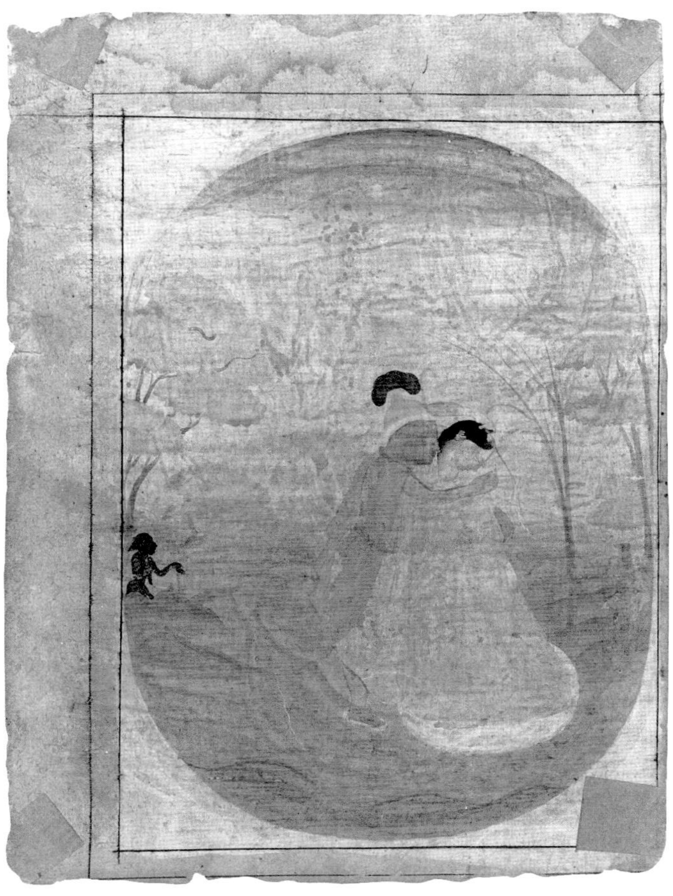

The identity of the Sikh ruler in this portrait remains uncertain. There is some facial resemblance with a representation from around 1840 of Raja Ranbir Singh (r. 1857–85) of Jammu (Brown 1999, pl. 16). The portrait in question is framed with a similar floral border. The strong nose and large eyes as well as the turban and attire all have the same sumptuousness. The ends of the moustache, here, however, curl upward; in the other, they rise vertically on the cheek. Riding a handsome chestnut steed, the prince is accompanied by three companions, one of whom holds the parasol over his head. While the rider and the lancer in the foreground are seen in profile, the other two turn their heads toward the viewer, uncommon for such representations but seen in a formal portrait of 1845–46 by Hasan-al-Zin, now in the British Library (Singh 1991, p. 54, cat. 6).

On the reverse is an unfinished sketch of Krishna and Radha embracing in a forest. They are watched by a small black ogress on the left edge of the oval frame. A more finished picture with the same subject and composition, but with reversed images, is in the Lahore Museum and has been attributed to a Kangra workshop of around 1825 (Aijazuddin 1977, pl. 72, fig. 37). This incomplete sketch must also be from the same workshop, and the sheet was likely used around 1850 to paint the equestrian portrait.

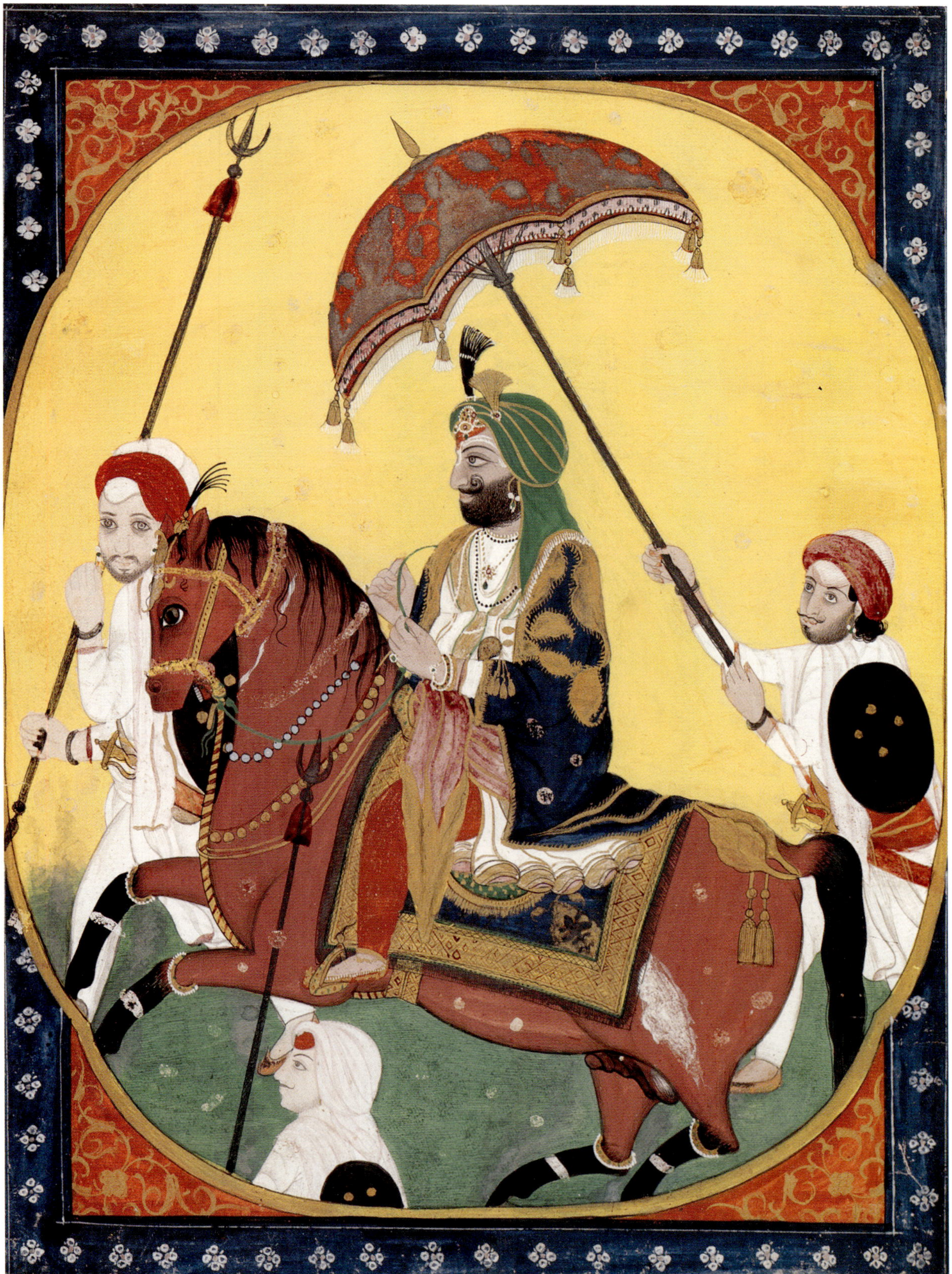

Spiritual Pursuits

74 Prithvisimha at Worship

Rajasthan, Bikaner, c. 1700
Opaque watercolor on paper
Sheet: 11 7/8 x 9 1/4 in. (30.2 x 23.5 cm)
Image: 10 x 7 3/8 in. (25.4 x 18.7 cm)
Promised gift of Ramesh and Urmil Kapoor

The Sanskrit verse above the picture is translated by Gautama Vajracharya as follows (personal communication, 2003): "Born as a son of Ruchi and Akuti, he performed many fire sacrifices in accordance with Vedic rituals. His name is Yajna, an incarnation of Vishnu, who is worshiped by the gods, sages and people as an embodiment of the Vedas. May he all the time protect Prithvisimha who performs the fire sacrifice." The same verse is annotated in Hindi in a longer passage on the back of the painting (see Appendix).

The characters mentioned in the verse, whose origin is unknown, are found in the puranic literature, all except for Prithvisimha. Akuti is a daughter of Svavayambhuva Manu, one of the fourteen mythological progenitors of mankind in Indian cosmology. She married Ruchi, a son of Brahma and one of the Prajapatis, or lords of creatures. Their son was Yajna, or sacrifice, an incarnation of Vishnu. However, Prithvisimha, who is seen here performing a sacrifice on the terrace outside a temple, remains unidentified. He could be a mythical figure or a mortal prince.

The painting is executed clearly, in a markedly different style from the kinds of pictures generally attributed to Bikaner early in the century. The pictorial touches evident in the handling of the internal space and the more realistic narrative strategies are derived ultimately from the Mughal tradition, which was introduced at the court, probably by Mughal-trained artists, during the reign of Karan Singh (1631–84). It was likely painted after the Karan Singh period. Lacking the finesse and rich coloring of that period, it is closer to Bikaner paintings of the end of the seventeenth century. The drawing is looser, the colors less intense and the ornamental details rendered more freely. For the largest group of published late-seventeenth-century Bikaner paintings, see Goswamy and Bhatia 1999, nos. 113–25.

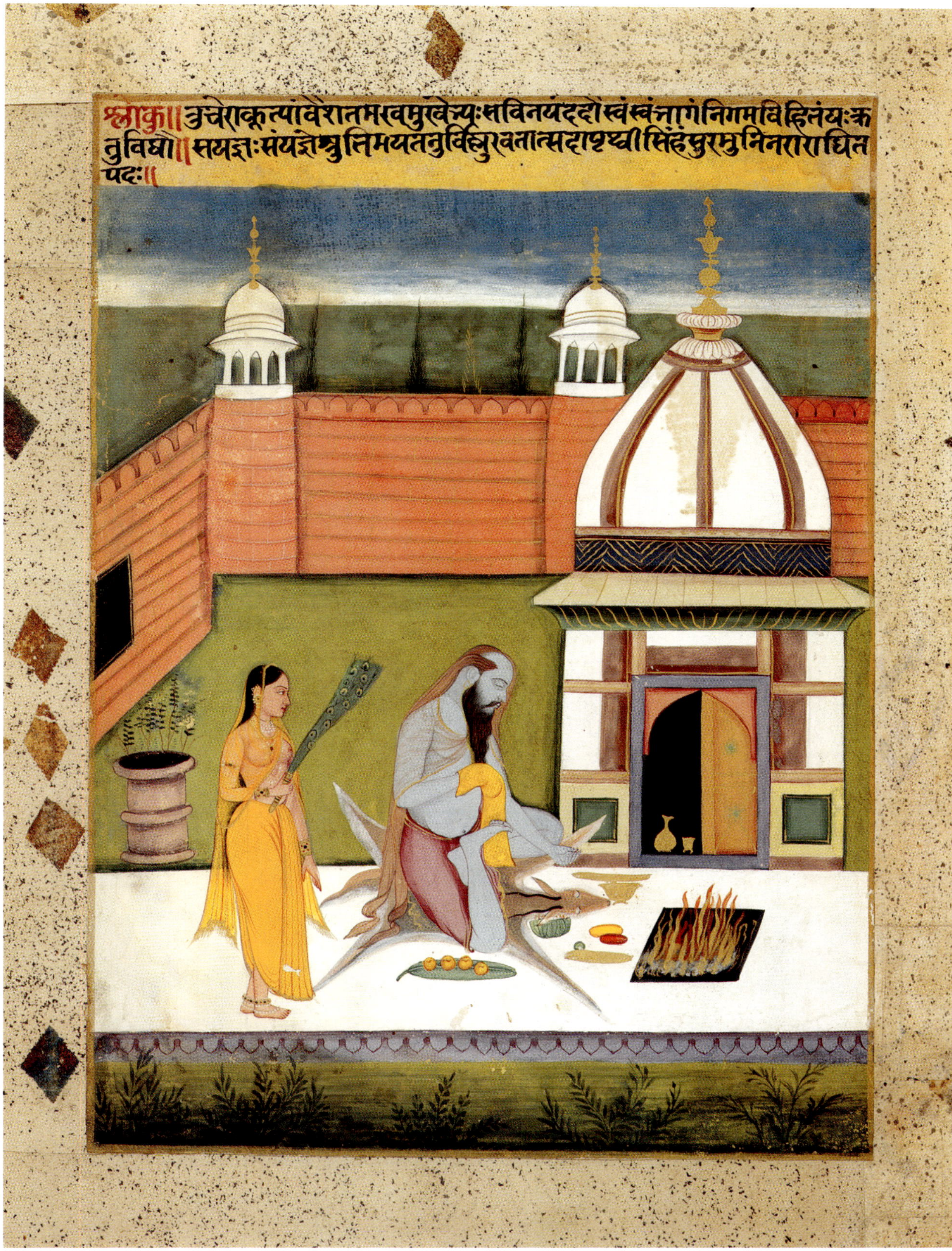

75 Maharana Sangram Singh Worshiping Krishna

Rajasthan, Mewar, c. 1725
Opaque watercolor on paper
Sheet: 22 ¾ x 17 ⅞ in. (57.8 x 45.4 cm)
Image: 21 ¼ x 16 in. (54 x 40.6 cm)
Lent by Ramesh and Urmil Kapoor

Sangram Singh II ruled the state of Mewar from its capital Udaipur from 1710 until 1734. He was a keen patron of painting and was particularly interested in having his durbars and entertainment recorded in meticulous detail (see Topsfield 2002, pp. 141–77 for an assessment of the paintings of his reign). Although the tradition of pictorial narrative of courtly events began in the reign of his father, Amar Singh II (r. c. 1670–1710), Sangram Singh brought to it a grandiosity and festive quality that remained a distinctive feature of Udaipur painting, unmatched for its opulence elsewhere.

The scene here takes place in the palace courtyard. Following the ancient Indian tradition of continuous narration, the ruler is shown thrice: in the rear center, worshiping an image of Krishna along with the priest in a temporary shrine; dancing with a group of courtiers on the left; and then pouring yellow liquid from a pot over other attendants. The women stand on either side as spectators, enjoying the *tamasha*, as such frolicking is called in India. The scene is likely an unusual rendering of the spring festival known as Holi, when colors, both in their solid and liquid forms, are poured over one another. The unusual color is the red *gulal* powder, which is usually the most striking feature of such Udaipur or Rajasthani pictures of the subject. Here, however, the unknown court artist has captured a more private ceremony that is both somber and celebratory, albeit with restraint.

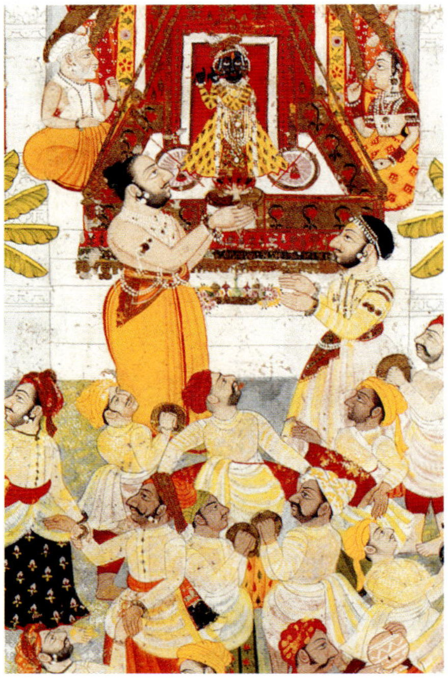

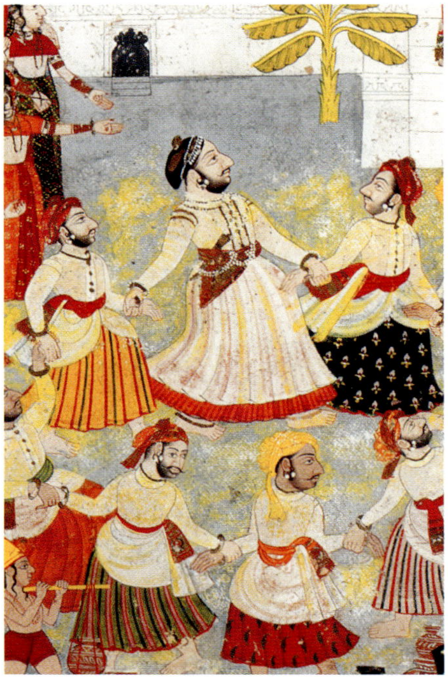

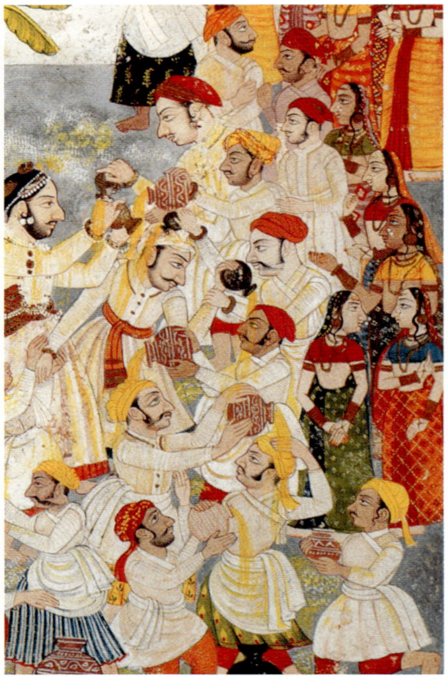

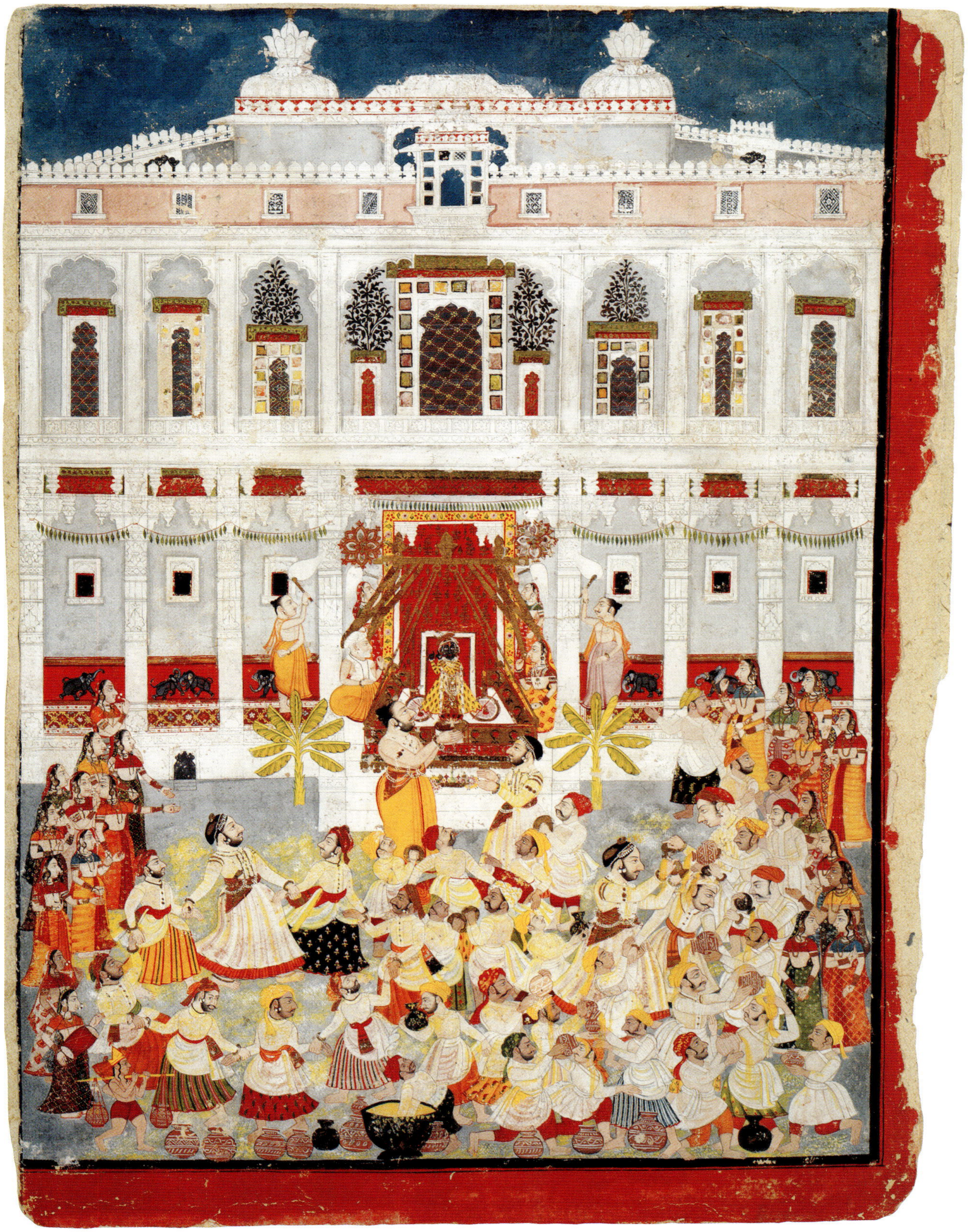

76 Woman Worshiping at a Shiva Shrine

Rajasthan, Devgarh, c. 1775
Opaque watercolor on paper
Sheet: 11 ½ x 9 ½ in. (29.2 x 24.1 cm)
Image: 6 ½ x 4 ⅜ in. (16.5 x 11.1 cm)
Promised gift of Ramesh and Urmil Kapoor

While the same theme is employed to represent the Ragini Bhairavi [57], here it probably depicts a genre that was popular with Rajput artists. It may have been rendered as a gift for a patron on a special occasion, as is the case with another picture in the collection [49]. Beside a lotus pond fed by water that streams out of the support of the image of Shiva, a beautiful young lady is seated with a lotus bud in her hand. While the torso of the deity faces the viewer, his four heads are turned sideways as if to look at the devotee and the bull, who also sits on the white platform placed below a banyan tree. On Shiva's head is a coiled serpent, and one wonders if the streaming water represents the descending river Ganga.

The woman's form and features as well as her transparent garments are delineated with great delicacy and with voyeuristic intent. Her large pneumatic breasts, the faces of Shiva, the impressionistic tree and the use of subtle shades of blue and green in the rolling hills are all characteristic of Devgarh pictures, especially those by the well-known artist Chokha, who worked for both the Udaipur and Devgarh courts. Devgarh was a *thikana*, or fiefdom, of the state of Mewar.

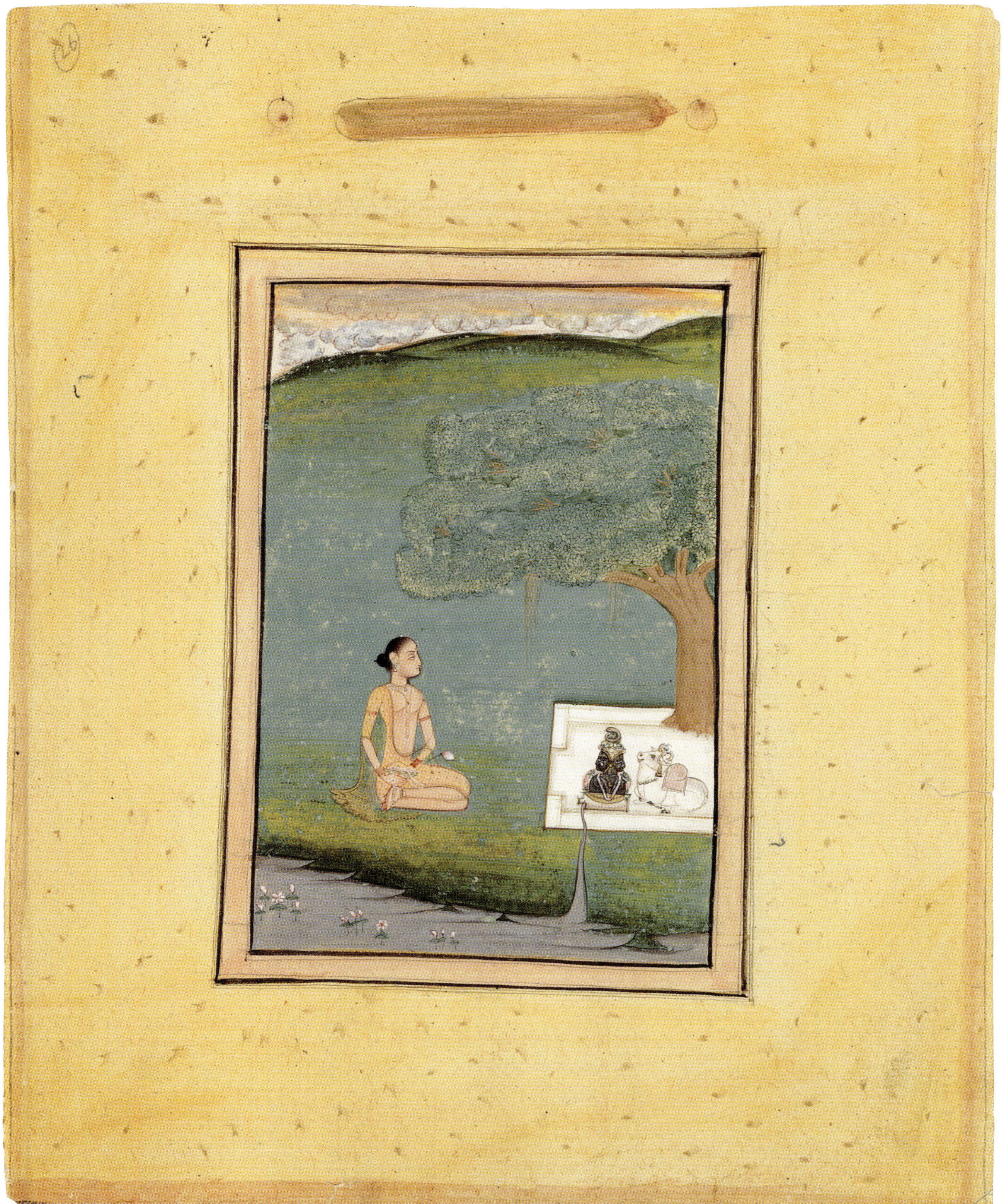

77 Vaishnava Teachers in Front of a Temple

Painted by Vichitra
Rajasthan, Kishangarh, c. 1800
Opaque watercolor and gold on paper
Sheet: 16 ¼ x 12 ⅞ in. (41.3 x 32.7 cm)
Image: 14 ¾ x 11 ⅝ in. (37.5 x 29.5 cm)
Lent by Ramesh and Urmil Kapoor

Not only is this one of the finest pictures from Kishangarh, but it is also important for its profusion of inscriptions (see Appendix). The inscription above the footprints constituting the icons of the shrine identify them as belonging to Radha (red) and Krishna (blue). The haloed principal figure is identified as Gosain or Goswami (a honorific title of a teacher-cum-mentor among Vaishnavas) Hitaruplal. Close to him but clearly of lesser importance is another Goswami whose name is Kisorilal. Lower still is Vrindavandas. Opposite beginning at the top are Gopaldas, Krishnadas, Premdas and Kasiram. Of the two unidentified devotees, one is stretched out on the floor doing an obeisance with all his limbs (*sashtanga pranama*) and the other plays the drum. In the last inscription at the bottom, the artist is named as the devotee (*sevaja* or *sevaka*) Vichitra. Thus the picture adds a new name, rather an unusual one, to the roster of Kishangarh artists.

The temple is very likely the shrine of the minor Vaishnava sect known as Radhavallabhis (beloved of Radha). The expression is also used in the inscription above the feet. In publishing a drawing of another Goswami of this sect, Chandlal, Goswamy and Bhatia comment that little is known of their religious beliefs, but that they are probably based in Mathura (1999, no. 139). They also point out that the Kishangarh ruler Sawant Singh (r. 1748–57) retired to Brindavan, where he died in 1764. A devout Vaishnava, he may well have been associated with the Radhavallabhis.

Though not as deep as the vista with lake and palace in another Kishangarh painting in the collection [52], the background shows a river, perhaps the Yamuna, followed by a distant view of rolling hills with trees and a gorgeous sunset sky of red and gold, glimpsed through the realistically rendered trees flanking the shrine. Typical of Kishangarh pictures, fact and fancy are mingled lyrically to create a tranquil and elegant composition. The rendering of the portraits is scrupulous and reflects not only the artist's familiarity with the subjects but also his meticulous skill in their characterizations. Even as he limned the figures with visual acuity and perceptiveness, he has added a touch of fantasy in placing them in a large, white, moon-like orb trimmed in gold.

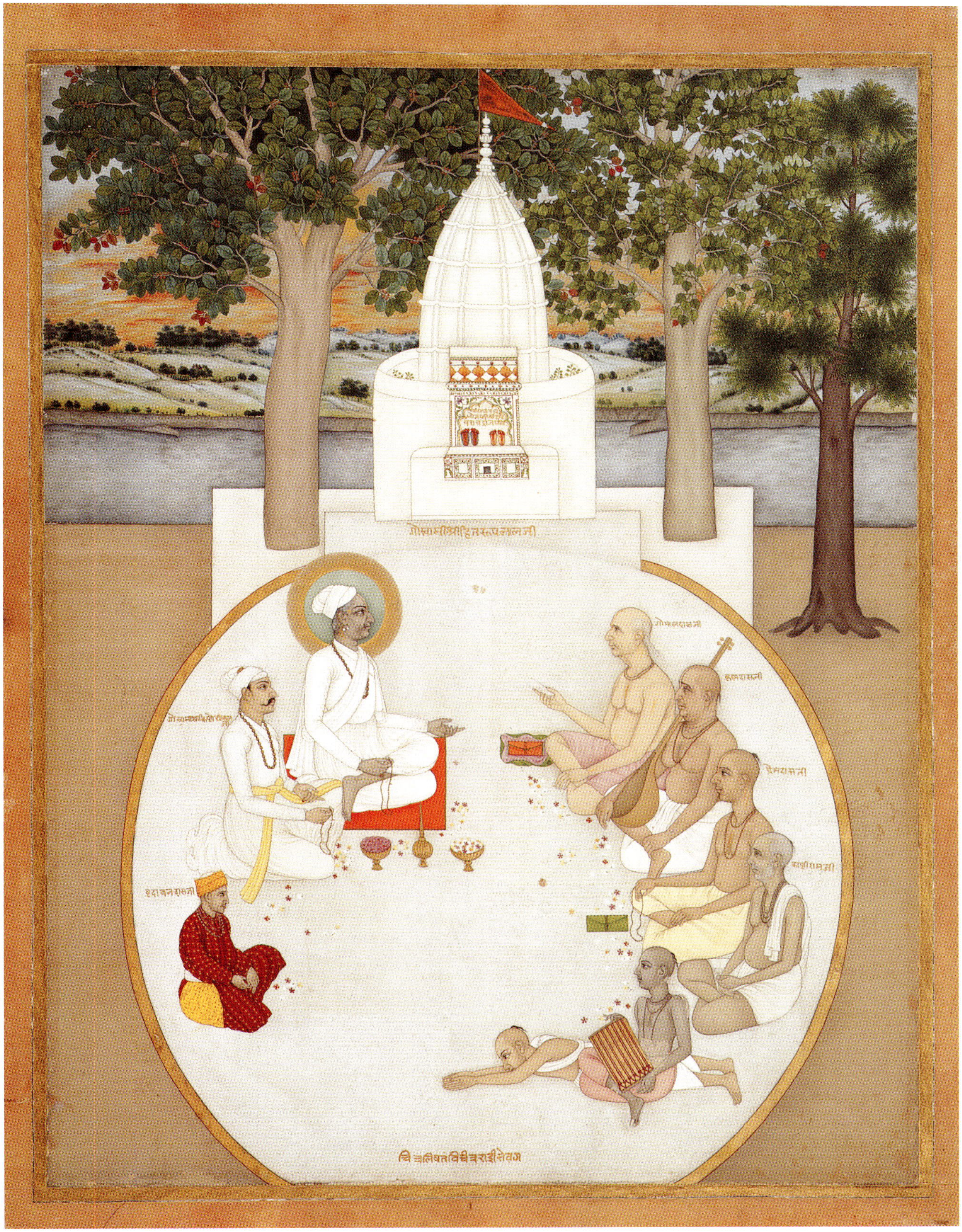
गोस्वामीश्रीहितरूपलालजी
चित्रलिषतं विचीत्रराई सेवग

78 Group of Inebriated Ascetics

Rajasthan, Kishangarh workshop, c. 1800
Opaque watercolor and gold on paper
Sheet: 8 ¾ x 7 ⅝ in. (22.2 x 19.4 cm)
Image: 7 ⅝ x 6 ⅝ in. (19.4 x 16.8 cm)
Gift of Suneet and Alka Kapoor; P.2002.4

With stark realism, an unknown artist of a Kishangarh workshop has recorded an unusual occasion. Several slim, gaunt men—each with an ascetic hairdo and wearing a dhoti with gold borders—seem to be in an inebriated and drugged state. Some appear to be more intoxicated than others. Their hookahs, however, are of the conventional form used for smoking tobacco rather than opium or hemp (*ganja*). Except for one in the lower right, all the hookahs are of the handheld variety still used on the subcontinent by the less affluent. One ascetic is in a bent upright position as he draws on the pipe, but the others are seated in a variety of postures. A couple of men are engaged in smashing something that may be bhang or opium. Small cups and pots are strewn all over the terrace. A few are unable to smoke on their own and are being helped by others who appear to be only marginally more sober. With one exception, all have long, rope-like braided hair, densely coiled on the head with some strands trailing on the ground. Interestingly, each is given differently colored hair, which probably reflects the artist's idiosyncrasy rather than reality.

Such subjects are rarely portrayed in art, which makes this an unusual and rare social document. Imbibing or smoking such narcotic products is common among the wandering holy men (*sadhu* or *sannyasi*) on the subcontinent. Its thematic interest aside, the painting is aesthetically appealing, both for its lively rhythmic composition and its appropriate mood.

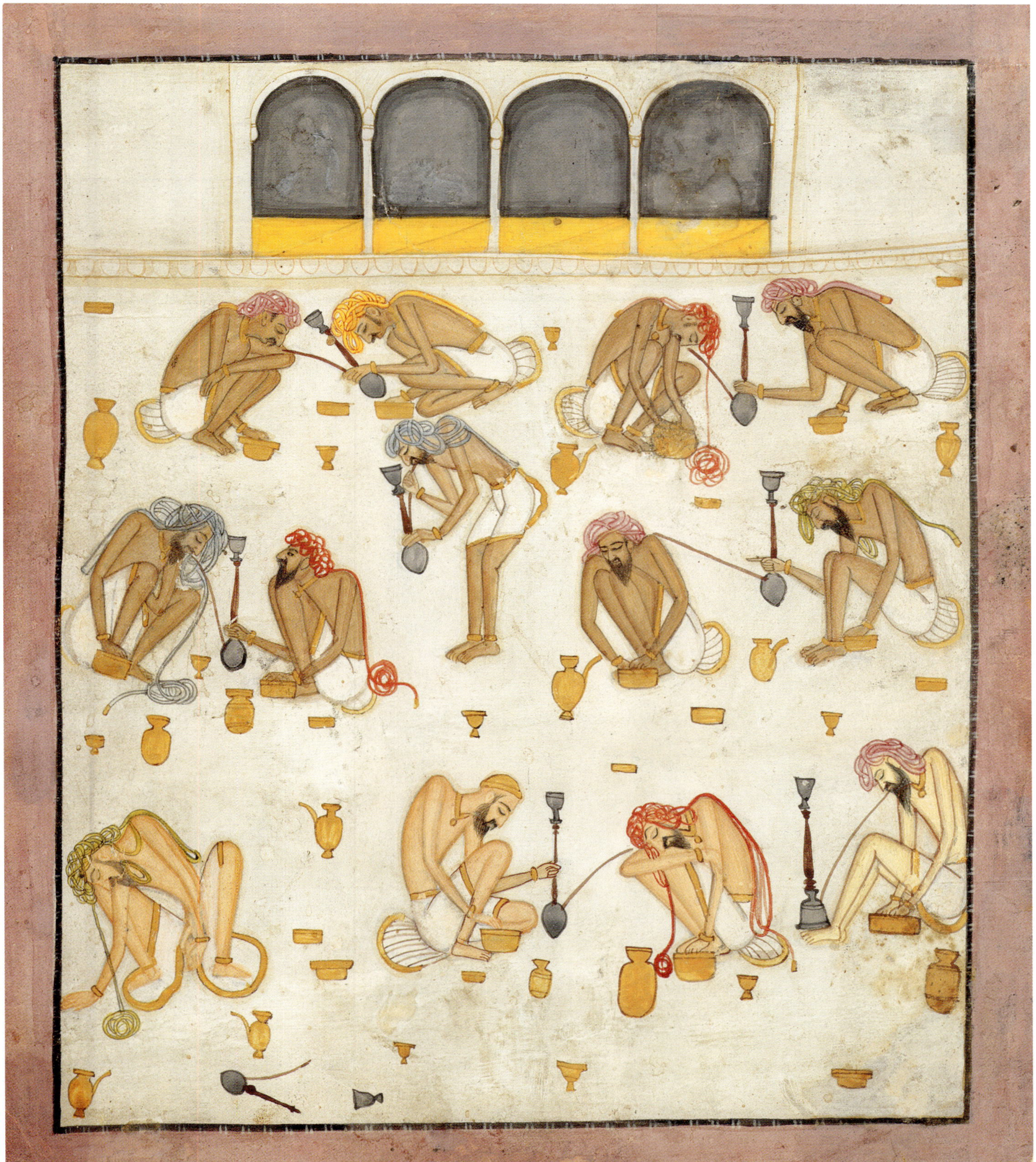

79 A Sikh Guru and a Prince in Conversation

Himachal Pradesh, Guler workshop, 1800–1825
Opaque watercolor on paper
Sheet: 11 ½ x 9 in. (29.2 x 22.9 cm)
Image: 8 ⅝ x 6 ⅜ in. (21.9 x 16.2 cm)
Gift of Ramesh and Urmil Kapoor; P.2001.13.1

Admired for their courage and physical prowess, the Sikhs form a distinct community in India. Concentrated mostly in the Indian state of Punjab, they are now encountered the world over and are easily distinguished from other Indians by their beards and the distinctive turbans covering their long hair. The word "sikh" is a colloquialism of the Sanskrit word *sishya*, meaning "disciple." Sikhs recognize ten gurus beginning with Nanak (1469–1539) and ending with Guru Gobind Singh, who died in 1708. Other than Nanak [80], all the Sikh gurus were both religious and martial leaders. They are portrayed as princely soldiers as opposed to the more ascetic Hindu gurus. Ironically, it was a Hindu holy man who converted to Sikhism and laid the foundation of Sikh political power. His name was Banda (1670–1716), and he valiantly fought the Mughals to establish a Sikh homeland.

This portrait shows a Sikh guru with a bow and arrow, as well as a sword, seated on a carpet below a baldachin, conversing with a young prince, perhaps a Mughal. Behind the guru stands an attendant holding a peacock-feather fan, or *morchal*, usually a regal emblem. Between the two hangs a shield, which is almost like a halo for the guru. Without an inscription, an exact identification is difficult, but a strong possibility exists that the figure represents the sixth guru Hargobind Singh (1595–1645). The face is similar to that seen in a portrait of the guru from around 1750 (Brown 1999, fig. 3). The young prince may well be Dara Shikoh, the eldest son of Emperor Shah Jahan, noted for his keen interest in non-Islamic religions. For this, he was unpopular among the orthodox Muslims of the Mughal court. Stylistically, the painting belongs to the same artistic milieu as a number of portraits of Sikh gurus now in the Lahore Museum that are considered to have been painted between 1815 and 1820 in Guler workshops (Aijazuddin 1977, pl. 57–58).

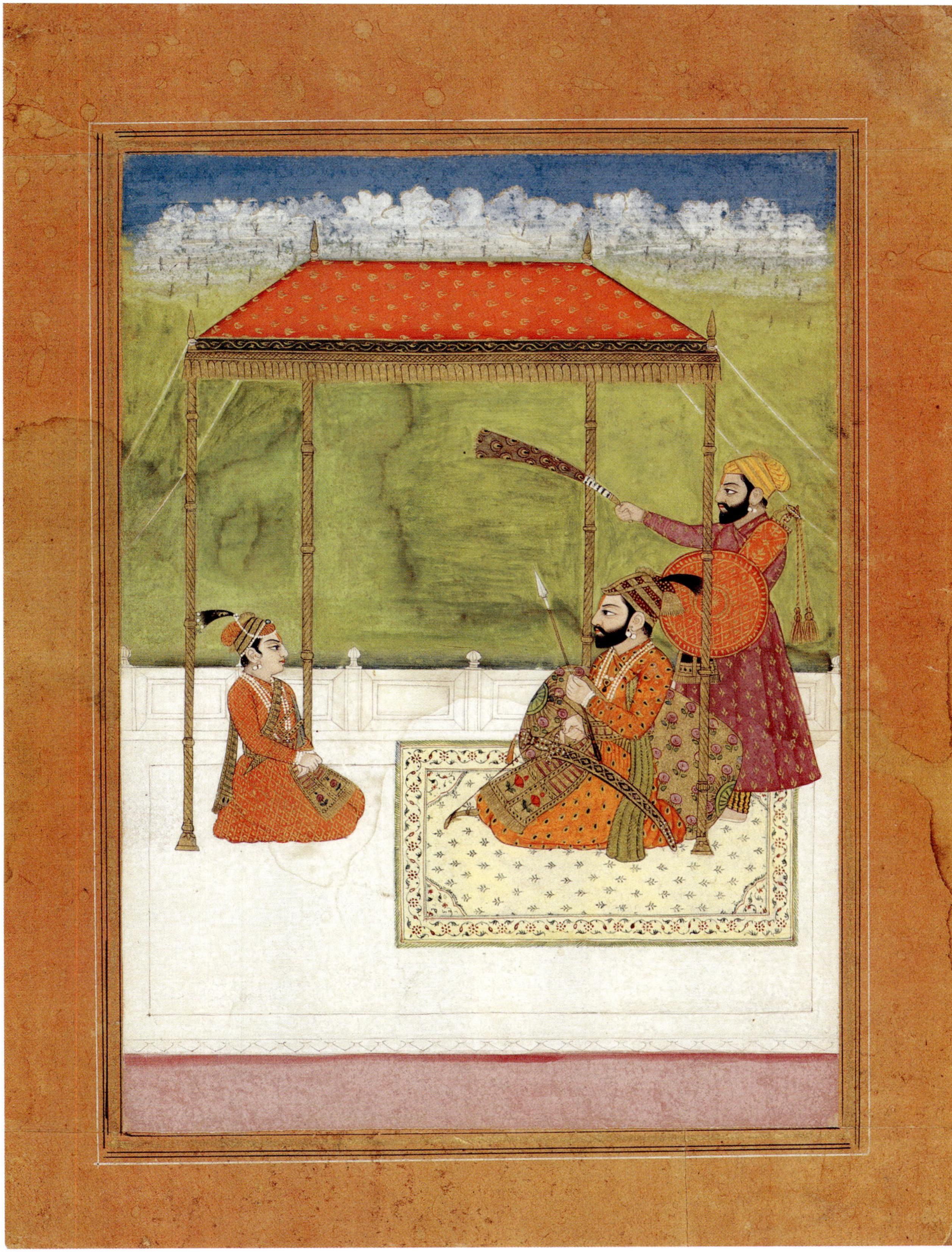

80 A Visitation to a Guru

Himachal Pradesh or Punjab, c. 1850
Opaque watercolor on paper
Sheet: 10 ¾ x 8 ½ in. (27.3 x 21.6 cm)
Image: 8 ¾ x 6 in. (22.2 x 15.2 cm)
Gift of Ramesh and Urmil Kapoor; P.2003.2.1

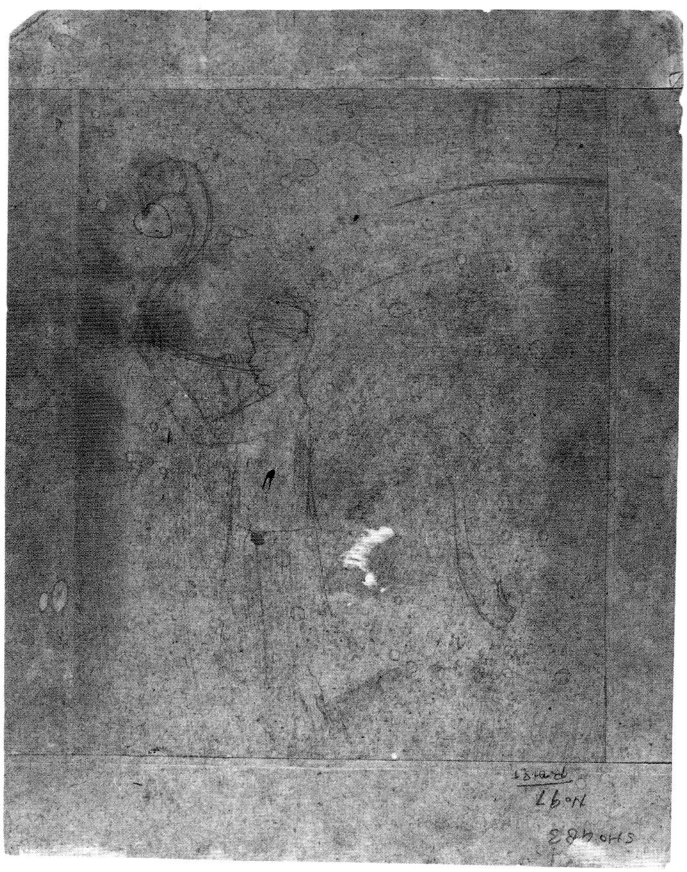

The scene takes place in the ashram of a guru, with two groups of people in two panels. In the foreground, a man with an armrest and his head turned to the left sits with his back to the viewer, separating the two pairs of men who face one another. The larger bearded figures are clearly the more important persons; the other pair are musicians, one playing a *sarangi* and the other a drum. While the frontal group sits directly on the grass, those above are seated on what is probably the paved section of a courtyard closer to the reed hut and the surrounding wall. A young man with a black beard like the ones of the two gentlemen directly below him sits under a caged parrot, while conversing with an older man with a flowing white beard and a rosary. An attendant stands behind him with a *morchal* fan, while four sit behind holding a plate of fruit as an offering. Three apples separate the two conversing figures.

Clearly the younger man, perhaps a companion of the two below, has come to visit the older man, who is most likely the first Sikh guru, Nanak (1469–1539). Not only is he usually accompanied by a *morchal*-bearer, but also by musicians (see Aijazuddin 1977, pl. 56 and Archer 1966, fig. 1). The identification is further confirmed by the presence of the patchwork shawl behind him, which is a distinctive attribute of Guru Nanak (see Boner et al 1994, no. 560). The visitor here is similar to the second figure in the two pictures published by Archer and Aijazuddin and has been identified by the former as Guru Gobind Singh, the tenth Sikh guru (1666–1708). If so, this would obviously be an imaginary meeting. It would be more likely for the figure to be identified with the second Sikh guru, Angad (1504–1552). In any event, this picture has more figures than the earlier versions of the meeting but lacks their acuity and technical finesse. While generally rendered in the Pahari style, the planes are flat and the colors somewhat lightly applied. It may have been rendered somewhere in the Punjab. On the back is a faint sketch of a trumpeter.

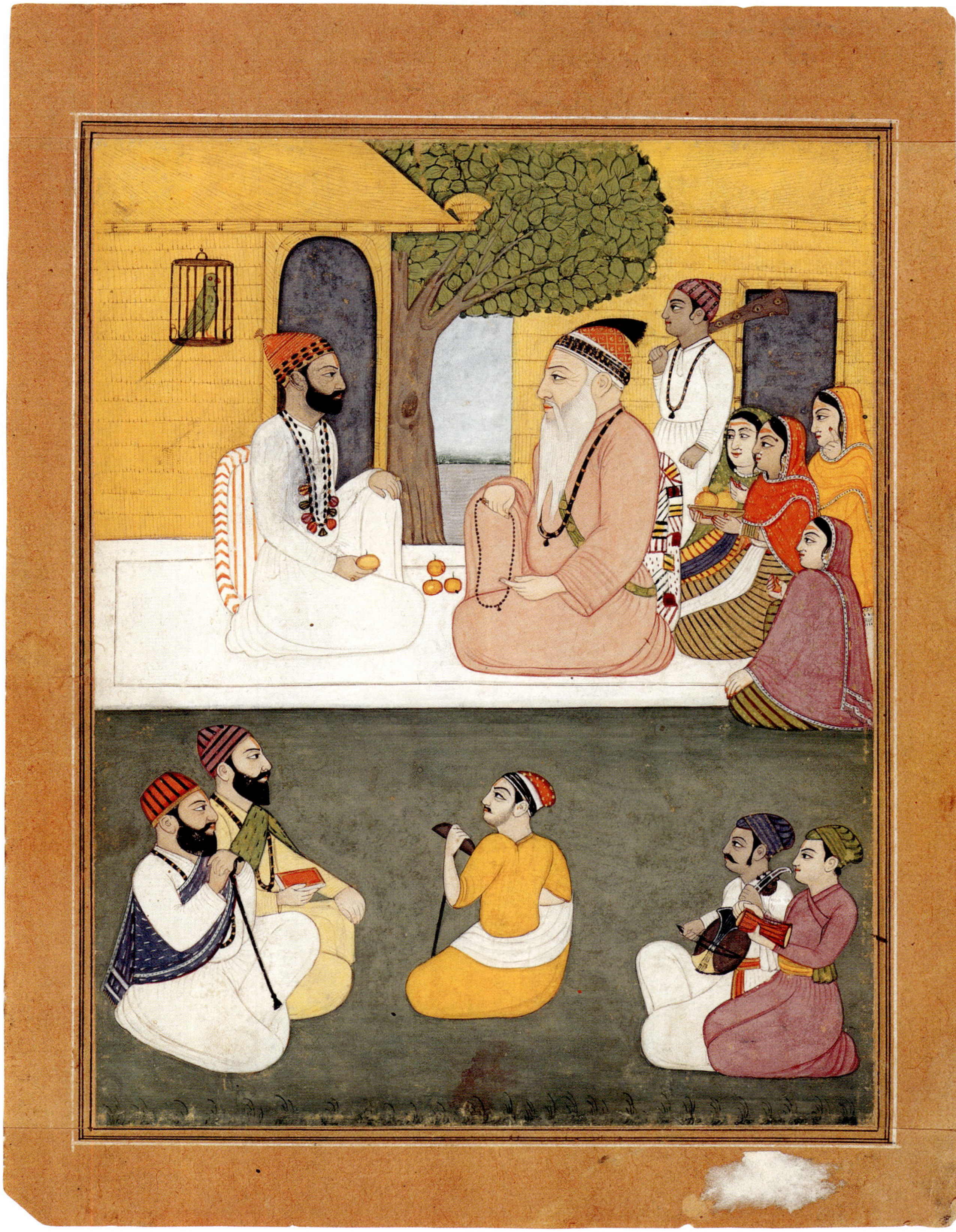

Appendix

G.B.	Gouriswar Bhattacharya
N.H.	Navina Haidar
N.K.	Naval Krishna
V.C.O.	V. C. Ohri
P.P.	Pratapaditya Pal
R.P.C.	Richa Pauranik-Clements
B.R.	Biswajeet Rath
G.V.	Gautama V. Vajracharya
A.N.W.	A. N. Walia

2 Folio from a *Samgrahanisutra* Manuscript: The Court of Indra

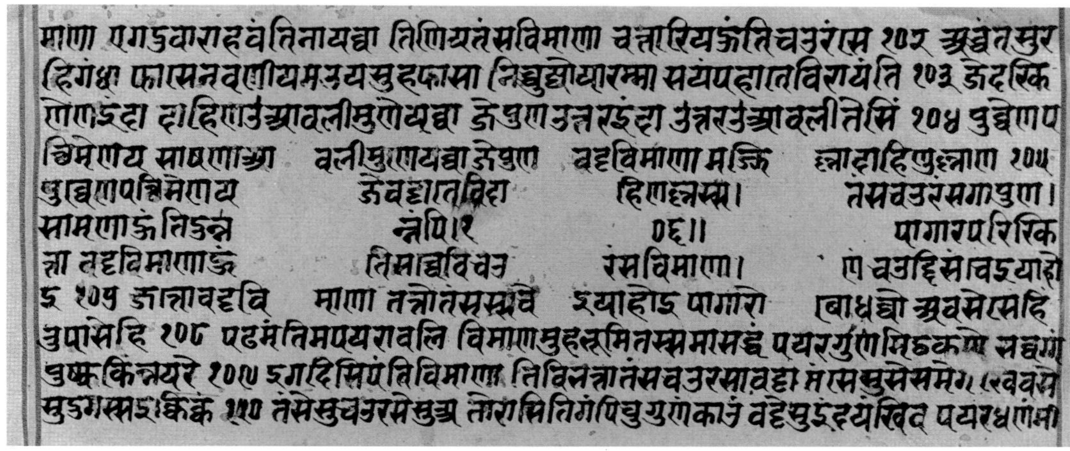

5 Shiva and Parvati with Companions

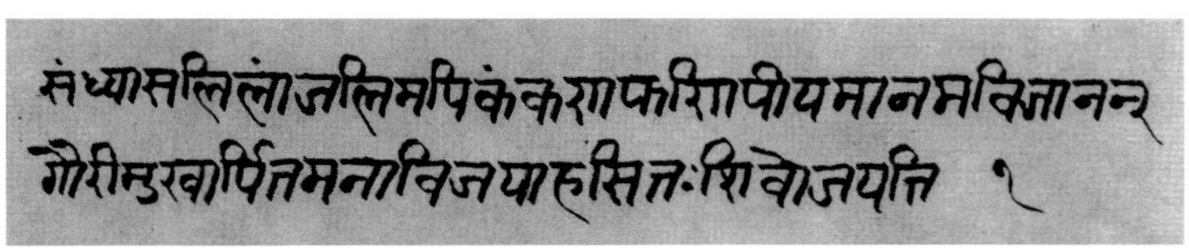
संध्यासलिलांजलिमपिकंकणफणिपीयमानमविज्ञानन्
गौरीमुखार्पितमनाविजयाहसितः शिवोजयति १

Let Shiva be victorious, who is so absorbed with the face of Gauri (his young bride) that he is unaware [of the fact] that the snake forming his bracelet has drunk all the water that she pours into his hands during the performance of the evening's ritual, seeing which [the maid] Vijaya laughs.—G.B.

12 Adoration of Ganesh

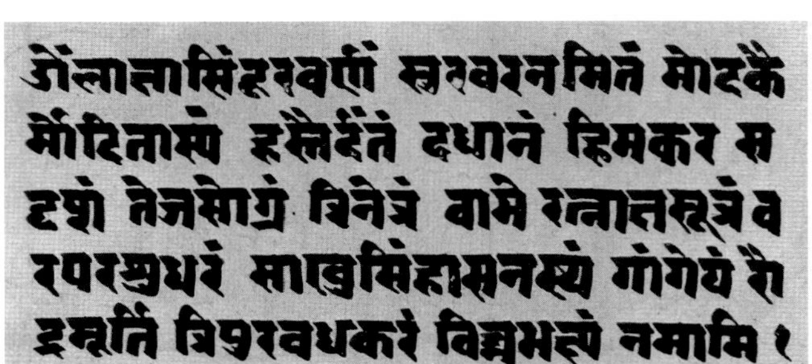
ॐलाक्षासिंदूरवर्णं सुरवरनमितं मोदकै
मोदितास्यं हस्तैर्दंतं दधानं हिमकर स
दृशं तेजसोग्रं त्रिनेत्रं वामे रत्नाक्षसूत्रं व
रपरशुधरं साखुसिंहासनस्थं गांगेयं रौ
द्रमूर्तिं त्रिपुरवधकरं विघ्नभर्त्रे नमामि १

Verse one: *I salute the destroyer of obstacles who has a red complexion like lac, who is saluted by the best of gods, who has a face delighted with sweets, who holds with hands his [own broken] tooth which is white like the moon, he has the third eye violent with glare, [he holds] in the left [hands] a jewel and a rosary, [and in the right hands] the gesture of boon and the battleaxe, [he is] seated on the throne with a rat; [he is] the son of Ganga [and he has] a frightful appearance destroying [the demon] Tripura.*

Comments: In the painting the deity is two-armed, but in the verse he is described as having four arms.—G.B.

13 Ganesh Enthroned

A leaf depicting Lord Ganesh, presented to the Maharaja on his birthday by the guild of Usta on the bright fortnight of July–August, Vikram Samvat 1911 [1854].

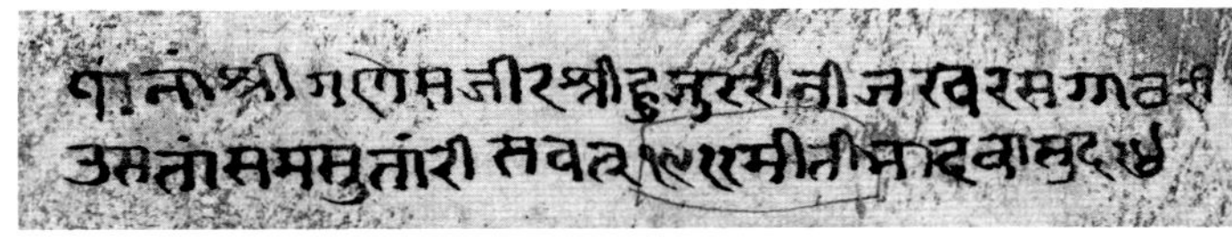

Comments: This painting was created by an Usta artist with Jaipur school influences. The Ustas were the established painters of the Bikaner court. In the mid–eighteenth century, a new group of painters called "Jaipura," artists from Jaipur, migrated to Bikaner and virtually overtook the Ustas.

The calligraphy does not match with that used in the contemporary account diaries as found in most of the Bikaner paintings. In contrast, it seems that it was written by one of the literate painters or a person of the guild with his painting brush.

A later inventory number (3442) is written in a circle and repeated in the rubber stamp area, which is a striking feature of the paintings that emerged from the collection of the Maharaja of Bikaner. This inventory was undertaken in 1963 by Mr. Khet Singh and completed in 1964, as the date of 15-6-1964 appears in the rubber stamp. —N.K.

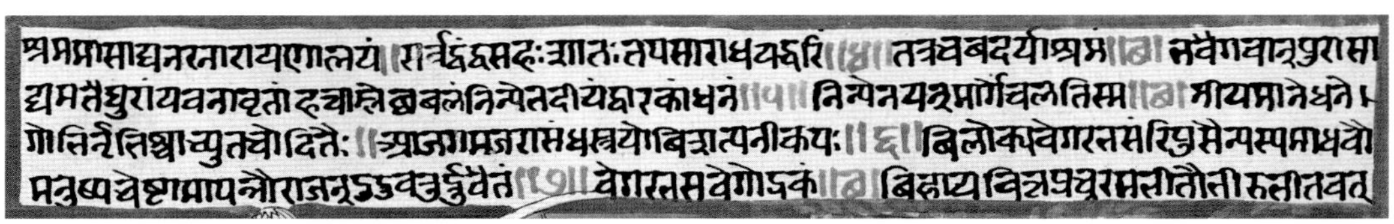

A

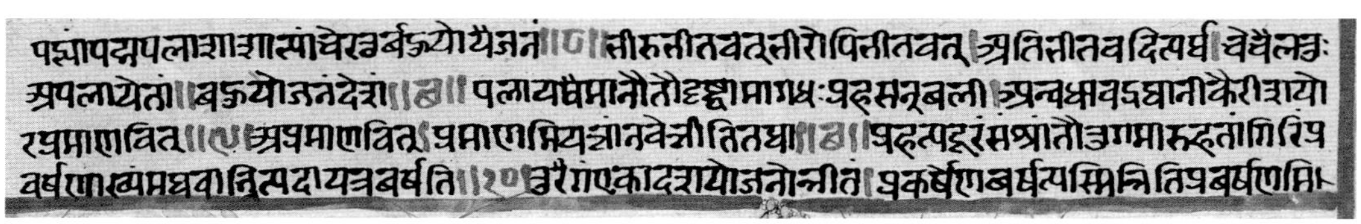

B

23 Folio Illustrating Episodes from the Jarasandha Story

[A] *Krishna reached Badaryasrama [Badarikasrama] where he practiced austerity. Then he invaded Mathura which was full of* yavana *[foreigners] and took the wealth of the city to Dvaraka. When Krishna was heading toward Dvaraka Jarasandha attacked him. The two Madhavas [Krishna and Balarama], seeing the army of the enemy chasing them, ran away just like ordinary mortals. Pretending to be extremely frightened, they left behind all their wealth.*

[B] *Jarasandha became very happy to see them fleeing because he was not familiar with the strength of these two brothers. He continued to chase them. Eventually they climbed a mountain called Pravarsana, which was eleven* yojana *[a unit of measurement of about two miles] tall.*

Comments: Although the story of Jarasandha appears in the *Mahabharata*, this seems to be a different version. The style of Sanskrit verses is close to that of later puranic literature.—G.V.

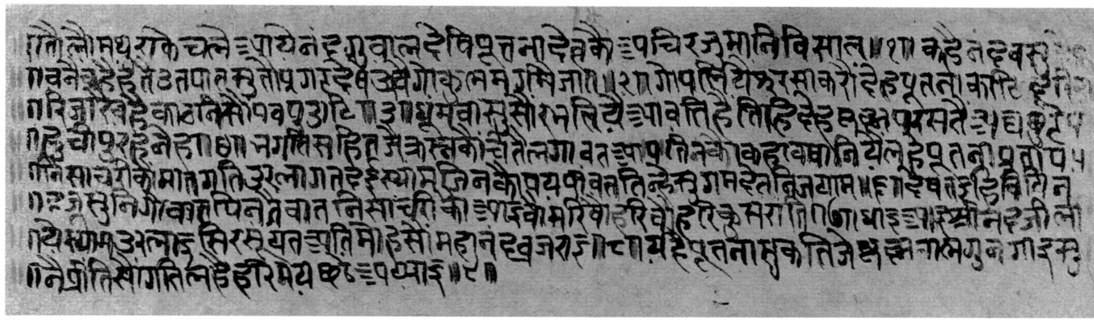

26 Emancipation of the Ogress Putana

Whoever would chant the story of Putana would receive salvation through God. During the middle of the night, Nanda and the milkmen returned home [they were away from Mathura when this incident occurred] and saw the gigantic body of Putana, the ogress, and were surprised.

Nanda tells Vasudeva that lots of nuisances and riots are occurring in Gokul. In order to burn the Putana's dead body, the milkmen begin to cut the body in pieces with axes. In bhakti, *[all are] embracing Krishna, O! Putana's killer! Unending miseries are hovering, how much we would complain! Krishna has bestowed the divine abode, as a mother feeds milk to her child. All the villagers chant or tell stories of various episodes connected to the arrival of Putana and her death.*

Comments: The inscription is in Soratha and Doha rhymes and is full of errors and illegible words and was written by a weak Brajbhasha poet. The inscription is from a Malwa *Ramayana* of 1688–90. A page of this episode is in Bharat Kala Bhavan, Varanasi, where Putana the ogress is lying at the bottom register and on the top register there are many scenes. —N.K.

33 Illustration from a *Bhagavatapurana* Series: Story of the Syamantaka Gem

At the top of the page is the number 25. Immediately below is the couplet of the twenty-fifth leaf. On the left margin is the number 10 followed by the number 301. Ten refers to the tenth book of the *Bhagavatapurana*. However, the text here is not in Sanskrit but in the Hindi dialect of Vrajabhasha. It narrates in eight verses a portion of the original text but is not a literal translation. The condensed verses are from chapter 56, in which the story of the magical Syamantaka gem is related (see Tagare 1976, pt. iv, pp. 1611–13, vv. 24–38).—N.K. & P.P.

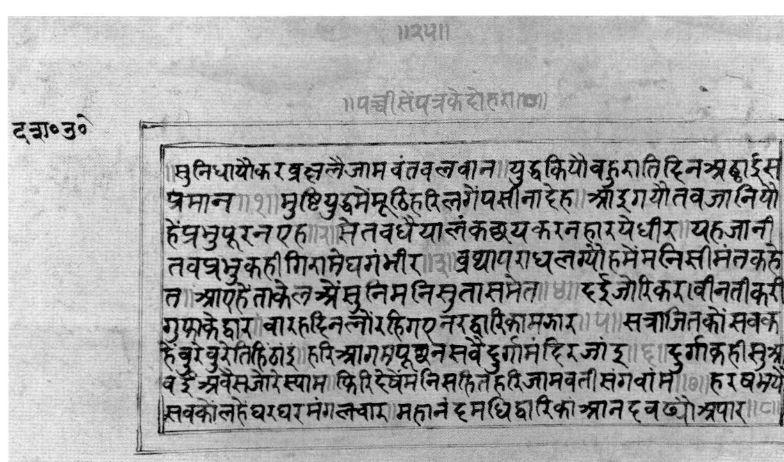

35 Sage Sukdeva and King Parikshit

Small, single-word inscriptions in Devanagari script above the two figures identify them as Sukdeva (on the left) and Parikshit (on the right). These inscriptions in white pigment were recorded by the painter. Several other known examples of Kangra paintings of the early nineteenth century bear inscriptions written with white pigment.

An inscription in Devanagari script taped to the back of the painting is not related to the subject matter of the painting.

Translation: Pictures total folios 113 were obtained through Padha Keshav for seeing on June 7, 1851.

Comments: The note in black ink is by the person who was in charge of the paintings as well as books and valuables. —V.C.O.

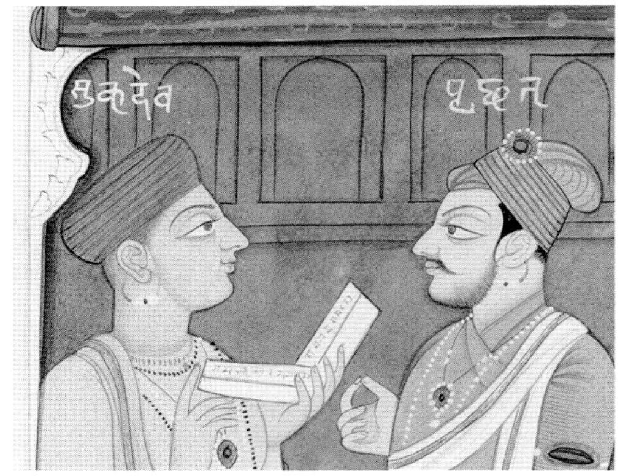

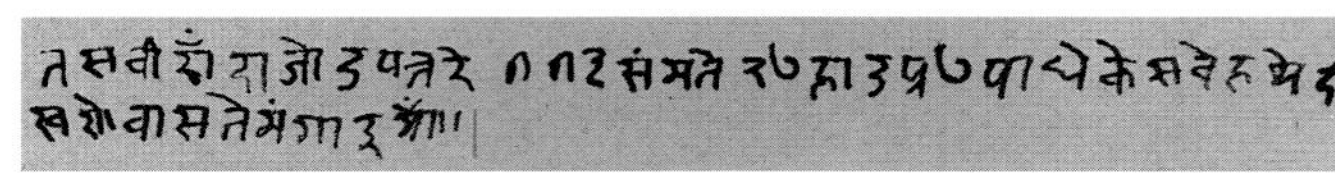

36 Folio from a *Bhagavatapurana* Series: King Yudhisthira Performs the Rajasuya Sacrifice

Inscriptions in Devanagari script are recorded within the painting for identifying the various figures and scenes.

1. *Sukdeva*
2. *Parikshit*
3. *Duryodhana*
4. *Karna*
5. *All the rajas and others are in service [to do the work]*
6. *Sahadeva*
7. *Draupadi*
8. *Sri Krishna*
9. *Bhimasena is the supervisor of the kitchen*
10. *Raja [King Yudhisthira, is bathing]*
11. *Raja [King Yudhisthira] is dressing himself*
12. *[They are] departing*

On the back of the painting is a sixteen-line text in Sanskrit, comprising 29 verses from chapter 75 of the tenth book of the *Bhagavatapurana* describing the performance of the Rajasuya sacrifice by King Yudhisthira (see Tagare 1976, pt. iv, pp. 1723–26 for an English translation).—V.C.O.

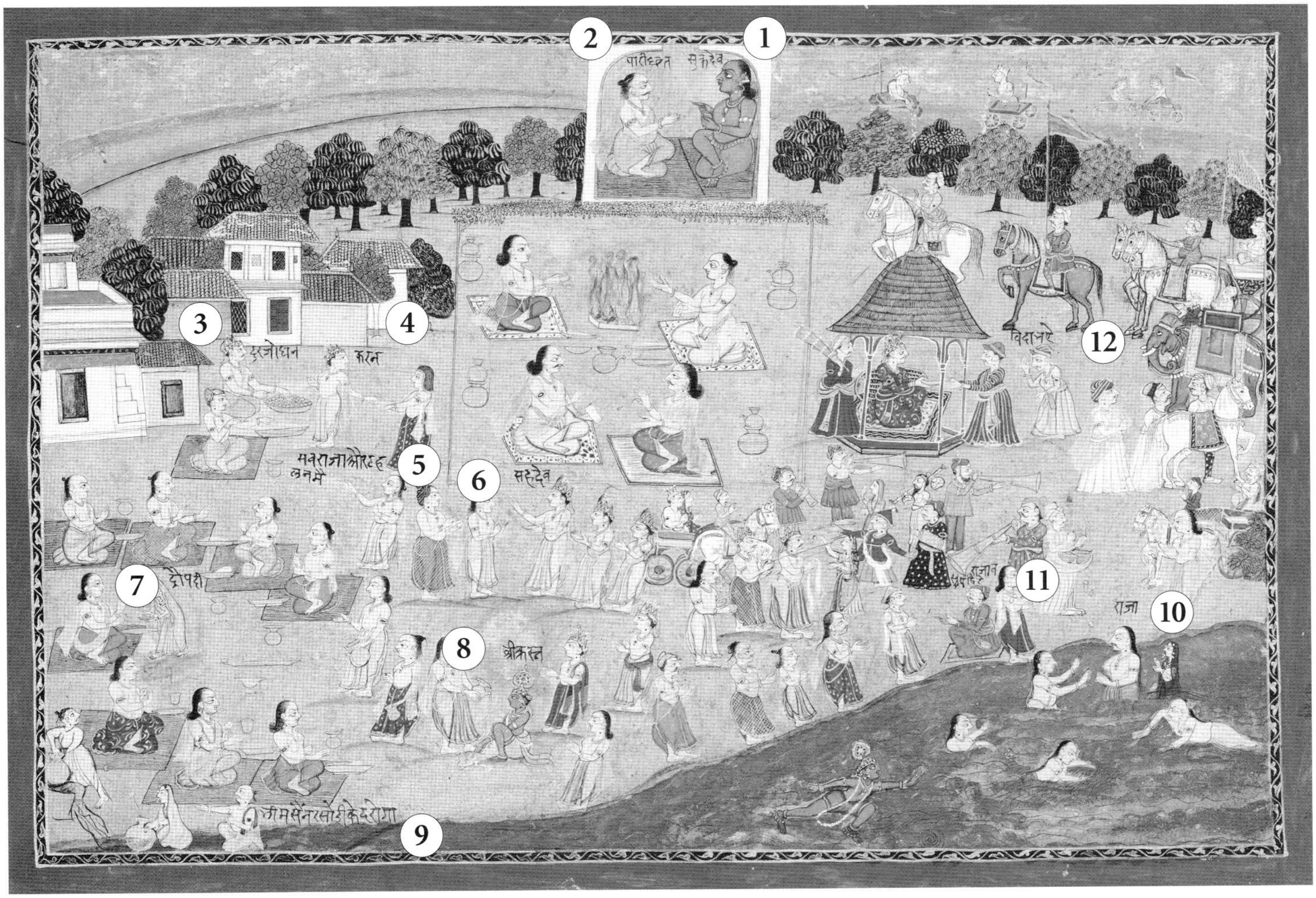

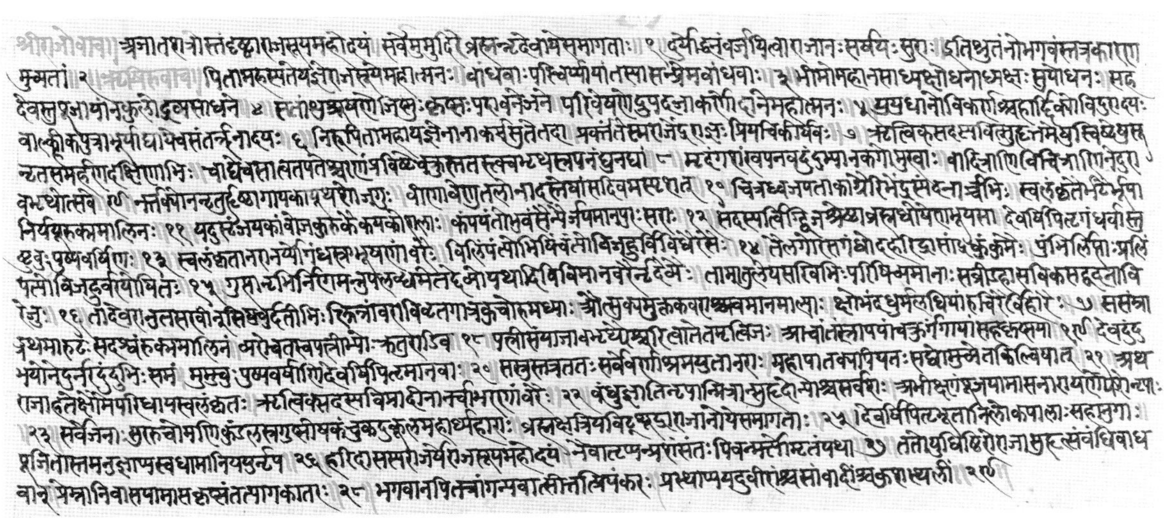
श्रीराजोवाच ॥ अजातशत्रोस्तं दृष्ट्वा राजसूयमहोदयं सर्वे मुमुदिरे ब्रह्मन्नृदेवा ये समागताः ॥ १ ॥ दुर्योधनं वर्जयित्वा राजानः सर्षयः सुराः इति श्रुतं नो भगवंस्तत्र कारण
मुच्यतां ॥ २ ॥ श्रीशुक उवाच ॥ पितामहस्य ते यज्ञे राजसूये महात्मनः बांधवाः परिचर्यायां तस्यासन्प्रेमबंधनाः ॥ ३ ॥ भीमो महानसाध्यक्षो धनाध्यक्षः सुयोधनः सह
देवस्तु पूजायां नकुलो द्रव्यसाधने ॥ ४ ॥ गुरुशुश्रूषणे जिष्णुः कृष्णः पादावनेजने परिवेषणे द्रुपदजा कर्णो दाने महात्मनः ॥ ५ ॥ युयुधानो विकर्णश्च हार्दिक्यो विदुरादयः
बाल्हीकपुत्रा भूर्याद्या ये च संतर्दनादयः ॥ ६ ॥ निरूपिता महायज्ञे नानाकर्मसु ते तदा प्रवर्तंते स्म राजेंद्र राज्ञः प्रियचिकीर्षवः ॥ ७ ॥ ऋत्विक्सदस्यबहुवित्सु सुहृत्तमेषु स्विष्टेषु सू
नृतसमर्हणदक्षिणाभिः चैद्ये च सात्वतपतेश्चरणं प्रविष्टे चक्रुस्ततस्त्ववभृथस्नपनं द्युनद्यां ॥ ८ ॥ मृदंगशंखपणवधुंधुर्यानकगोमुखाः वादित्राणि विचित्राणि नेदुरा
वभृथोत्सवे ॥ ९ ॥ नर्तक्यो ननृतुर्हृष्टा गायका यूथशो जगुः वीणावेणुतलोन्नादस्तेषां स दिवमस्पृशत् ॥ १० ॥ चित्रध्वजपताकाग्रैरिभेंद्रस्यंदनार्वभिः स्वलंकृतैर्भटैर्भूपा
निर्ययू रुक्ममालिनः ॥ ११ ॥ यदुसृंजयकांबोजकुरुकेकयकोशलाः कंपयंतो भुवं सैन्यैर्यजमानपुरःसराः ॥ १२ ॥ सदस्यर्त्विग्द्विजश्रेष्ठा ब्रह्मघोषेण भूयसा देवर्षिपितृगंधर्वास्तु
ष्टुवुः पुष्पवर्षिणः ॥ १३ ॥ स्वलंकृता नरा नार्यो गंधस्रग्भूषणांबरैः विलिंपंत्योऽभिषिंचंत्यो विजह्रुर्विविधै रसैः ॥ १४ ॥ तैलगोरसगंधोदहरिद्रासांद्रकुंकुमैः पुंभिर्लिप्ताः प्रलिं
पंत्यो विजह्रुर्वारयोषितः ॥ १५ ॥ गुप्ता नृभिर्निरगमन्नुपलब्धुमेतद्देव्यो यथा दिवि विमानवरैर्नृदेव्यो ता मातुलेयसखिभिः परिषिच्यमानाः सव्रीडहासविकसद्वदना वि
रेजुः ॥ १६ ॥ ता देवरानुत सखीन्सिषिचुर्दृतीभिः क्लिन्नांबरा विवृतगात्रकुचोरुमध्याः औत्सुक्यमुक्तकवराच्च्यवमानमाल्याः क्षोभं दधुर्मलधियां रुचिरैर्विहारैः ॥ १७ ॥ स सम्रा
ड्रथमारूढः सदश्वं रुक्ममालिनं व्यरोचत स्वपत्नीभिः क्रतुराडिव ॥ १८ ॥ पत्नीसंयाजावभृथ्यैश्चरित्वा ते तमृत्विजः आचांतं स्नापयांचक्रुर्गंगायां सह कृष्णया ॥ १९ ॥ देवदुंदु
भयो नेदुर्नरदुंदुभिभिः समं मुमुचुः पुष्पवर्षाणि देवर्षिपितृमानवाः ॥ २० ॥ सस्नुस्तत्र ततः सर्वे वर्णाश्रमयुता नराः महापातक्यपि यतः सद्यो मुच्येत किल्बिषात् ॥ २१ ॥ अथ
राजाहते क्षौमे परिधाय स्वलंकृतः ऋत्विक्सदस्यविप्रादीनानर्चाभरणांबरैः ॥ २२ ॥ बंधुज्ञातिनृपान्मित्रसुहृदोऽन्यांश्च सर्वशः अभीक्ष्णं पूजयामास नारायणपरो नृपः
॥ २३ ॥ सर्वे जनाः सुररुचो मणिकुंडलस्रगुष्णीषकंचुकदुकूलमहार्घ्यहाराः ब्रह्मक्षत्रियविट्शूद्रा राजानो ये समागताः ॥ २५ ॥ देवर्षिपितृभूतानि लोकपालाः सहानुगाः
पूजितास्तमनुज्ञाप्य स्वधामानि ययुस्ततः ॥ २६ ॥ हरिदासस्य राजर्षे राजसूयमहोदयं नैवातृप्यन्प्रशंसंतः पिबन्मर्त्योऽमृतं यथा ॥ २७ ॥ ततो युधिष्ठिरो राजा सुहृत्संबंधिबांध
वान्प्रेम्णा निवारयामास कृष्णं च त्यागकातरः ॥ २८ ॥ भगवानपि तत्रांग न्यवात्सीत्तत्प्रियंकरः प्रस्थाप्य यदुवीरांश्च सांबादींश्च कुशस्थलीं ॥ २९ ॥

37 Folio from a *Bhagavatapurana*: Priests Perform a Sacrifice

The king respectfully and with folded hands said, Oh, the brahmans and the followers of Lord Krishna, the rice cooked by the milkman and sent by Lord Rama has come. Lord Krishna himself who was immersed in devotion has accepted the rice from Bidur. Oh great priests and highly knowledgeable in religious scriptures, please accept the rice if you are interested. There is no taboo in accepting the rice from a jajamana *[host of a sacrifice] during the solemnization and* yajna *ceremonies. Thus the brahmans heard the prayers of the* jajamana.

Those ignorant people who for little gain work very hard and those who boast that they know the time and space, good and evil, recitals and other religious activities besides treating the Supreme Personality of Lord Vishnu as a human being do not realize that all mortals are subject to death and will fall into death's trap one day. In other words, they disregarded Lord Vishnu.—B.R.

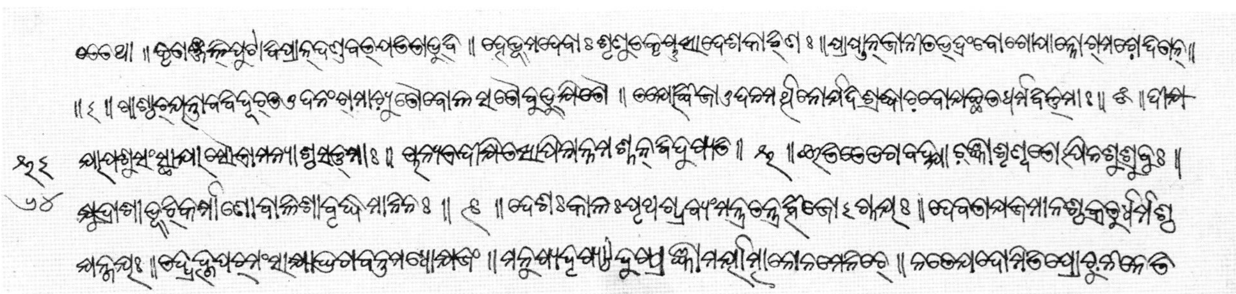

42 Parvati Extolling Punyaka Rite to Wives of the Sages

Summary of the long text on the back:
Parvati [Uma] is narrating the importance and the merits of the Punyaka Vrat (fast) to Arundhati (spouse of the *rishi* Vasishta), who is seen seated with her hands joined in front of the narrator (Uma). Other virtuous women, devoted to their husbands, are also present. Uma says, I with the blessings of my spouse (Lord Shiva) know everything, yet He had told me the merits of the Punyaka Vrat which I had observed in accordance with the ancient tradition. The fast, when observed according to the prescribed process and following the rituals, brings happiness to the woman and her husband. Devotion to one's husband is emphasized. Vidhi and Vidhan (rituals of the Punyaka fast) are described in detail.

Details of the *udyapana* (final ceremony of the fast) are also described in this passage. The woman observing the prescribed fast and her husband give valuable gifts to brahmans and organize a feast for them as well as the kinsmen of the husband. Details and importance of some other fasts for begetting offspring are further described in this text. The text recorded here is a part of the Parijata-harana story. Parijata is a celestial flowering tree [which Krishna seized from Indra's garden].

The sage Narada had brought a flower of the Parijata tree from the heaven which he gave to Krishna. Rukmini, Krishna's chief queen, had observed the fast and, upon performing the *udyapana* ceremony at the Revataka mount, was seated beside Krishna. Krishna gave the flower to Rukmini. Narada described the special and unusual qualities of the flower to Rukmini. The flower never fades and maintains its rare pleasant fragrance for a year. It fulfills all one's wishes, Narada told Rukmini, and after a year the flower would fly back and reattach at its original place on the tree. These facts were reported by the maids to Satyabhama, another queen of Krishna, who became jealous and expressed annoyance. Krishna brought the Parijata tree from Indra's heaven to please Satyabhama. Freed thereafter from jealous and negative feelings, she lived happily along with other queens of Krishna.

COMMENTS: The Sanskrit text is from the *Harivamsa-Purana*, which is part of the appendices of the *Mahabharata*. The chapter numbers of the text written on the painting are different from those used in the published text. The chapters mentioned in the books are: 78 to 81 (17). The *Harivamsa-Purana*—published by the Gita Press Gorakhpur (12th impression) with its Sanskrit text along with its translation in Hindi—has been consulted.—V.C.O.

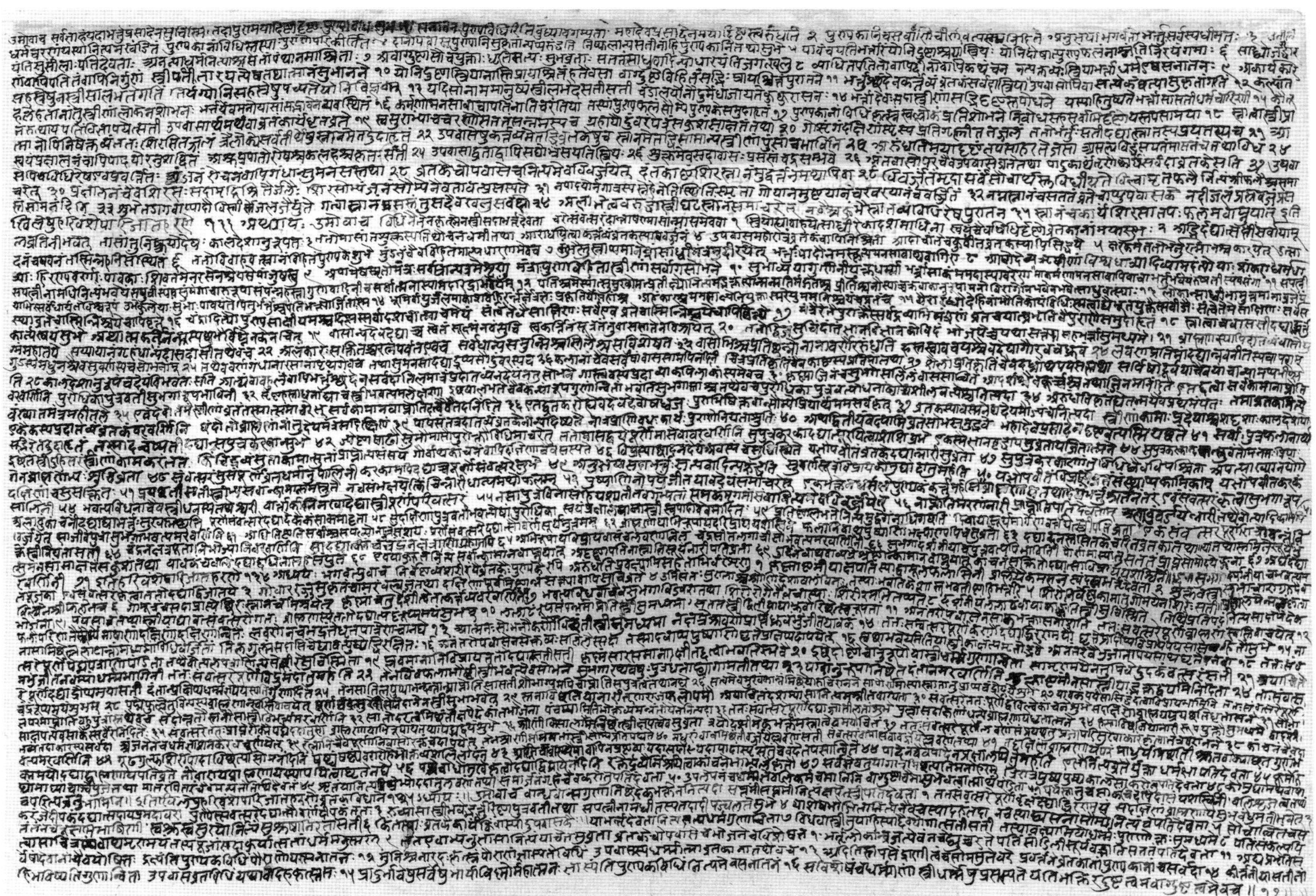

44 Illustration to a Verse from Jayadeva's *Gitagovinda*: The Charming Flautist

May blessings be bestowed by the sound of the flute of Kamsa's foe,
The sound of the flute removing the difficult grief of the gods by the danavas *[demons] humbled,*
The sound of the flute, the great invitation to the deer-eyed women, stirring, delighting, and making them bold,
The sound bringing down from the crests of the dwellers of heaven, swaying with pleasure, the mandara *flowers!*

Translated by George Kyt and quoted in John B. Alphonso-Karkala, ed., *An Anthology of Indian Literature*, Penguin Books, 1971, p. 523.

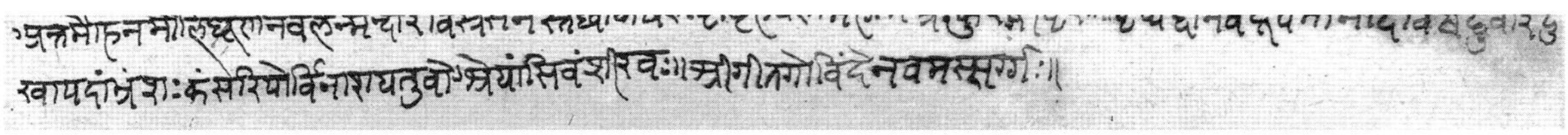

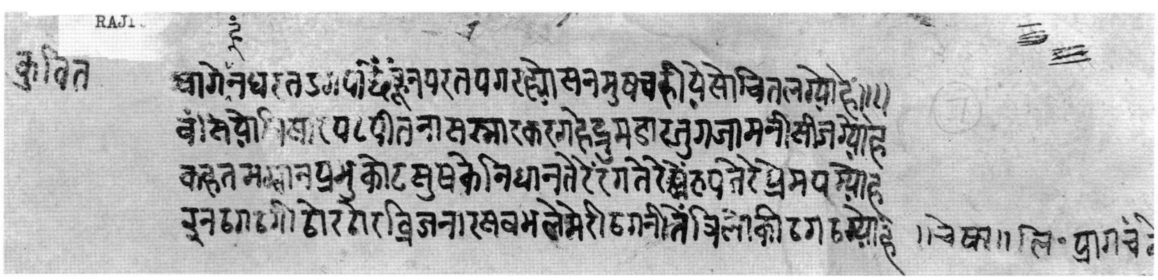

47 The Captive Krishna

Neither can he move forward nor step backward. His heart is completely occupied [and] wishes her to remain before his eyes. Not aware of his flute [and] his yellow garment, not held properly, holding a branch of the tree, his effulgence is making the night glittering and awake. [Here the poet uses a word with two meanings to hint of the flash of lightning, also.] Bhagwan [the poet], says our lord, the treasure of endless happiness, is captivated by the charm of her beauty. His maya *[illusion], which befools the denizens of the three worlds, is himself befooled by the [simple] women of Braj.*

Comments: Bhagwan, the author of the above verses, is not known from any published work. The language, content and style of the metrical composition suggest that he flourished in the period of the Ritikala Hindi poetry (1700–1850). Numerous poets using the dialect of Braj were active throughout north India from Bengal in the east to Punjab in the west. Many poets of this period who lived in obscure places or were attached to the courts of petty chiefs are not known. A carpenter/painter named Praga (Prag Chand) living in the village Chari in the Kangra-Beas valley is known from the records of the priests at Hardwar. Praga visited Hardwar in 1820. This information has been discovered recently by Vijay Sharma of Chamba.—V.C.O.

49 The Hour of Cowdust

Now [about] the signs of confusion: Where, because of love, words and ornaments are contrary.

Verse: *[She] wrapped the garland around the curve of [her] waist [and], taking the belt of sweet-sounding small bells, [she] hung it across the breasts. Without a blouse, having forgotten the care of the hem [of her garment], [she] adorned her ankles with bracelets. Having stained [her] lovely cheeks with collyrium and enhanced the beauty of [her] eyes with red lac dye, [and] hearing the arrival of the Ornament-of-Braj [Krishna], adorned with ornaments, [she] got up and ran to look.*

Now [about] the attractive mannerisms of Krishna:

Verse: *Krishna—[yellow] garments like lightning, radiant peacock-feathered crown setting off the rainbow's beauty—is coming, singing softly [and] playing the flute, making [his] friends dance like peacocks. O sister! Get up and fill your eyes with the sight, [for] he puts out the fire in [every] Catak bird's heart. [Says] Kesava, in this way comes Cloud-dark Krishna, as a rain-filled dark cloud, from the forest to Braj. Thus, according to* Rasikapriya.—R.P.C.

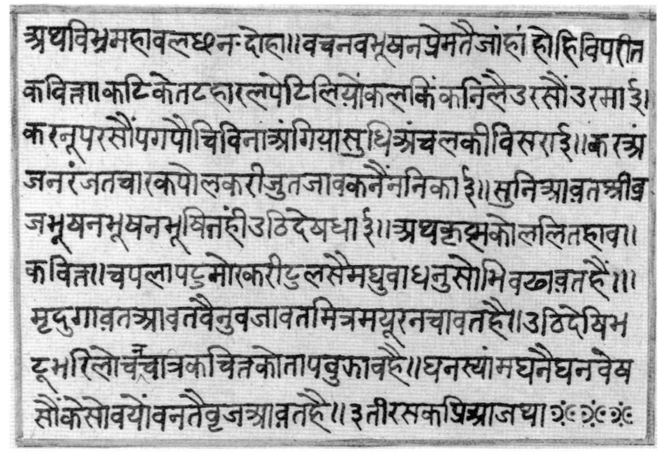

अथविभ्रमहावलछन दोहा॥वचनवभूखनप्रेमतेजांहां होहिविपरीत
कवित्त॥कटिकेतटहारलपेटिलियोकलकिंकनिलैउरसौंउरमाइ।
करनूपरसौंपगपौंचिबिनाअंगियासुधिअंचलकीबिसराइ॥करत्र
जनरंजतचारुकपोलकरीजुतजावकनैंननिकाइ॥सुनिआवतश्रीव्र
जभूखनभूखनभूखितह्वैउठिदेखधाइ॥अथकुतूहलकोललितहाव॥
कवित्त॥चपलापटुमोरकरीटुलसैमधुवाधनुसोभिवढावतहैं॥
मृदुगावतआवतवेनुवजावतमित्रमयूरनचावतहैं॥उठिदेखिभ
रूभरिलोचनचातककोचितकोतापवुझावहैं॥घनस्यामघनैघनवेस
सौंकेसोवयोंवनतैंव्रजआवतहैं॥इतीरसकप्रियाजया

50 A Folio from the *Satsai* (?): Ravishing Revelation

What he said to her companion:
When I saw her lovely ankles my valiant heart unfalteringly remained transfixed to them until it was crushed to powder under her anklets. (27)
What one of her companions said to another:
Drunk with his love night and day, his beauty's splendor so haunts her mind each moment.
That, heedless of her elders, she keeps blurting out words she should not. (28)
What she said to her companion:
Though I am trying to banish Krishna's remembrance from my mind, friend, his sweet ways of love perpetually haunt me, sleeping or awake, or dreaming; in joy, anger, repose, or agitation. (29)
What her companion said:
Dear girl, drunk with the vanity of your wisdom you do not heed my counsel; still I will caution you not to surrender your heart to your lover if he wants to seize it by force. (30)
What one of her companions said to another:
It seems she has vowed to listen to no other sound except of Krishna's flute. Day and night she strains her ears to catch their notes when he is piping in the forest. (31)

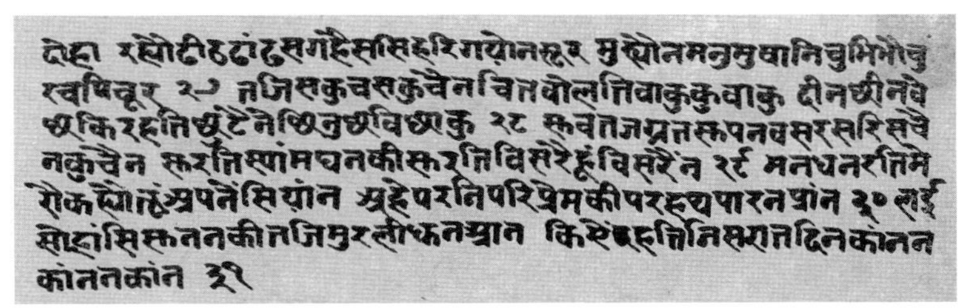

Comments: The above *dohas* (couplets) of Bihari's *Satsai* are written in Devanagari characters on the back of the painting. The translation of each *doha* is by Krishna P. Bahadur (1992, pp. 62, 64–66, 68). The illustration, however, is of a *doha* (mentioned below) that is not written on the painting. The picture was correctly identified by M. S. Randhawa (1966, pp. 68–69, pl. xii). He quotes two *dohas* related to the picture, while Bahadur (1990, p. 68) has translated only one *doha*, as given below.

What he said to her companion:
No sooner than she reached her porch she turned back on some pretence, and, glancing at me, smiled. She had come for sour curd to cast into milk for curdling, but instead cast love in my heart!—V.C.O.

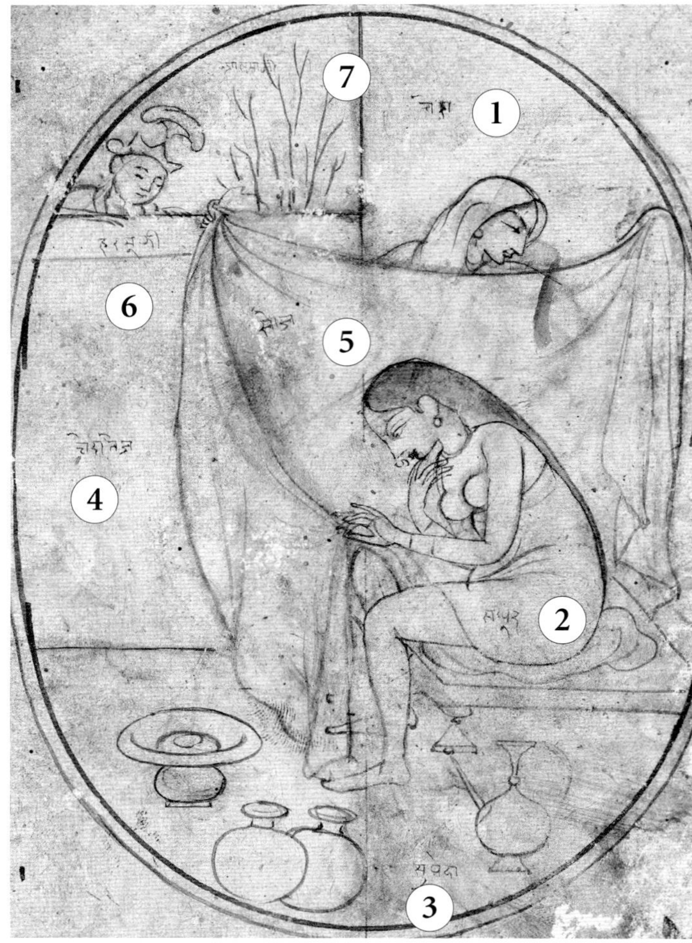

51 A Sketch for a *Satsai* Illustration (?): Peeping Tom

The names of colors are written in Devanagari script on the drawing:

1. Chehra — color of the face
2. Sandhur — red lead
3. Sapeda — white
4. Chehra tej — color of the face in a deeper tone
5. Soj — green
6. Harmunji — dark red clay
7. Asmani — light blue of the sky

—V.C.O.

52 Toilette on a Terrace

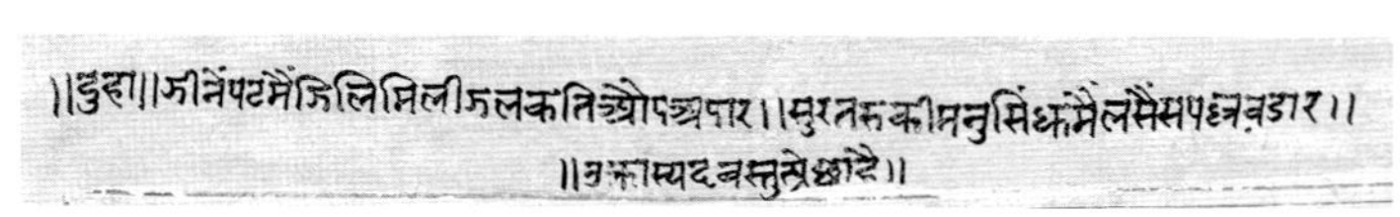

Behind the translucent textile, the grace of the Nayika's body glitters similarly as the grace of leaves of the Kalpa tree along with its branches in the ocean.

Comments: The verse is from the *Lalachandrika* by the poet Lallulala (1763–1825), a brahman from Gujarat. It was composed in Vikram Samvat 1857 [1799/1800].

For the original verse see Sudhakar Pandey, *Bihari Satsayi* [LalChandrika yukta] Vikram Samvat 2034 [1977], Varanasi, p. 178, *doha* (couplet) 482—N.K.

53 The Month of Bhadon (August–September)

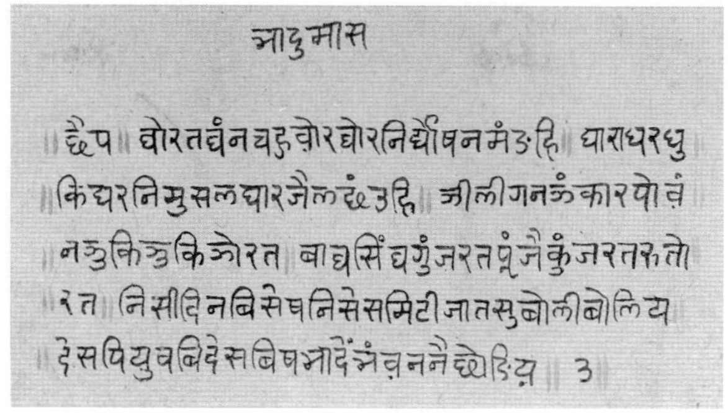

59 Illustration from a *Ragamala* Album: Saranga Raga

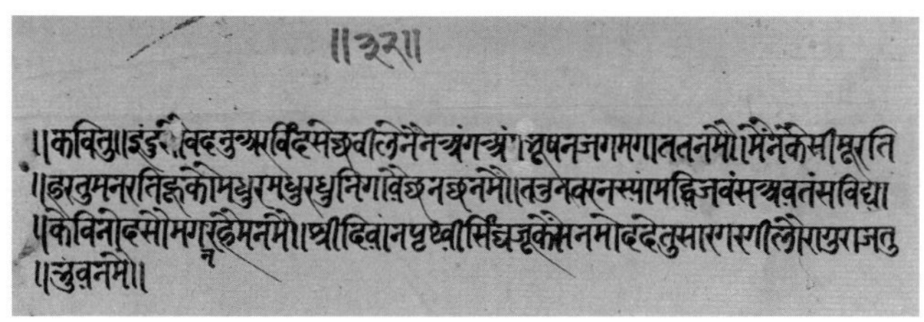

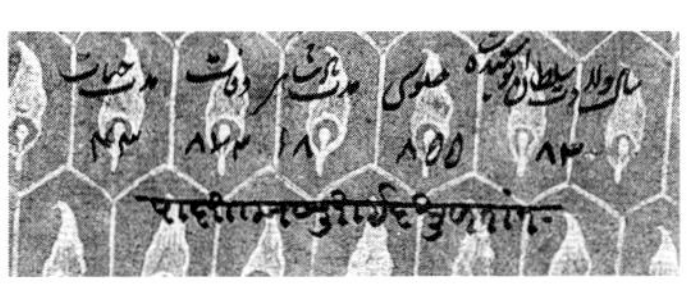

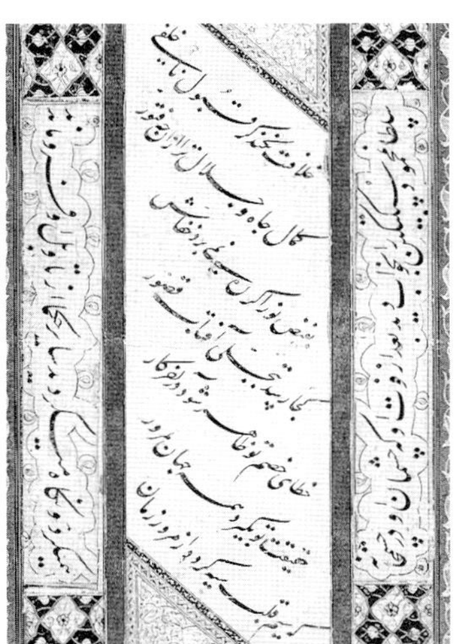

60 Leaf from an Album: Sultan Abu Sa'id

Persian inscription on the front:

Sultan Abu Sayyid Shah was born in A.H. *830 [1427]. He ascended to the throne in* A.H. *855 [1451/52] and reigned for 18 years. He died in* A.H. *873 [1469] at the age of 43.*
—V.C.O.

Persian calligraphy (incomplete verse) on the back:

Sultan Mahmood saw Subakatgin in a dream after the latter's death. His eyes were still moving in their sockets and watching. All the wise men (consulted by Mahmood) were unable to suggest any interpretation of the dream.

If an undutiful son does not accept (your) office of Caliphate, what harm could there be to your glory and exalted position. If the bat does not receive fine rays of light what is the fault of the brilliance of the Sun. The mistake of your enemy would be exposed at last (and) your reality would prevail upon the changing world (times). That the heart of silver (purity of heart) becomes black with the passage of time
—A.N.W.

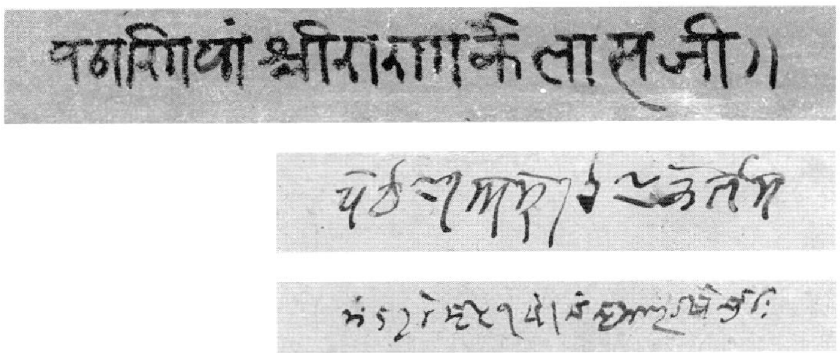

64 Raja Kailash Pal of Nurpur

Inscription in Devanagari on the front:
Rana Kailash the Pathania

Inscription in Takri on the back:
Rana Kailash the Pathania

An inscription at the bottom is in another hand and unintelligible. It seems to record the date of 1708.—V.C.O.

66 Raja Ranjit Sen of Suket and Family

Inscriptions in Persian script on the front identify the sitters, from left to right:
Mian Bishan Singh, son of Mian Kishan Singh
Mian Kishan Singh, the real brother of Raja Ranjit Singh
Raja Ranjit Singh
Raja Bikram Sen, the worthy son of Ranjit Singh

Inscription in Devanagari script on the back: (right)
Sukhetad [of Suket] Sri Raja Ranjit Singh
Mian Kishan Singh
Suket ke [of Suket] Raja Ranjit Sen

Comments: The work seems to be a contemporary study of the subjects and must have been done around 1775–80. The identifying names recorded in Persian script are correct. These were written at a later date during the reign of Bikram Sen, who succeeded his father Raja Ranjit Sen in 1791. This fact is suggested by the use of the title "Raja" with the name of Bikram Sen. This is also suggested by the fact that the ruling Rajas of Suket were known by the royal family name "Sen," but here the word is used with the name of the son (Bikram Sen) and not with the name of the father. In the identifying names recorded in Persian script on the front of the painting, his name is given as Ranjit Singh. Mian Kishan Singh's daughter was married to Raja Sansar Chand of Kangra.—V.C.O.

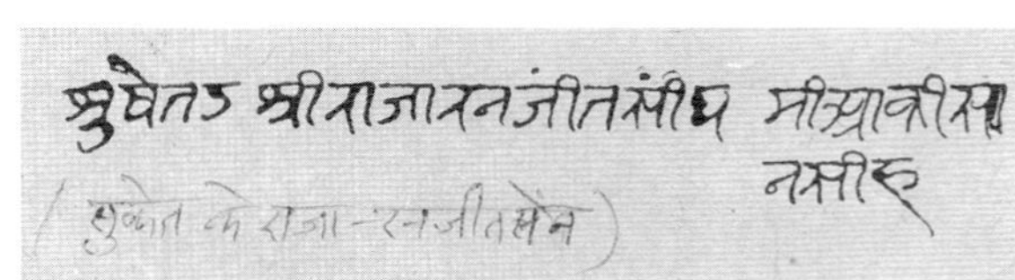

67 Maharao Basant Singh and Maharaja Sahab Prithivi Singh

Inscription in white brush on the top of the front of the painting:
Maharav Raja ji Shri Basant Singh ji [and] Maharaja Sahab Prithivi Singh ji

Comments: There are several inventory numbers on the front and back of this painting, as this leaf went through the various hands of royalty or dealers. The words "Kanayaa," perhaps the name of a twentieth-century inventory clerk, and "Gopivallabh," perhaps the name of a late-nineteenth-century inventory clerk, appear also on the backs of [68–70] with different inventory numbers. There are also notations in Urdu and English.—N.K.

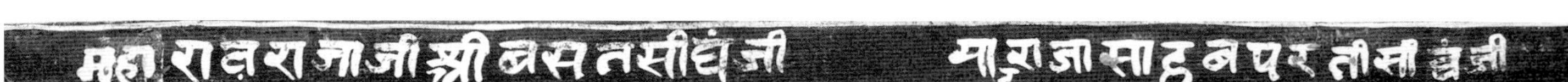

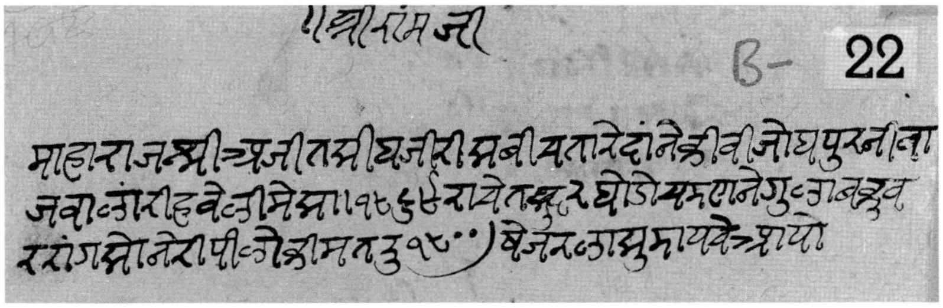

72 Ajit Singh of Ghanerao

The portrait of Maharaj[a] Ajit Singh ji painted by Chitara Dana in a mansion called Nivajwala Haveli, in Chaitra, Sud, Vikram Samvat 1869 [1812]. He is mounted on a mare [named] Gulab Kunvar, her complexion is yellow as gold, her price [current] is Rs. 1800/, from Khejarla's "Dayave."

Comments: Chitara Dana was a famous painter of the court of Maharaja Man Singh of Jodhpur. Nivajwala Haveli is a *thikana* (fiefdom) of Jodhpur. Names like Gulab Kunvar were usually given to Rajput ladies, so it is surprising that this one should be for a mare. Since the name precedes the description/complexion and price of the animal, it should be the name of the mare. "Dayave"may be a misspelling for "Dayaje," meaning part of a dowry, which seems unlikely since the price is given.—N.K.

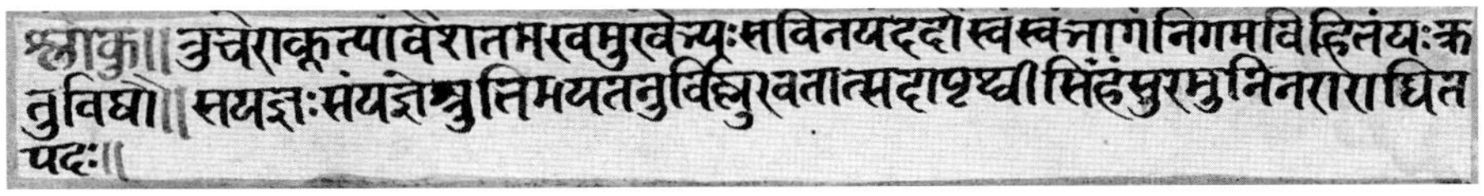

74 Prithvisimha at Worship

Inscription on front: (right)
A verse. Born as a son of Ruchi and Akuti, he performed many fire sacrifices in accordance with Vedic rituals. His name is Yajna, an incarnation of Vishnu who is worshipped by the gods, sages and people as an embodiment of the Vedas. May he all the time protect Prithvisimha who performs the fire sacrifice.—G.V.

Inscription on back: (below)
In Dandaku chhanda: The one of sacred and beautiful form, whatever he makes is beautiful, his mother is also of cultivated taste, he is the incarnation of all enjoyments. He is well versed, is the form of good Yagya, as if married to the 'dakshina' [of the Yagya, i.e. her wife is like 'dakshina'], is like the 'yupa' [the stump fixed in the Yagya site—forerunner of Ashoka's pillars], who offers gifts like an ocean, who is born in the form of Dev, who has troubled the demons, has cleared the paths of sins, thus eradicated the sorrow of the three worlds. Who has been incarnating through Yugs [compare Gita], [all must keep] the same Kunwar Bahadur in the form of Hari [the god] in their hearts.
—N.K.

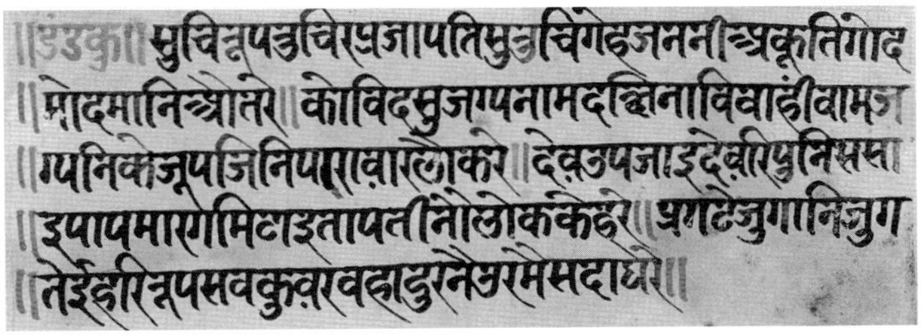

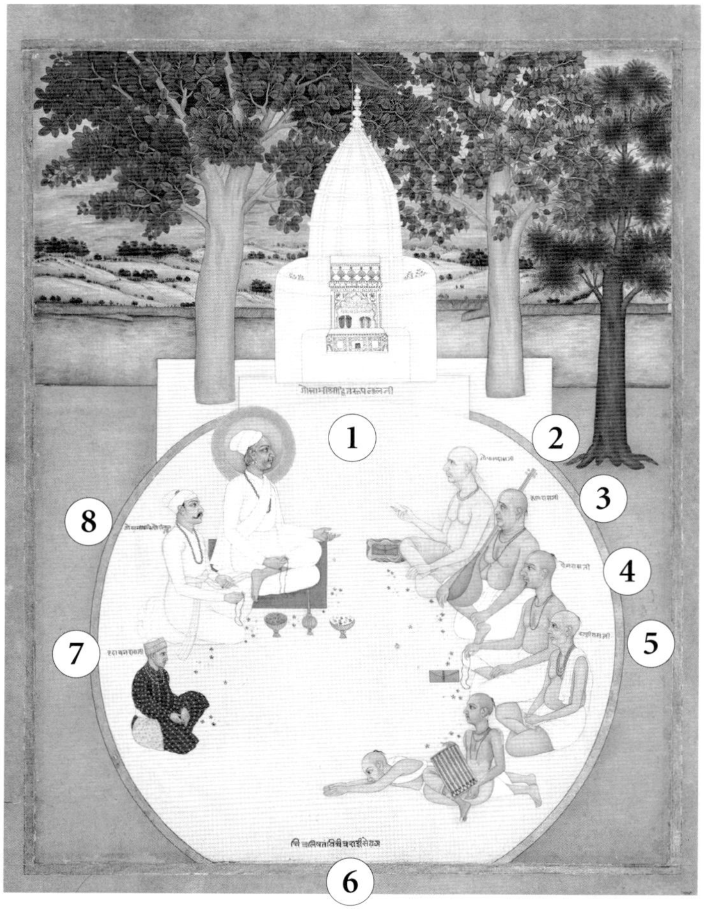

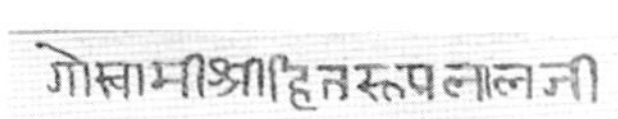

1 *Gosain or Goswami Hitaruplal*

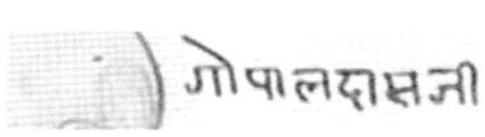

2 *Gopaldas*

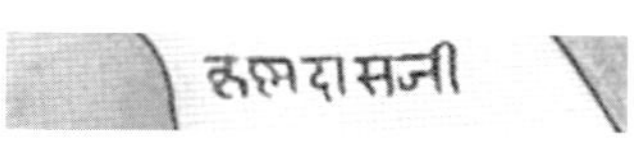

3 *Krishnadas*

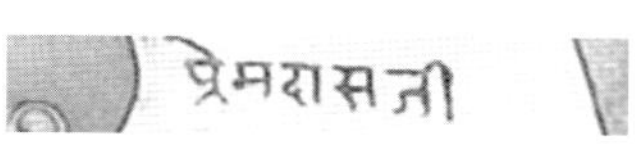

4 *Premdas*

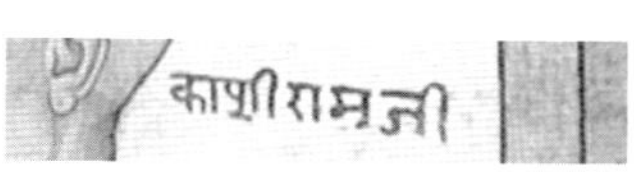

5 *Kasiram*

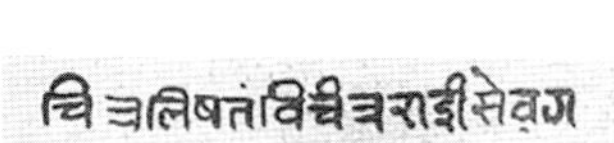

6 *Painting done by Vichitra in the service of the king (or court painter).*

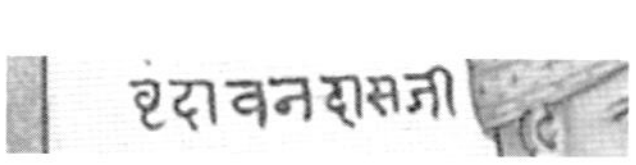

7 *Vrindavandas*

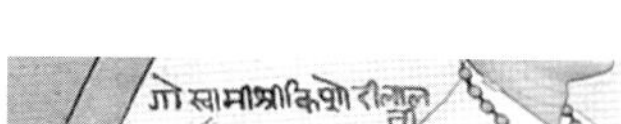

8 *Kisorilal*

77 Vaishnava Teachers in Front of a Temple

This painting portrays a group of Radhavallabi *bhaktas*, or devotees, who are identified with inscriptions.

Premdas was a disciple of Ruplal Goswami and the author of the most popular commentary on the Hit Cauraasi. He died in 1757 in Vrindaban in Ahmadshah's massacre. Vrindavandas was known as "Chaachaa" Hit Vrindavandas and was one of the most prolific writers of the eighteenth century. Ruplal Goswami was Vrindavandas' guru and died in the same massacre in 1757.

Comments: The inscriptions on this painting are not typical of Kishangarh paintings—most of the early inscriptions tend to be dual Persian-Hindi. But from about 1800 or so, Hindi alone was favored, and for religious subjects like this, would have been a natural choice. The inscription on the temple at the top of the picture is the characteristic "slogan" of the sect and is very standard.
—N.H.

Bibliography

Aijazuddin, F. S. 1977. *Pahari Paintings and Sikh Portraits in the Lahore Museum.* London and New York: Sotheby Parke Bernet.

Archer, William G. 1966. *Paintings of the Sikhs.* London: Her Majesty's Stationery Office.

——. 1973. *Indian Paintings from the Punjab Hills: A Survey and History of Pahari Miniature Painting.* 2 vols. London and New York: Sotheby Parke Bernet.

Bahadur, Krishna P., trans. 1992. *The Satasai.* London and New York: Penguin Books.

Banerjee, P. 1978. *The Life of Krishna in Indian Art.* New Delhi: National Museum.

Basak, Radhagovinda. 1971. *The Prakrit Gatha-Saptasati.* Calcutta: Asiatic Society.

Beach, Milo Cleveland. 1974. *Rajput Painting at Bundi and Kota.* Ascona: Artibus Asiae Publishers.

Boner, Georgette, Eberhard Fischer and B. N. Goswamy. 1994. *Sammlung Alice Boner: Geschenk an das Museum Rietberg Zürich.* Zürich: Museum Rietberg Zürich.

Brown, Kerry, ed. 1999. *Sikh Art and Literature.* London and New York: Routledge in collaboration with the Sikh Foundation.

Caillat, C. and R. Kumar. 1981. *The Jain Cosmology.* Basel: Ravi Kumar.

Coomaraswamy, Ananda K. 1916. *Rajput Painting.* 2 vols. London and New York: Oxford University Press.

——. 1926. *Catalogue of the Indian Collections in the Museum of Fine Arts, Boston. Part 5: Rajput Painting.* Boston: Museum of Fine Arts.

——. 1927. *History of Indian and Indonesian Art.* London: Edward Goldston; New York: E. Weyhe; Leipzig: Karl W. Hiersemann.

Crill, Rosemary. n.d. [2000] *Marwar Painting: A History of the Jodhpur Style.* Mumbai: India Book House.

Dallapiccola, Anna L., ed. 1982. *Krishna, the Divine Lover: Myth and Legend through Indian Art.* Contributions by B. N. Goswamy. London: Serindia; Boston: D. R. Godine.

Doshi, Saryu. 1985. *Masterpieces of Jain Painting.* Bombay: Marg Publications.

——, ed. 1995. *The Royal Bequest: Art Treasures of the Baroda Museum and Picture Gallery.* Bombay: India Book House.

Dye, Joseph M., III. 2001. *The Arts of India.* Richmond, Va.: Virginia Museum of Fine Arts.

Ebeling, Klaus. 1973. *Ragamala Painting.* Basel and New Delhi: Ravi Kumar.

Elvehjem Art Center. 1971. *Indian Miniature Painting: The Collection of Earnest C. and Jane Werner Watson.* Madison, Wisc., Elvehjem Art Center, University of Wisconsin: University of Wisconsin Press.

Fabri, Charles Louis. 1974. *History of the Art of Orissa.* Bombay: Orient Longman.

Fischer, Eberhard and Dinanath Pathy. 1990. *Die Perlenkette dem Geliebten, Elf illustrierte Palmblatter zur Rasika Haravali-Romanze des Dichters Upendra Bhanja von Orissa, aus der Sammlung Alice Boner im Museum Rietberg Zürich.* Zürich: Museum Rietberg Zürich.

——. 1998. "Laharu and Mahesh: Two Master Painters of Chamba." In Ohri and Craven 1998, pp. 28–45.

Fogg, Sam. 2003. *Divine Pursuits: Indian Painting Traditions from the 15th to the 19th Centuries.* Sam Fogg: London.

Galloway, Francesca. 2000. *Asian Textiles, Indian Miniatures and Works of Art.* Francesca Galloway: London.

Goswamy, B. N. and Usha Bhatia. 1999. *Painted Visions: The Goenka Collection of Indian Paintings.* New Delhi: Lalit Kala Akademi.

Goswamy, B. N. and Eberhard Fischer. 1992. *Pahari Masters: Court Painters of Northern India.* Supplementum XXXVIII. Zurich: Artibus Asiae Publishers and Museum Rietberg Zürich.

——. 1997. *Pahari Masters: Court Painters of Northern India.* Delhi: Oxford University Press.

Gupta, S. P., ed. 1985. *Masterpieces from the National Museum Collection.* New Delhi: National Museum of India.

Holland, Barron Gregory. 1969. "The Satsai of Bihari: Hindi Poetry of the Early Riti Period." Ph.D. dissertation, University of California-Berkeley.

Hutchison, J. and J. Ph. Vogel. 1933. *History of the Panjab Hill States.* Lahore.

Jain-Neubauer, Jutta. 1998. "Fattu: A Rediscovery." In Ohri and Craven 1998, pp. 81–97.

Kandalavala, Karl. 1958. *Pahari Miniature Paintings.* Bombay: New Book Company.

Krishna, Anand, ed. 1981. *Chhvavi-2: Rai Krishnadasa Felicitation Volume.* Banaras: Bharat Kala Bhavan.

Krishna, Naval. 1985. "Bikaneri Miniature Painting Workshops of Ruknuddin Ibrahim and Nathu." *Lalit Kala* 21, pp. 23–27.

Lal, Mukandi. 1968. *Garhwal Painting.* New Delhi: Publications Division, Ministry of Information and Broadcasting, Government of India.

Mathur, Girija Kumar, ed. 1973. *The Veiled Moon: Translations of Bihari Satsai by Amar Nath Jha.* New Delhi: Indian Council for Cultural Relations.

Miller, Barbara Stoler, trans. and ed. 1977. *Love Song of the Dark Lord: Jayadeva's Gitagovinda.* New York: Columbia University Press.

Ohri, Vishwa Chander and Roy C. Craven Jr., eds. 1998. *Painters of the Pahari Schools.* Mumbai: Marg Publications on behalf of the National Centre for the Performing Art.

Okada, Amin and Roselyne Hurel. 2002. *Pouvoir et Desir: Miniatures Indiennes du San Diego Museum of Art.* Paris: Paris-Musées.

Pal, Pratapaditya. 1967. *Ragamala Paintings in the Museum of Fine Arts, Boston.* Boston: Museum of Fine Arts.

——. 1976. *The Flute and the Brush: Indian Paintings from the William Theo Brown and Paul Wonner Collection.* Newport Beach, Calif: Newport Harbor Art Museum.

——. 1978. *The Classical Tradition in Rajput Painting: From the Paul F. Walter Collection.* New York: Pierpont Morgan Library and The Gallery Association of New York State.

——. 1993. *Indian Painting, Vol. I: A Catalogue of the Los Angeles County Museum of Art Collection.* Los Angeles: Los Angeles County Museum of Art.

——. 1994. *The Peaceful Liberators: Jain Art from India.* New York: Thames and Hudson; Los Angeles: Los Angeles County Museum of Art.

——, et al. 1997. *Dancing to the Flute: Music and Dance in Indian Art.* Sydney: Art Gallery of New South Wales.

——. 2001. *Desire and Devotion: Art from India, Nepal, and Tibet in the John and Berthe Ford Collection.* Baltimore and London: Walters Art Museum.

Pal, Pratapaditya and Betty Seid. 2002. *The Holy Cow and Other Animals: A Selection of Indian Paintings from the Art Institute of Chicago.* Chicago: Art Institute of Chicago; Seattle: Distributed by University of Washington Press.

Poster, Amy G. 1994. *Realms of Heroism: Indian Paintings at the Brooklyn Museum.* New York: Brooklyn Museum in association with Hudson Hill Press.

Randhawa, M. S. 1959. *Basohli Painting.* New Delhi: Publications Division, Ministry of Information and Broadcasting, Government of India.

——. 1960. *Kangra Paintings of the Bhagavata Purana.* New Delhi: National Museum of India.

——. 1962. *Kangra Paintings on Love.* New Delhi: National Museum of India.

——. 1963. *Kangra Paintings of the Gita Govinda.* New Delhi: National Museum of India.

——. 1966. *Kangra Paintings of the Bihari Sat Sai.* New Delhi: National Museum of India.

Ryder, Arthur W., trans. [1912] 1933. *Shakuntala and Other Writings by Kalidasa.* New York: E. P. Dutton and Co.

Singh, Khushwant, Nima Poovaya-Smith and Kaveri Ponnapa. 1991. *Warm and Rich and Fearless: A Brief Survey of Sikh Culture.* Bradford, England: Bradford Art Galleries and Museums.

Sotheby's. *Important Indian Paintings from the Gloria Katz and Willard Huyck Collection.* Catalogue of an auction held in New York on 22 March 2002.

Spink, Walter. 1971. *Krishnamandala, a Devotional Theme in Indian Art.* Ann Arbor, Mich., Center for South and Southeast Asian Studies, University of Michigan.

Tagare, Ganesh Vasudeo, trans. 1976. *The Bhagavata-purana.* 4 vols. Edited by J. L. Shastri. Delhi: Motilal Banarsidass.

Topsfield, Andrew. 1980. *Paintings from Rajasthan in the National Gallery of Victoria: A Collection Acquired through the Felton Bequests' Committee.* Melbourne: National Gallery of Victoria.

——. 1981. "Sahibdin's Gita Govinda Illustrations" in A. Krishna, ed., 1981, pp. 231–38.

——, ed. 2000. *Court Painting in Rajasthan.* Mumbai: Marg Publications.

——. 2002. *Court Painting at Udaipur: Art under the Patronage of the Maharanas of Mewar.* Supplementum XLIV. Zürich: Artibus Asia Publications. Museum Rietberg Zürich.

Vajracharya, Gautama V. 2002. *Watson Collection of Indian Miniatures at the Elvehjem Museum of Art: A Detailed Study of Selected Works.* Madison, Wisc.: Elvehjem Museum of Art.

Vatsyayan, Kapila. 1980. *Miniatures of the Gita-Govinda: 17th Century Manuscript of North Gujarat.* Jaipur: Maharaja Sawai Man Singh II Museum.

Vaudeville, Charlotte. 1986. *Barahmasa in Indian Literatures: Songs of the Twelve Months in Indo-Aryan Literatures.* Delhi: Motilal Banarsidass.

Waldschmidt, Ernst and Rose Leonore. 1967. *Miniatures of Musical Inspiration in the Collection of the Berlin Museum of Indian Art. Part I: Ragamala Pictures from the Western Himalayan Promontory.* Bombay: G.R. Bhatkal for Popular Prakashan.

——. 1975. *Miniatures of Musical Inspiration in the Collection of the Berlin Museum of Indian Art. Part II: Ragamala Pictures from Northern India and the Deccan.* Berlin: Museum für Indische Kunst Berlin.

Welch, Stuart Cary, ed. 1997. *Gods, Kings, and Tigers: The Art of Kotah.* New York: Asia Society Galleries and Harvard University Art Museums.

Map of India

The maps indicate modern states and regional painting schools that are the focus of the Ramesh and Urmil Kapoor Collection.

▲ painting schools
■ major cities

1 Pahari Painting Schools

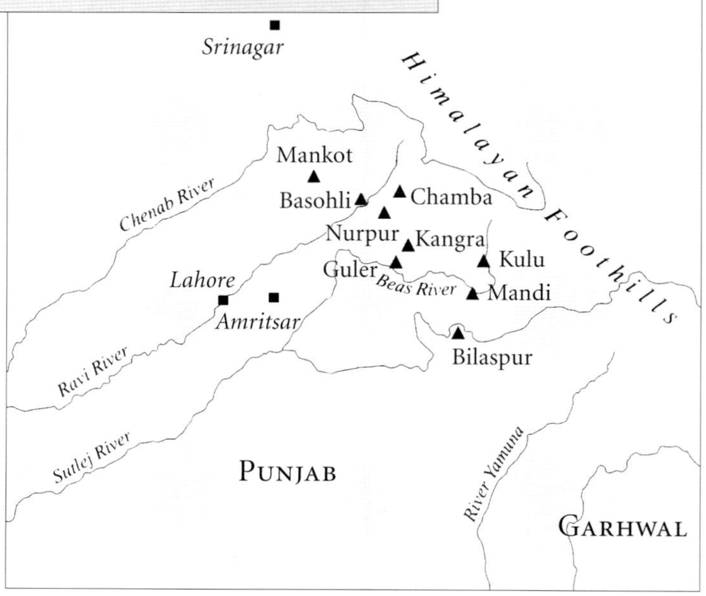

2 Rajasthan Painting Schools

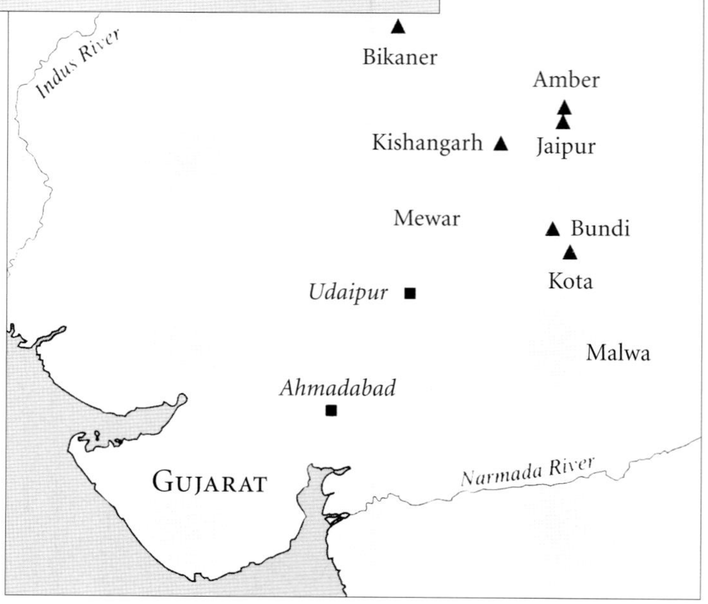

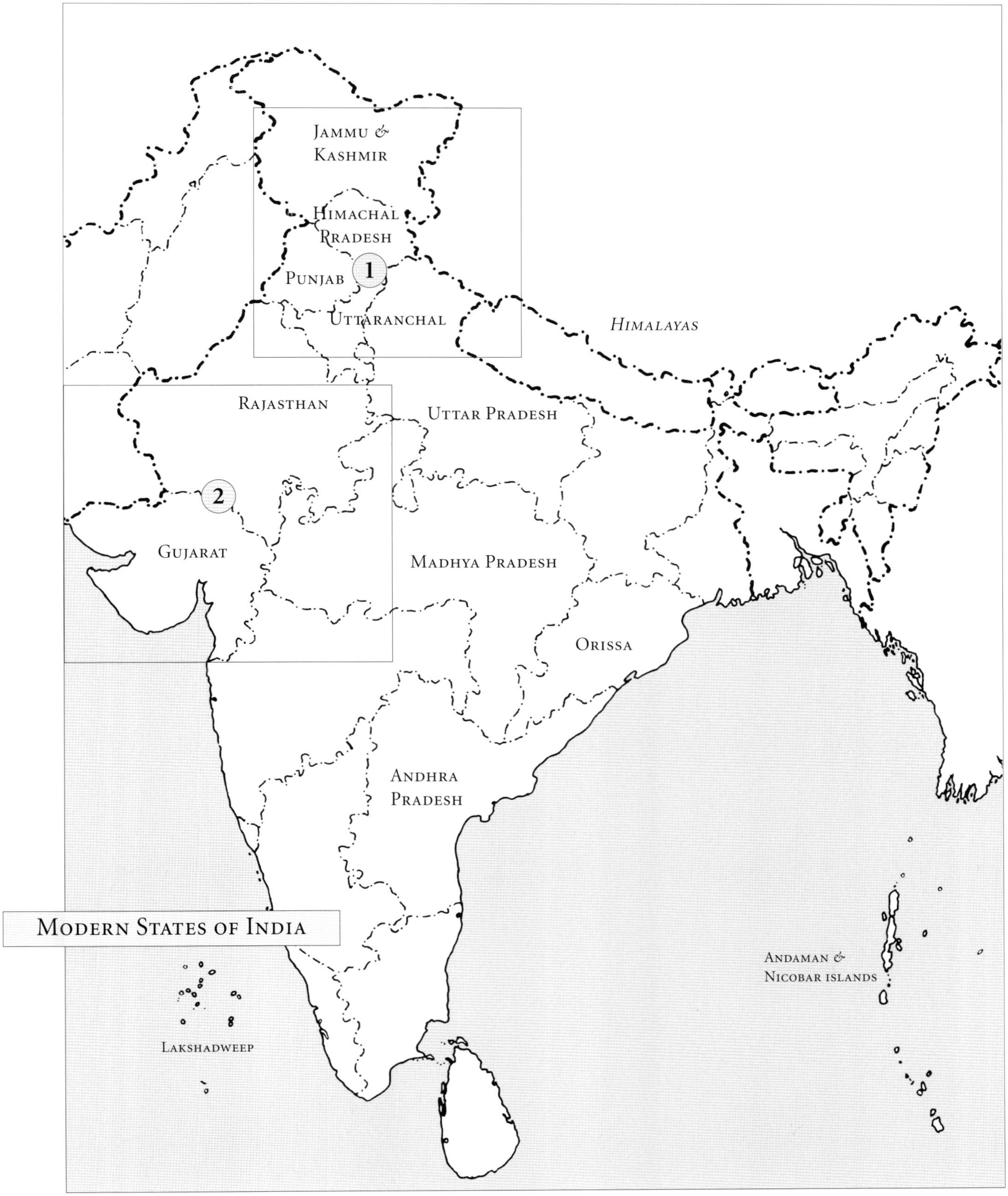
Jammu & Kashmir
Himachal Pradesh
Punjab
1
Uttaranchal
Himalayas
Rajasthan
Uttar Pradesh
2
Gujarat
Madhya Pradesh
Orissa
Andhra Pradesh
Modern States of India
Andaman & Nicobar islands
Lakshadweep